Classrooms That Work

THIRD EDITION

Classrooms That Work

They Can *All* Read and Write

Patricia M. Cunningham
Wake Forest University

Richard L. Allington
University of Florida

Boston   New York   San Francisco
Mexico City   Montreal   Toronto   London   Madrid   Munich   Paris
Hong Kong   Singapore   Tokyo   Cape Town   Sydney

Series Editor: Aurora Martínez Ramos
Editorial Assistant: Beth Slater
Marketing Manager: Amy Cronin
Editorial Production Service: Omegatype Typography, Inc.
Composition and Prepress Buyer: Linda Cox
Manufacturing Manager: Megan Cochran
Cover Administrator: Linda Knowles
Electronic Composition: Omegatype Typography, Inc.

For related titles and support materials, visit our online catalog at www.ablongman.com.

Library of Congress Cataloging-in-Publication Data
Cunningham, Patricia Marr.
    Classrooms that work : they can all read and write / Patricia M. Cunningham, Richard
L. Allington.—3rd ed.
        p. cm.
    Includes bibliographical references (p.) and index.
    ISBN 0-205-35541-2 (alk. paper)
        1. Language arts (Elementary)—United States.   2. Reading (Elementary)—United States.
I. Allington, Richard L.   II. Title.

LB1576 .C855 2003
372.6'0973—dc21

2002016307

Printed in the United States

10   9   8   7   6   5   4   3   RRD-VA   07   06   05   04   03

Text on p. 213 used with permission. From *Brown Bear, Brown Bear, What Do You See?* by Bill Martin Jr., © 1967, 1970 by Harcourt Brace & Company, renewed in 1995 by Bill Martin Jr. Reprinted by permission of Henry Holt & Co., LLC.

Photos were taken by Rosalyn D. Morgan, who graduated from the WFU Elementary Education program in 1992 and is currently teaching first grade in the Atlanta area. Some of the art was drawn by Tracy Seiler, who graduated from Wake Forest in 1994 and is currently teaching second grade in Winston Salem, North Carolina.

This book is dedicated to all the teachers who work tirelessly and enthusiastically every day to provide good balanced literacy instruction for *all* the children they teach. In spite of constant criticism and little appreciation, these teachers create classrooms that really do work (most of the time!) in which all children learn to read and write.

BRIEF CONTENTS

CONTENTS

INTRODUCTION

Ten years ago, when we wrote the first edition of *Classrooms That Work: They Can All Learn to Read and Write,* we wanted to convey our firm belief that all children could learn to read and write and that the single most important variable in achieving that goal was what each classroom teacher did, day by day, minute by minute, in the classroom. A decade later, we are still convinced that the goal of getting all children reading and writing well is achievable, but we are worried about how that goal is being pursued. Most states now have "high-stakes" testing programs. Children who do not achieve at grade level are often retained in the current grade. High school students not only must pass their courses but, in most states, must pass a graduation competency test to get a diploma.

High standards and high expectations are important. Our technological society does require a high level of thinking and literacy for almost every job. The link between high expectations and standards and high-stakes testing, however, is a dubious one. Test scores on the state-mandated tests have improved in many states, but scores on the NAEP (National Assessment of Educational Progress) have not. How can this be? Which test is truly a test of increased learning? Following are some of the strategies implemented by schools "under the gun" to improve test scores (Allington, 2000).

Some school administrators suggest to parents that certain students be kept at home during the testing days so that their children will not have to experience the "stress" of the test. Other schools schedule a field trip for all the Title 1 remedial reading students! Some high schools expel students or encourage certain students to "drop out" just before the test is given. San Francisco, for example, recently reported increased enrollment, higher test scores, and fewer test takers. Some states exclude students with disabilities from the testing or allow accommodations such as reading the reading test to them if they are reading disabled. Scores go up but so do the numbers of children identified with disabilities.

Some schools, in an attempt to achieve the highest possible number of children who pass, target certain children for intensive instruction. Unfortunately, the targeted children are not apt to be the ones most in need of acceleration. One school reportedly decided that about one-third of its students would pass with no trouble, one-third were very unlikely to pass, and one-third would pass if they were given most of the teacher's instructional time and energy. Students were identified and teachers were told to concentrate on the students in the middle third. If the teachers followed this dictum strictly (and many probably did not), the high achievers would coast through that year and the low-achieving students would be even further behind next year.

Of course, some schools spend a lot of time and money doing "test prep." It is, however, well documented that practicing the type of item to be given on the test and learning how to use syntax to ferret out distracters will raise test scores but won't increase learning or reading levels. In many states, the tests are given in March. Some school districts have changed the school calendar so that students return to school in July and thus have an extra month or two of instruction before the test. Of course the children get out of school a few months earlier than they used to. No additional weeks or months of learning have been added—only additional time before the test. This exemplifies, again, efforts being aimed at improving test scores, not increasing learning.

Now, consider the intriguing issue of how state test scores could show remarkable gains when scores on the nationally administered NAEP hold steady. NAEP tests are not given to all students. Rather, schools and children within schools are randomly selected and given the test. Many times, administrators don't know until the NAEP testers arrive that their school was chosen, and no one knows which children will be chosen. Most NAEP questions require higher-level thinking and some extended answers. Test prep would probably not significantly improve NAEP scores, and no one is going to go to all the expense and trouble to prep their students for a test most of them will never take. NAEP scores probably come as close as is possible to actually evaluating student literacy levels.

Classrooms That Work is a positive and (we hope) uplifting book. It is all about what we can do and how our daily efforts can increase learning and raise reading and writing levels for all children. Why then did we choose to begin this book with this discouraging description of the problems created by the high-stakes testing movement? The tests and the questionable gains made by certain schools, districts, and states have become so much a part of our world that it is easy to get caught up in this and forget what really matters in teaching children to read and write. High-quality instruction in a good balanced reading program, provided by smart, caring teachers, day in and day out, result in all our children reading and writing to their highest potential. More children at all different entering levels can achieve higher levels of literacy. They also score better on whatever test they are given. Our experience with high-stakes testing so far seems to indicate that we cannot raise the reading and thinking levels of all our children if we set our sights on higher test scores. If we set our sights on raising reading and thinking levels for all our children, we can accomplish that and raise test scores.

This book is about teaching all our children to read and write better. We have tried hard to pull together the very best of what is known about how to do that and to make the strategies and activities as workable in real classrooms as we can. Chapter 1, "Reading and Writing Real 'Things,'" is based on the simple but true idea that the more children read and write, the better they will read and write. Children who find reading and writing pleasurable and entertaining read and write a lot more than children who find reading and writing boring and onerous. Lots of ideas are suggested in this first chapter for getting kids turned on to reading and writing. When readers find their own particular kind of wonderful book and authors find their own voices, they read and write willingly. Lots of self-selected reading and writing are the cornerstones of classrooms in which all children learn to read and write.

In addition to self-selected reading and writing, children need to be taught strategies to be good readers and writers. Chapter 2, "Words," focuses on helping children learn to read and spell fluently and automatically the most common words and to use patterns to decode and spell other words. Chapter 3, "Comprehension," describes a variety of activities that promote thoughtful literacy for both story and informational text. Chapter 4, "Writing," describes ways to promote both self-selected and focused writing.

Chapter 5, "Multilevel Instruction," is a completely new chapter in this third edition. Multilevel instruction is instruction that includes multiple things to be learned, depending on what the child is ready to learn. When instruction is multilevel, learners at every level can experience success. A variety of whole-class and small-group formats are described, which teachers use to provide support for struggling readers and challenges for advanced readers. Chapter 6, "Assessment," is also a completely new chapter in this edition. This chapter describes how teachers can make assessment an integral part of their instruction and contains a variety of practical checklists and other assessment suggestions. Chapter 7, "Science and Social Studies Matter to Struggling Readers," reminds us that prior knowledge and meaning vocabulary are huge factors in comprehension and suggest many ways to integrate these subjects with literacy instruction. Chapter 8, "Extra Support for Students Who Need It Most," provides ideas for "above and beyond" support for those students who are most likely to fall through the cracks.

Chapters 9, 10, and 11 are three of our favorite chapters. Chapter 9 describes a sample day in a Building Blocks kindergarten. Chapter 10 describes a sample day in a Four Blocks primary classroom. Chapter 11 describes a sample week in a Big Blocks intermediate classroom. We have tried in these chapters to show how all the important components of a balanced literacy program can be combined and to capture the best of what we have seen in the many outstanding kindergarten, primary, and intermediate classrooms we have been privileged to visit. The final chapter, "Beyond the Classroom: Things Worth Fighting For," describes some of the schoolwide, districtwide, and communitywide efforts that we believe are most needed and effective and that we all should get behind and push for.

These are difficult times in schools. The problems that must be solved and the "false solutions" are evident to all of us. But classroom teachers can still close their doors and do their very best for all their children, and most of them do! This book is our small effort to make your efforts more productive and—don't tell anyone—more fun!

ACKNOWLEDGMENTS

We are most indebted to the thousands of teachers with whom we have worked and who have shared their concerns, their ideas, their insights, and their "tricks of the trade." We wrote this book for them and with their help and support.

We are grateful to our colleagues with whom we share ideas and who challenge us to think more deeply and clearly about the important issues. We are especially grateful to Dottie Hall, director of the Four Blocks Center at Wake Forest University, who volunteered (sort of!) to revise the Building Blocks chapter and who made it much more lively and representative of the Building Blocks framework. Thanks, Dottie. We owe you! As always, we are grateful for the support, encouragement, patience, and criticism (always constructive!) of our spouses and professional colleagues, Anne McGill-Franzen and Jim Cunningham.

We express thanks to all our students and teachers who read and commented on various sections of the book and to the reviewers who made suggestions for changes to the previous edition: Brenda Bradshaw, Southwest Missouri State University; Jan Buswell, Metropolitan State College of Denver; Deborah E. Doty, Northern Kentucky University; Susan McBride, California Polytechnic State University; Kouider Mokhtari, Oklahoma State University; Lynn Romeo, Monmouth University; Donna H. Topping, Millersville University; and April Whatley, University of New Orleans. The suggestions were very helpful. We tried to incorporate them all. Unfortunately, we could not find a way to incorporate the changes of one reviewer who suggested many additions, a larger font size, and finished with the clear admonition, "Whatever you do, don't increase the length of the book!"

Classrooms That Work

CHAPTER 1

Reading and Writing Real "Things"

Walk into a classroom where all the children are destined to succeed in learning to read and write and what do you see? There will be lots of books and other reading materials, along with evidence that the teacher and the children read and write (Allington, 2001; Pressley, et al., 2001). Stay in that classroom as the children enter and the day begins and ask yourself, "How much time will the teacher and the children spend reading and writing real things?" Notice that the teacher reads a variety of real things to the children at different points in the day—not just a story after lunch. The teacher may begin the day by showing a cartoon from yesterday's paper or by reading an account of a local football game that many of the students attended. A math lesson may even begin with the teacher reading an advertisement from the newspaper and asking the students, "How much would you really be saving by buying now?"

As the day goes on, several books or parts of books are read or referred to. Some weather poems are read as a springboard into a science unit on weather. Pictures and captions from an art book or magazine are shared as students begin an art lesson. After lunch, the teacher reads from the chapter book currently being read to the class. As the social studies lesson begins, children are reminded of a chapter book that was read aloud earlier in the year and that was set in the historical era about to be studied. Later in the day, after self-selected reading time, the teacher selects several children to share the books they are currently reading. The children simply introduce the book, comment on it and on why they selected it (often, it was recommended by a friend). Each response is brief and is focused on the reader's opinion of the book.

Also notice that the teacher and the children write. The morning begins with the teacher writing a "morning message" on the board. The children watch eagerly to see what interesting event might be planned for the day. Notice also that the walls of the room are literally covered with print. Children's writing is displayed along with posters, maps, time lines, newspaper clippings, and other written material. The teacher creates a bulletin board on which the children may display some of their ideas. Each child has a mailbox into which the teacher or other children may put messages.

Now focus on the children. Observe the real things that they read and write. During self-selected reading, everyone reads. During writing time, everyone writes. Notice the other things that children read and write. Notice how some children pick up the newspaper from which the teacher has read and read a different part of it. Also notice how the children work with a partner using encyclopedias and other information sources to find the answers to some "weather expert" questions. Observe the references children make to books they have read when various topics come up. Note that writing takes many forms. Children may come up with some "weather expert" questions to try to stump their classmates, or may compose book reviews and responses to books. They may create summaries of science and social studies materials and caption artwork. Some composing activities are brief "quickwrites" just to jot down what they already know before they read about a topic or about what they would really like to learn. Children create their own chapter books during a 3- or 4-week period. In creating these, they write, revise, edit, and publish.

Children who are successful at becoming literate view reading and writing as authentic activities from which they get information and pleasure, and by which they communicate with others. They know what reading and writing are really for and they want to be successful at it. The literacy-rich classroom communicates the importance of real reading and writing activities by engaging children in a variety of print activities and not relegating reading and writing to a brief period. The teachers know that it is important to take the time to read to children each day. They know it is important to have a time each day in which children read materials that they have selected for themselves. In addition to self-selected reading, the teachers know it is critical that they schedule time each week to engage the children in reading lessons that teach essential reading strategies. The teachers know that writing takes time, so they schedule blocks of time for children to write. They know that sharing reading is important, so they set aside time to allow children to share their books and writing with each other. In short, these teachers know that if no time is scheduled in the school day for real reading and writing, children get the powerful message that reading and writing have no value. The first and most basic component of classroom instruction is offering children a variety of real reading and writing encounters.

This principle is so logical and makes so much common sense that it is often overlooked in planning instruction. In many classrooms students engage in little reading of real things and have even fewer opportunities to write real things. Oddly, this problem seems to increase as children advance through the grades! Why is it that second-grade teachers typically have students spend more time reading and writing than sixth-grade teachers do? The older students are able to read a wider array of texts and able to write in a greater variety of genres, but, often, older students are given fewer opportunities to read and write than younger students. It is just as important that fifth and sixth graders have lots of opportunities to read and write real things during the school day as it is for first and second graders. In this vein, another oddity is that schools with higher-achieving students usually schedule more opportunities for real reading and writing than schools with many lower-achieving students! All students need these daily opportunities to engage in real reading and writing, regardless of grade level or achievement level.

But not all students have equal access to books in and out of school, and limited access to engaging, appropriate books limits real reading opportunity. Children who attend school in wealthier communities have more books in their classrooms and their school libraries than do children from less-advantaged communities. Children from economically more advantaged families have larger numbers of books available in both their homes and their classrooms (Smith, Constantino, & Krashen, 1997). Some children come from homes in which books, magazines, newspapers, paper, pencils, pens, markers, typewriters, and computers abound—homes where bedroom libraries of 100 books are common and where parents and older siblings read and write regularly. Such homes provide children with models of authentic reading and writing experience, materials to read and write with, and time during which reading and writing are the expected activities. These experiences and resources seem to account for some of the achievement advantage so often reported for more advantaged students. Although we would love to wave a magic wand and magically transform the homes of all children into literacy-rich environments, this is not within our power. What is within our power is the ability to create literacy-rich environments within our classrooms. In the remainder of this chapter, specific suggestions are made for providing models, materials, and motivation at various grade levels.

MODELS, MATERIALS, AND MOTIVATION IN KINDERGARTEN AND FIRST GRADE

Kindergartens have undergone dramatic changes in the last decade, and the debate concerning the socialization/play kindergarten versus the academic kindergarten continues. We would like to suggest a third and different role for kindergarten. We would like kindergartens to simulate what happens in the homes of children in which books and writing tools have been a part of childhood from birth. Children from such homes spend more than 1,000 hours actively engaged in some kind of reading and writing before they come to school—more hours than most children spend in kindergarten! We cannot (and do not want to) spend all our hours reading and writing, but we must provide as much "quality" time as possible.

A Peek into Literate Homes

Before describing our kindergarten, imagine the home environment that we are trying to simulate. If we visited the home of one of the lucky children who have had all those reading and writing encounters, what would we see? What kind of encounters would they be?

The first thing we would probably notice is reading material. The child's bedroom would probably have shelves housing 30–50 books (or more). Among these books would be certain favorites that the child would insist on having read over and over until the parent (or older brother, sister, grandparent) could not stand to read again! We would observe the bedtime story ritual—a parent reading books aloud after the child is tucked in. During this reading, the parent would ask questions about the pictures ("Can you find the mouse now?"), comment on words and phrases ("Listen, these two words rhyme"), and cue predictions and responses ("What is he going to do now?" "How do you think she feels?"). The parent may read three or four books each night before turning out the light. If we peeked into that bedroom when the lights were supposed to be out, we might see the child "reading" one of those often-read books to a stuffed animal! We put the word *reading* in quotes because, in reality, the child knows what to say on each page and has memorized some repetitive parts of the book. Pretend reading of a familiar book is one of the most common occurrences for children who have had the luxury of books and a captive adult reader.

In addition to the bookshelf of "owned" books, we would probably also see a stack of four or five library books. Weekly or biweekly trips to the library to pick out some great new books would be scheduled along with gymnastics lessons and soccer practice. While at the library, the adult who took the child might also pick up some books for pleasure reading along with some functional books, such as *How to Compost, Paying for College,* and *Getting Your Child Ready for Kindergarten.*

In addition to a permanent bedroom library and a changing collection from the lending library, many other less obvious sources of reading materials impact the lives of 3- and 4-year-olds. The newspaper is present, and even though the child does not read it, someone may read the comics to her or him. In addition, children see adults reading the newspaper and hear them discussing what they read. "Can you believe they finally caught the guy who broke into the Donahues' house?" "I think we should go car shopping this weekend. The dealers are outdoing themselves with rebates and financing that can't last forever."

Other materials are read, too. Various family members check on their favorite programs in a TV guide. Bills and announcements come in the mail and people react and often read information from them aloud. Birthday cards, letters from Granny, and postcards from friends are sifted out from the junk mail, read, and taped to the refrigerator. Magnetic letters stick to the refrigerator and spell out an older brother's name.

Mealtimes and trips to the grocery store become literacy events as the child's attention is drawn to the barrage of words available. The child observes that the cook is reading a recipe or directions on the back of a package. An older brother reads the back of the cereal box. The adult shopper reads the ingredients and refuses to buy the cereal because it is all sugar! Trips to and from the grocery store become opportunities to read as well. Signs are read along the way and many 4-year-olds begin their journeys into reading by recognizing words such as *Kmart, McDonald's,* and *Pizza Hut.* In many of these homes, children have access to computers and educational software, including games.

So far, we have been focusing on the omnipresence of reading material, models, and opportunities in the day-to-day life of a preschool child from a literate environment. If we look closely, we also see writing material. We see paper—lined and unlined—and we see young children experimenting with a combination that we call *driting* (drawing and writing). They do this in their own inimitable 4-year-old fashion and what they write is decipherable only to them. They know what they have written and then ask some poor adult to read it! (The savvy adult says, "That's wonderful! I don't have my glasses. Why don't you read it to me!") In other cases, an adult provides the caption for an illustration or simply prints the child's name on the artwork.

They write with real pencils that have erasers on the ends (not those awful fat ones with no erasers which, for no good reason but tradition, they are subjected to once they arrive at school!), with pens, markers, crayons, and chalk. They write on paper, index cards, checks, envelopes, chalkboards, and (alas) walls! They write the things they have seen others write—thank-you notes, shopping lists, directions, letters, and memos! Their writing is posted around the home (with the refrigerator doing especially heavy duty here). Parents also mail the writing to Grandma and Grandpa who inevitably write back. The children write not just for themselves but for others too. The writing is shared with adults who offer supportive advice about writing when asked.

Take an imaginary journey into the life of a lucky preschooler and you will be overwhelmed by how many reading and writing encounters these young children have. From these encounters, they develop four critical understandings:

1. They know that ideas and words can be written down.
2. They know that when you read or write you are trying to understand or communicate a story or some information.
3. They know that reading and writing are two important things that bigger people do, and because they want to be big too, they must learn.
4. They know from overwhelming adult pleasure and approval of them making fledgling attempts at pretend reading, of them reading some signs and labels, and of them writing that they are succeeding at mastering this mysterious code.

When children come to the classroom with an understanding of what reading and writing are, with a strong desire to do them, and with a history of successful beginning attempts, it is no surprise that we can teach almost all of them to read and write. Our literate home simulation kindergartens must provide reading and writing encounters in which all children can develop these four critical concepts.

Building Blocks Kindergartens

We call kindergartens that provide children with the literacy experiences that take place in literate homes *Building Blocks kindergartens*. In Building Blocks kindergartens, you find a substantial classroom library, a comfortable reading area, and a special place for the books that the children and teacher have checked out from school or the public library. Newspapers and magazines are present, and perhaps a bulletin board is available on which cartoons, pictures, advertisements, announcements, or something else of interest to kindergartners can be posted daily. Both the teacher and the children bring in interesting items to add to this board.

On charts, language experience stories, favorite poems, and finger plays are recorded. Class books with fascinating titles, such as *The Favorite Foods of Ms. J.'s Big Eaters* and *Room 112 Goes to the Zoo,* record with photos, drawings, and short sentences the preferences and adventures of this kindergarten class. Cereal boxes and other packages are part of the home and grocery center. Traffic signs also are part of the block's center.

In addition to a multitude of reading materials, our literate home simulation kindergarten has lots of writing implements. Paper and pencils (with erasers) are always available. Each week some unique writing materials (colored pencils, markers, chalk, finger paint, chocolate pudding, purple stationery, free hotel post-cards, wallpaper samples, etc.) also are featured that everyone wants to use and that are in the classroom for a "limited engagement." There are also individual chalkboards and magic slates as well as a couple of old typewriters. (Many people have one to give away as we all switch to computers!) The big chalkboard in the classroom is divided into thirds, and three children each day may role-play teacher and write on the real chalkboard.

Once the materials for reading and writing are available for children to use, we must turn our attention to the models of reading and writing. Of course, the teacher reads—and not just a book after lunch. The teacher reads many types of materials—something from the newspaper (to be added to the newspaper board), the lunch menu, a simple recipe from a cookbook, a counting book as math begins, a rain poem as it begins to rain, and so on.

Often the teacher draws the children into a story circle to read to them and bring them up close to see the book, the artwork, and the print. This is especially necessary when reading from a regular-sized book, but even when reading from big books, proximity matters. The teacher knows that although the story is important and enjoyment is critical, for many children the proximity to the actual text is also critical. This proximity allows the children to see the words as they are read and to notice how the teacher moves from left to right and from top to bottom as the book is read. In addition, the teacher often comments on the artwork, the words, the rhymes, and the language as she reads the big books aloud. The teacher's talk sounds much like the bedtime story talk that is found in the homes of the lucky children.

The teacher also writes down many things, such as adding those foods to the class foods book that the children tell her they like best, a list of questions the children want to ask the police captain so they don't forget anything, or a note to the child's parent explaining how the child skinned her knee. The teacher writes on the chalkboard and on chart paper. She writes while the children watch her turn their spoken words or her spoken words into print. She may even use a magnetic letterboard (reminiscent of those letters on the refrigerators in some homes) to illustrate words, spellings, and how the words are put together. Most of all, the teacher talks about her own writing as she writes. She explains what she is writing and how and why she is writing it.

In addition to teacher models of real reading and writing, children need to see that other "big people" read and write. Some savvy teachers get guest readers to come in and read something to the children. Some young children actually express amazement when they discover that the custodian, the lunchroom manager, or the secretary can read. If the police captain is coming to talk about safety, he or she might be flattered if asked to read one of his or her favorite books from childhood.

One model available in all schools is the "big kids." Many schools have "buddy" programs in which each fourth or fifth grader is paired with a kindergarten child. Once a week, big buddies come to the kindergarten and read a book (which they have practiced ahead of time) to their little buddy. Big buddies can also write a short note to their little buddy or record something their little buddy dictates to them. Sometimes these reading sessions are followed by playground or gym time in which the big kids teach a physical skill to the little kids. Schools that have put these buddy systems in place report that they do as much for the self-esteem of the big kids as they do for the literacy development of the little kids.

Finally, time must be scheduled in each kindergarten day for reading and writing. One kindergarten teacher asks the children to get a large piece of drawing paper as they walk in the door: "Draw and write about something you want to tell us this morning" is the standard way every day begins. Children are encouraged to draw and write (drite) in whatever way they can. No words are spelled for them and no corrections are made. The morning then begins with the children sitting in a circle. Each child shows what she or he has dritten and tells the others about it. Because kindergartners always come in the door with something they want to talk about, they are highly motivated to draw and write something each day.

The kindergarten teachers schedule time each day to read to the children and let the children read to themselves or to each other. After reading several books to the children—including rereading some constantly requested favorites—they then help the children select a book to read. When this procedure is followed from the first day of school, kindergartners do not usually object or protest that they cannot read. If they do, teachers simply tell them, "Tell the story as you remember it from the pictures" or, "Pretend that you are the teacher and you are reading the book." Children who want to read with a friend are allowed to, as long as they use quiet voices. Kindergarten children are also very motivated to read if they are allowed to pick a stuffed animal or a doll to read to!

In addition to the daily writing or reading time that is scheduled, a print-rich kindergarten classroom provides many opportunities for children to read and write throughout the day. They provide children opportunities to learn the letters of the alphabet and how words are written and read. Our literate home simulation

RECOMMENDED RESOURCES ——

You can read lots more about Building Blocks kindergartens in *The Teacher's Guide to Building Blocks* (Hall & Williams, 2000) and *Month-by-Month Reading and Writing for Kindergarten* (Hall & Cunningham, 1997).

kindergartens are not just for play and socialization. Neither are they "watered-down" first grades. Rather, they try to simulate natural reading and writing activities that occur in the homes of more fortunate preschoolers, and that are critical to success in beginning reading and writing, while providing the kinds of instructional support that these lucky children receive at home. Observations made in the homes of children who come to school ready for reading and writing instruction reveal that these children have materials to read and write with, have other people in the home who read and write, and have others who offer support as their reading and writing develop. Literate home simulation kindergartens provide this foundation for all children and help to narrow the gap between the children who arrive with the least- and the most-advantaged backgrounds.

First-Grade Classrooms

If you are a first-grade teacher whose children have arrived at school from a literate home simulation kindergarten, you will notice that the children all value reading and writing and see themselves as readers and writers. Not all first-grade teachers are so fortunate, however. Many first graders lack the understandings developed through a literate home environment or a literate home simulation kindergarten. These unlucky children do not have a clear sense of what reading and writing are for. They have not gone through the pretend reading and driting stages that develop an "of course I can" attitude. They have not had lots of "bigger people" models to convince them that a person has to learn reading and writing if he or she wants to be big. They have not had the kind of support that helps children acquire an understanding of just how our alphabetic writing system works. What do first-grade teachers do when faced with this problem?

First, they blame the parents; then they blame the kindergarten teachers; finally, they decide that if the problem has not been addressed already, they will have to address it! Once again, real reading and writing materials must be available. Models of bigger people reading—the teacher, other adults, and big kids—must be provided along with rich, supportive instruction that occurs throughout the day. Time for self-selected reading and writing must be part of the daily schedule.

Providing the materials, models, and the time in first grade, however, is sometimes easier said than done. Unlike kindergarten teachers, almost all first-grade teachers work under the constraints of a standard curriculum with goals and objectives. Often certain skills must be checked off, books covered, and tests taken. First-grade teachers realize the need for developing the foundations described in the kindergarten section but sometimes feel that they just can't afford the time to do it. The truth is that when children come to you without the critical understandings, you cannot afford to not take the time needed to develop them. Lacking clear knowledge of what reading and writing are for, and lacking a firm desire to learn how to do them, most of these children fail. Once determined to provide materials, models, and time, most first-grade teachers discover that adding the "real" reading and writing component is worth the effort. The universal excitement and enthusiasm of first graders renders them eager readers and willing writers, if the teacher accepts their pretend reading and driting as valid beginning points.

Children still love to role-play teacher and read to each other or to a stuffed animal. They love to have reading parties on Friday afternoons when they meet in groups of four or five and each child gets to read or tell about a few favorite pages of a book. If you have a mixed class in which some children are reading early in first grade, you can pair these readers with your fledgling readers and let them choose a book to read together. First graders have not yet developed self-consciousness about not being able to read, and they gladly accept the teaching of a more proficient child just as they accept another child's instruction in a new game or song.

When writing is coupled with drawing and a show-and-tell sharing session, all first graders can write! When children are at the early scribbling and driting stages, no emphasis should be placed on spelling or handwriting. Children become able to cope with handwriting/spelling/revising demands when they have figured out what writing is and when they have developed some control and proficiency. Think about how you would respond to the first writing efforts of your first graders by imagining how you would respond if your 4-year-old niece proudly presented you with a paper, saying "Look what I wrote!" You would probably try to decipher which direction was "up" and respond, "Wonderful. Why don't you read it to me!" Regardless of age, children who are going to become writers must go through scribbling/driting stages. If they have not done this before first grade, we must allow and encourage their efforts when they get there.

MODELS, MATERIALS, AND MOTIVATION
IN SECOND AND THIRD GRADES

If children come to second or third grade and have not been successful in learning to read and write, the task of getting them to engage in real reading and writing becomes more difficult. By second or third grade, good readers are reading 10 times as many words each day as poor readers (Allington, 1983). Many teachers of struggling readers acknowledge that children who read nothing but the few pages they are forced to read during a reading group, and who write almost nothing but one-word or one-sentence responses to questions, will never become truly literate. Children who come to second and third grade with a history of failure behind them have lost their "I can do anything" attitude to reading and writing and begin to develop avoidance behaviors and the "reading and writing are stupid" attitude. This attitude can be overcome, however, if the second- or third-grade teacher makes a commitment to models, materials, and time.

Reading to Children

When children come to second or third grade with negative attitudes toward reading, the teacher must make more of an effort to show the children that reading is a source of pleasure and information and that writing is another mode of communication. Four types of material should be read to children every day. The first type is something informational. Informational material can come from newspapers, magazines, encyclopedias, *The World Almanac, The Guinness Book of World Records,* or nonfiction books. Ideally, the teacher would find an opportunity to read from all these sources of information over a month's time. This reading often takes place at different times of the day as it fits in with something else that the teacher is doing. Regardless of when the teacher reads this information to the children, the attitude for the teacher to model is one of wonderment:

"Isn't this fascinating!"

"Imagine how frightened these people must have been!"

"Imagine a whale that would fill this whole room!"

"I was reading this magazine last night and I just couldn't wait to get here this morning and share it with you!"

These informational reading encounters do not have to take very long. In fact, they can lose their effectiveness if they become long, tedious lessons. They should, however, take place frequently—at least once a day—and the source from which the teacher reads should be made available for children to read once their appetites are whetted. During the school year, the children would hear the teacher use a variety of words and show/read a variety of informational tidbits, all conveying the message, "I read because there are fascinating things to find out."

RECOMMENDED RESOURCES

Magazines for Children

Classrooms should have magazines as well as books available for children (see *Magazines for Kids and Teens* by Donald Stoll, available from the International Reading Association for magazine reviews and ordering information). Four wonderful informational magazines for second and third grade are

Ranger Rick, National Wildlife Federation

3-2-1 Contact, Children's Television Workshop

Kid City, Children's Television Workshop

Chickadee, Owl Communications Group

The second type of material that should be read each day is traditional second- and third-grade favorites. Some books are just part of being 7 or 8 years old and should not be missed by any child. Some of these books use sophisticated language and are a little hard for second and third graders to read themselves, but all children can enjoy listening to them. Teachers should not neglect to include easier books in their read-alouds as well. The reading of these books—often a chapter or two each day—should take place at a regular time so that children can look forward to daily escape into literary worlds (much the same way that adult readers read a chapter or two of some escape fiction before turning out the light each night).

 RECOMMENDED RESOURCES

Most-Loved Second- and Third-Grade Read-Aloud Books

It is impossible to list all the best read-aloud books but here are a few to get you started.

Alexander and the Terrible, Horrible, No Good, Very Bad Day, Judith Viorst

Amelia Bedelia, Peggy Parrish

Aunt Flossie's Hats, Patricia Fitzgerald Howard

Back Home, Gloria Jean Pinkney

Charlotte's Web, E. B. White

Chicken Socks, Brod Bogert

Eruption! The Story of Volcanoes, Anita Ganeri

Finding Providence: The Story of Roger Williams, Avi

Flossie and the Fox, Patricia McKissack

In the Tall, Tall Grass, Denise Fleming

James and the Giant Peach, Roald Dahl

Julian's Glorious Summer, Anne Cameron

Knots on a Counting Rope, Bill Martin and John Archambault

Miss Nelson Is Missing, Harry Allard

Momo's Kitten, Taro Yashima and Mitsu

Nate the Great, Marjorie Sharmat

Owl Moon, Jane Yolen

Tell Me a Story, Mama, Angela Johnson

The Beast in Mrs. Rooney's Room, Pat Reilly Giff

The Polar Express, Chris Van Allsburg

Spiders, Gail Gibbons

The preceding list contains some books that feature children of various ethnic backgrounds as main characters. There is a treasure trove of good multicultural children's literature. The best source for finding these books is Violet Harris's *Using Multiethnic Literature in the K–8 Classroom* (1997). Specific chapters are devoted to detailing the history, well-known authors, and recommended books of African American, Asian Pacific American, Native American, Puerto Rican American, Mexican American, and Caribbean children's literature.

Poetry is the third daily must! The poetry available to children today is wonderful and varied. Much of it is funny, and the language, rhyme, and rhythm are delightful. Keep a poetry book handy and read one or two poems to the children when you have a few empty minutes. When appropriate, reread the poem and have the children chime in on the rhyme or refrain. For the poems that really interest your children, write them on a piece of chart paper and let the children read them with you when you have time. In almost every culture, childhood is a time for chants and songs. Poetry appeals to children's affinity for rhyme and rhythm.

Some children who don't care about information and who are bored by stories find poetry to be a real reason for reading.

Finally, many struggling readers have not experienced the pleasure of reading at home or in first and second grade. This is one good reason that a time should be set aside each day for the teacher to read some "easy books" to the children and a time for the children to read easy books themselves. To help you understand the need for this activity and to commit yourself to this goal, imagine yourself peeking into the room of a fortunate second or third grader as she or he is going to bed. Even though the child is now a reader, an adult probably reads aloud a chapter or two of a book that is a little beyond the child's level. The child is then allowed to read to himself or herself for 15 minutes before turning out the lights. The child may read a recently acquired book but is also likely to pick up from the shelf an old favorite, such as *Are You My Mother?*, *Goldilocks and the Three Bears*, or *Caps for Sale*, and read it just for fun! A large classroom supply of easy books is absolutely critical though, if we want second and third graders who are experiencing difficulty to pick up books and read.

Classrooms that can turn reluctant second and third graders into readers are classrooms in which many and varied materials to read are accessible. A few of these materials—most importantly the easy-to-read books—are permanent fixtures in the classroom. Other materials—newspapers, magazines, informational books, chapter books, poetry books, and so forth—come and go as teachers and children bring them in and return them. Teachers read both whole books and lots of little snippets of things to children. From the wealth and variety of materials as well as the teacher modeling the pleasure and information to be gained, children develop (or redevelop, if they have tried and failed) the desire to learn to read.

Children should be encouraged to reread books they enjoy several times. (Our best readers who learn to read easily often reread books until they have virtually memorized them!) The teacher can model this by rereading favorite books to the class, particularly books with wonderful descriptions, powerful words, or repetitive phrases. During guided reading, teachers can engage children in repeated readings. Echo and choral reading of plays, poetry, and stories with refrains are enjoyable activities that lead to fluent reading. Fluent readng is reading that "feels easy and effortless." Struggling readers seldom experience what fluent reading feels like. Repeated reading of familiar text allows struggling readers to experience the joy of effortless reading.

Self-Selected Reading

Once the models and materials are in place, children must be allowed time to spend in self-selected reading. All second and third graders should spend at least 20 minutes each day engaged in reading materials they have chosen to

RECOMMENDED RESOURCES ——

You can find lots more practical suggestions for self-selected reading at all grade levels in *Self-Selected Reading the Four Blocks Way* (Cunningham, Hall, & Gambrell, 2002).

read. This time should not include the time spent looking for a book. In fact, some teachers have children choose several pieces of reading material before the time begins and do not allow children to get up and change material until the time ends. In other classrooms, a crate of books is placed on each table and the children choose from that crate. The book crates rotate from table to table so that all the children have access to lots of different books within arm's length.

When setting up the self-selected reading time, most teachers circulate around the room and have whispered conversations with individual children about their books. Once the self-selected reading time is well established, teachers often schedule conferences with one-fifth of their children each day. They use this time to monitor each child's reading, to encourage them in their individual reading interests, and to help children with book selection if they need that help.

Although at least 20 minutes daily for self-selected reading is the goal, most teachers start with a shorter period of time and increase the time gradually as children establish the reading habit and learn to look forward to this daily "read what you want to" time. Some teachers use a timer to signal the beginning and end of the self-selected reading time. (A timer also keeps the teacher from shrinking the time to 5–10 minutes of reading when the teacher is behind and "the tests"

RECOMMENDED RESOURCES ——————

Favorite Series Books

Series books, such as those listed below, are wonderful materials for use with struggling readers. Series books are easier than a variety of books because the reader builds up a store of information about the characters and the author's style that make the books predictable. Kids often devour series books—not just because they are easier, but because they like them!

Norman Bridwell's Clifford, the Big Red Dog series

H. A. Rey's Curious George books

Mercer Mayer's Little Critters

Pat Reilly Giff's Polk Street School Kids

Judy Delton's Pee Wee Scouts

Else Minarik's Little Bear books

Cynthia Rylant's Henry and Mudge books

James Marshall's George and Martha books

Marc Brown's Arthur books

Barbara Park's Junie B. Jones books

Mary Pope Osborne's Magic Tree series

Dave Pikey's Adventures of Captain Underpants

David Adler's Cam Jansen mysteries

Louis Sacher's Marvin Redpost books

are to be given in a few days!) When we engage regularly in activities, we establish natural time rhythms. Using a timer to monitor the self-selected reading time helps children establish these rhythms. When the timer sounds at the end of the session, the teacher should probably say something like, "Take another minute if you need to get to a stopping point."

Some teachers take a few minutes after self-selected reading to let children share something they have read. Other teachers schedule a weekly time to have the children share comments in small groups. Many classrooms have TGIF celebrations late Friday afternoon, which include having some goodies to munch on and time for everyone to read or tell about the best thing they read all week. Teachers find out that the time invested in this weekly activity is more than paid back as they observe children reading what certain children had raved about the Friday before. (Many teachers invite parents to these celebrations and the parents come because their children all have starring roles!)

Self-Selected Writing

Getting second and third graders to write is sometimes easier than getting them to read. In fact, observational data suggest that children do more writing in second grade than at any other grade level. Most second and third graders have developed some ability to spell and write, and they have lots of things they want to write about. Teachers at the second- and third-grade level are usually willing to accept whatever writing children are able to produce and focus on their ideas rather than on their mechanics. Many teachers find that it helps for each child to have a writing notebook—preferably spiral bound and reserved exclusively for writing. Providing time each day for children to write about "anything they choose," accepting and encouraging their beginning efforts, and providing some time for children to read what they have written are usually all the motivation that children need. One of the biggest problems faced by teachers whose classrooms are involved with writing something daily is that everyone wants to read what they have written; there is seldom time for this to happen. One teacher solved this problem by designating a fifth of the class as Monday children, a fifth as Tuesday children, and so on. (The teacher was a Wednesday person, so she read something she had written every Wednesday.) Just before lunch every day, the children whose day it was would get to sit in the "author's chair" and read something they had written or that they were in the process of writing. Other children commented on what they liked or on questions they had. This sharing only took a few minutes each day, but it motivated the children to write and assured that everyone got a fair chance to be in the spotlight.

Even though some children come to second and third grade without having experienced the pleasures of reading and writing, almost all of them can still be lured into literacy. They enjoy stories—listening to them, telling them, reading them, and writing them. Their early childhood curiosity is still intact and they want to know how things work and what really happens. They are fascinated by all there is to know about this vast world that we live in. Teachers who make the effort to provide models, materials, and time for daily self-selected reading and writing are usually rewarded by seeing all their children become readers and writers.

MODELS, MATERIALS, AND MOTIVATION IN FOURTH, FIFTH, AND SIXTH GRADES

If you have children who have been reading and writing for years and are successful at these activities, the intermediate grades will be the "reaping" years. You reap the rewards of the seeds sown in all those previous years. Your children know that books are sources of pleasure and information and they are developing some control and fluency in their writing. If you make time and materials available and continue to model positive attitudes, you can turn them loose on many student-initiated reading and writing projects. If, however, your children come to you with poor reading and writing abilities and even worse reading and writing attitudes, these will not be the reaping years, but rather, the "weeping" years.

The greatest difference in the instructional program provided for good and poor readers becomes evident in grades 4, 5, and 6. Children who are successful at these grade levels spend more and more time engaged in real reading and writing. On the other hand, children who have been unsuccessful with reading for many years will be discouraged, so we should not be too surprised when they spend almost no time engaged in reading activities either in or out of school (and often their science and social studies books are simply too difficult for them).

The difficult challenge faced by the intermediate teacher of struggling readers is not only to develop positive attitudes toward reading and writing, but also to transform the negative and often hostile attitudes these children bring along with them. This is not an easy task and can require a great deal of determination and stamina. Even with a concerted effort, the attitudes of all children may not be turned around. But many will be! The knowledge that some children—even after 4 or 5 years of failure—can become readers and writers is what must fuel your fire of determination.

In this section, we are going to envision a class with a lot of resistant readers and writers. They aren't good at it, don't do it except when forced, and don't want to do it because they think it is "sissy, dumb, and stupid!" (If this does not describe your struggling readers, count your blessings and go on to the next chapter!) Just as in earlier grades, models, materials, and time are the keys to success. All three need different twists, however, if they are to succeed with intermediate-aged children who have a history of failure.

Reading to Older Children

The teacher as a reading and writing model is even more critical at these grades than at the lower grade levels. Intermediate teachers must continue the practice of reading chapter books aloud to the class, and books must be chosen with the highest possible appeal for children of this age.

RECOMMENDED RESOURCES

Teacher Read-Aloud Books for Older Readers

Across Five Aprils, Irene Hunt

Anastasia Krupnik, Lois Lowry

Bridge to Terabithia, Katherine Paterson

Class Clown, Johanna Hurwitz

Dear Mr. Henshaw, Beverly Cleary

Dinosaur Detectives, Peter Chrisp

Dogsong, Gary Paterson

Faithful Elephants, Yukio Tsuchiya

Fast Sam, Cool Clyde and Stuff, Walter Dean Myers

Favorite Greek Myths, Mary Pope Osborne

Going Home, Nicholasa Mohr

Maniac Magee, Jerry Spinelli

Mississippi Bridge, Mildred Taylor

Pearl Harbor! Wallace B. Black and Jean F. Blashfield

Rosa Parks: My Story, Rosa Parks (with James Haskins)

Ruby the Copycat, Peggy Rathmann

Sarah, Plain and Tall, Patricia MacLachlan

Sign of the Beaver, Elizabeth Speare

Stone Fox, John Gardiner

Streams to the River, Return to the Sea, Scott O'Dell

Tales of a Fourth Grade Nothing, Judy Blume

The Black Stallion, Walter Farley

The Indian in the Cupboard, Lynn Reid Banks

The Lion, the Witch and the Wardrobe, C. S. Lewis

The Little Prince, Antoine Saint-Exupery

Zeely, Virginia Hamilton

Teachers must make an extra effort to bring real-world reading materials, such as newspapers and magazines, into the classroom, and to read tidbits from these with an "I was reading this last night and I just couldn't wait to get here and share it with you" attitude. The savvy teacher also keeps a book of poetry handy and reads one or two poems whenever appropriate. No intermediate-aged student can resist the appeal of Jack Prelutsky's or Judith Viorst's poems. In addition to poetry, you need your own personal copy of *The Guinness Book of World Records* and a collection of joke and riddle books.

Imagine that you are reading daily from a "grabber" chapter book and that four or five times throughout the day, you read a short article from a newspaper, magazine, or informational book, or share a little poem, joke, riddle, or phenomenal fact with your students. Multiply those five or six reading encounters times 180 school days and you have demonstrated more than 1,000 times, for your resistant readers, that reading is a source of information, pleasure, humor, and wonderment!

Even with the saturation suggested above, the teacher as model may not be enough to convince some intermediate-aged students of the value and benefit of reading. It is still true that most elementary teachers are women and that most struggling readers are boys. A lot of struggling readers believe that "real men" do not read books! Many schools have reported an increased motivation to read when they were able to find real men to read books to their classes. Finding these men

Here are just a few of the many easy-to-read joke, riddle, and "do something" books that even intermediate-aged resistant readers cannot resist!

and getting them to come to school regularly is not easy, but if you are on the look-out for them, they can often be found. Service organizations such as the JAYCEES and Big Brother groups are places to begin your search. City workers, including policemen and firemen, may be willing to help. Would the person who delivers something to your school each week be flattered to be asked to come and read to your class? If you have some construction being done in your neighborhood, the construction company may feel that it is good PR to allow its workers to volunteer to come into your classroom for a half hour each week and read to your class.

Big Reader Buddies

In the kindergarten section of this chapter, we suggested "buddy" programs in which big kids are paired with kindergarten children. Once a week, the big buddies come to the kindergarten and read a book (which they have practiced ahead of time) to their little buddy. Arranging such a partnership allows your older struggling readers to become reading models. The buddy system also serves another critical function in that it legitimizes the reading and rereading of very easy books. Once you have a buddy system set up, you can have the kindergarten teacher send up a basket of books from which each of your "big readers" can choose. Tell them that "professional" readers always practice reading a book several times before reading it to an audience. Then, let them practice reading the book—first to themselves, then to a partner in the classroom, and finally to a tape recorder.

FOOTBALL PLAYERS AS READING MODELS

Cindy Visser, a reading specialist in Washington, reports how her school formed a partnership with the local high school football team (1991). Football players volunteered to come once a month and read to elementary classes. Appropriate read-aloud books were chosen by the elementary teachers and sent to the high school ahead of time. Interested athletes chose a book and took it home to "polish their delivery." Then, on the last Friday of the month, the athletes donned their football jerseys and rode the team bus to the elementary school. The arrival of the bus was greeted by cheering elementary students, and the players were escorted to their classes where they read to the children and answered questions about reading, life, and, of course, the big game. This partnership, which was initiated by an elementary school in search of male reading models, turned out to be as profitable for the athletes as it was for the elementary students. The coach reported a waiting list of athletes who wanted to participate and a boost in the self-esteem of the ones who did.

Repeated readings of easy material has long been demonstrated to improve the reading ability of poor readers. Finding easy material that appeals to big kids is very difficult, however. Convincing poor readers to read "baby books" over and over is, under normal circumstances, almost impossible. By setting up a buddy–reader partnership with a kindergarten teacher, you solve the problem of finding easy books by borrowing them from the kindergarten or the library. Once you have a "big reader" program set up, you have transformed the act of reading and rereading simple books into a purposeful, self-esteem-building activity.

Materials

In addition to newspapers, magazines, poetry, joke and riddle books, and the easy books your students are preparing to read to their buddies, you might try to add other relatively easy but appealing materials to your classroom collection. The best list currently available can be found in Marianne Lanino Pilla's *The Best High/Low Books for Reluctant Readers* (1990). In this book, she describes 374 books that she has found to be accessible and appealing to reluctant readers. Of course, new books are being published at a phenomenal rate, so you should constantly be on the lookout for books that appeal to your children.

Collecting appealing books that are easy for reluctant preteens requires determination, cleverness, and an eye for bargains. In addition to obvious sources, such as getting free books from book clubs when your students order books, asking parents to donate, begging for books from your friends and relatives whose children have outgrown them, and haunting yard sales and thrift shops, less obvious sources exist as well. Libraries often sell or donate used books and magazines on a regular basis. Some bookstores will give you a good deal on closeouts and may even set up a donation basket in which they will collect used books for you. (Take some pictures of your eager readers and have your children write letters

RECOMMENDED RESOURCES

Books Even Struggling Readers Cannot Resist!

There are so few books "just" right for reluctant upper-elementary-grade readers that we have to mention a couple of our favorites.

How to Eat Fried Worms, Thomas Rockwell

My Teacher Is an Alien, Bruce Coville

The Chewing Gum Book, Robert Young

Beetles Lightly Toasted, Phyllis R. Naylor

telling what kind of books they like to read for the store to display above the donation basket.) In some schools, collections of the high/low books are stored in the remedial reading room and can be borrowed on a rotating basis for use in the classroom.

Self-Selected Reading

Now that you have models and materials, you must make sure that each child has time every day to engage in self-selected reading. Teachers provide this time by setting aside at least 20–30 minutes each day for reading. If this independent reading time is new to your students, you might give them a little pep talk so that they realize the importance of the time they spend reading.

Use an analogy to help your children understand that becoming good at reading is just like becoming good at anything else. Compare learning to read with learning to play the piano, tennis, or baseball. Explain that to become good at anything, a person needs three things: (1) instruction, (2) practice on the skills, and (3) practice on the whole thing. To become a good tennis player, a person needs to (1) take tennis lessons, (2) practice the skills (backhand, serve, etc.), and (3) play tennis. To become a good reader, a person also needs instruction, needs to practice the important skills, and needs to read! Point out that sometimes we get so busy that we may forget to take the important time each day to read and, therefore, we must schedule it just like anything else we do. (Until we make time to read in school, we have no reason to expect children to make time to read out of school.)

To have successful self-selected reading, it is crucial that students choose their own reading materials and have lots of materials from which to choose. It is also critical that no students are wandering around the room looking for things to read. Most teachers have a book/magazine selection time before the beginning of the self-selected reading time and require students to have several texts they want to read within arm's reach so that no one has any excuse to be going from place to place. (To make doubly sure of this, a crate of good reading material is often placed at each student grouping just in case anyone needs something additional to read.) Students need to understand that reading requires quiet and concentration and that people wandering around are distracting to everyone.

Teachers who report the most success with self-selected reading set up this time as a special time when there is no work to do, no questions, and no reports, and you get to read anything you like. The only requirement is to read and to talk occasionally with you, their teacher, about the books they are reading.

Once the self-selected reading time gets up and running and children know where they are to be and how they are to read during this time, teachers can spend time holding individual conferences with children. Most teachers designate the

THE ROTATING BOOK CRATES SOLUTION

The goal of every fourth-, fifth-, and sixth-grade teacher of struggling readers should be to have a variety of appealing reading materials constantly and readily available to the children. In one school, four intermediate teachers became convinced of the futility of trying to teach resistant children to read with almost no appealing materials in the classroom. The teachers appealed to the administration and the parent group for money and were told that it would be put in the budget "for next year"! Not willing to "write off" the children they were teaching this year, each teacher cleaned out her or his closets (school and home), rummaged through the book room, and used other means to round up all the easy and appealing books they could find. Then they put these materials into four big crates, making sure that each crate had as much variety as possible. Mysteries, sports, biographies, science fiction, informational books, cartoon books, and so forth were divided up equally.

Because they did this over the Christmas holidays, they decided that each classroom would keep a crate for 5 weeks. At the end of each 5-week period, students carried the crate of books that had been in their room to another room. In this way, the four teachers provided many more appealing books than they could have if each teacher kept the books for a single classroom.

The four-crate solution was one of those "necessity is the mother of invention" solutions to try to get through the year without many books; fortunately, it had serendipitous results. When the first crate left each classroom at the end of the 5-week period, several children complained that they had not read certain books, or that they wanted to read some again. The teacher sympathized but explained that not enough "great" books were available to go around and that their crate had to go to the next room. The teacher then made a "countdown" calendar to be attached to the second crate. Each day, a child tore a number off so they would realize that they had only 10, 9, 8, 7 . . . days to read or reread anything they wanted from this second crate. Reading enthusiasm picked up when the students knew that they had limited time with these books.

When the third crate arrived, students dug in immediately. A racelike atmosphere developed as children tried to read as many books as possible before the books moved on. When the fourth (and final) crate arrived, children already knew about some of the books that were in it. Comments such as "My friend read a great mystery in that crate and I am going to read it too" let the teachers know that the children were talking to their friends in other classes about the books in the crates!

Although the enthusiasm generated by the moving crates of books had not been anticipated by the teachers, they realized in retrospect that it could have been. We all like something new and different, and limited time–only offers are a common selling device. The following year, even with many more books available, the teachers divided up their books into seven crates and moved them every 5 weeks so that the children would always have new, fresh material.

children as Monday, Tuesday, Wednesday, and so forth. and then conference with them on their day, spending 3 or 4 minutes with each child. Children know that on their day they should bring one book that they have selected to share with the teacher. They read a few pages to the teacher and discuss the book and why they chose it. Thus each child gets a short but dependable conference time with the teacher each week to share what they like about books. Most students look forward to their weekly one-to-one time with the teacher, and the teacher has a chance each week to monitor their reading growth and encourage their reading interests.

In a recent research study Ivey and Broaddus (2001) surveyed 1,765 sixth graders to determine what motivates them to read. The response of this large group of diverse preteens indicated that their major motivation for reading came from having time for independent reading in books of their own choosing and teachers' reading aloud to them.

Sharing and Responding

Children who read also enjoy talking to their classmates about what they have read. In fact, Manning and Manning (1984) found that providing time for children to interact with one another about reading material enhanced the effects of sustained silent reading on both reading achievement and attitudes. One device sure to spark conversation about books is to create a classroom bookboard. Cover a bulletin board with white paper and use yarn to divide it into 40 or 50 spaces. Select 40 to 50 titles from the classroom library and write each title in one of the spaces. Next, make some small construction paper rectangles in three colors or use three colors of small sticky notes. Designate a color to stand for various reactions to the books.

- Red might stand for "Super—one of the all-time best books I've ever read."
- Blue could indicate that a book was "OK—not the best I've ever read but still enjoyable."
- Yellow could stand for "Yucky, boring—a waste of time!"

Children were encouraged to read as many of the bookboard books as possible and to put their "autograph" on a red, blue, or yellow rectangle and attach it to the appropriate title. Once a week, the teacher led the class in a lively discussion of the reasons for their book evaluations. Some books were universally declared reds, blues, or yellows, but other books collected evaluations in all three colors. As the weeks went on, everyone wanted to read the red books and some children chose the yellow books to see whether they were "really that bad." When most children had read these books, a new bookboard was begun. This time each child selected a book title or two to put on the bookboard and labeled/decorated the spot for that book.

In some classrooms the self-selected block ends with a "reader's chair" in which one or two children each day do a book talk. They show a favorite book and read or tell a little about the book, and then try to "sell this book to the rest of the class." Their selling techniques appear to be quite effective because these books are usually quickly seen in the hands of many of their classmates.

Other teachers have reading parties one afternoon every 2 or 3 weeks. Children's names are pulled from a jar and they form a group of three or four in which everyone gets to share their favorite book. Reading parties, like other parties, often include refreshments such as popcorn or cookies. Children develop all kinds of tasty associations with books and sharing books! Still other teachers arrange outings for their children to read to younger children in the school. Each child selects a favorite book and then reads it to a younger reading buddy.

Finding time for children to talk about books is not easy in today's crowded curriculum. However, a part of each day is not well used in most elementary classrooms—the last 15 minutes of the day. Many teachers have found that they can successfully schedule weekly reading sharing time if they utilize the last 15 minutes. Here is how this sharing time works in one fifth-grade classroom.

Every Thursday afternoon, the teacher gets the children completely ready to be dismissed 15 minutes before the final bell rings. Notes to go home are distributed. Bookbags are packed. Chairs are placed on top of the desks. The teacher then uses index cards and writes each child's name on a card. The index cards are shuffled and the first five names—which form the first group—are called. These children go to a corner of the room that always serves as the meeting place for the first group. The next five names that come out form the second group and go to whichever place is designated for the second group. The process continues until all five or six groups are formed and the children are in their places. Now, each child has 2 minutes to read, tell, show, act out, or otherwise share something from what they have been reading this week. The children share in the order that their names are called. The first person called for each group is the leader. Each person has exactly 2 minutes and is timed by a timer. When the timer sounds, the next person gets 2 minutes. If a few minutes remain after all the children have had their allotted 2 minutes, the leader of each group selects something to share with the whole class.

Teachers who have used such a procedure on a regular basis to ensure that children have a chance to talk with others about what they read find that the children are more enthusiastic about reading. Comments such as "I'm going to stump them with these riddles when I get my 2 minutes" or "Wait 'til I read the scary part to everyone" are proof that sharing helps motivate reading. The popularity of the books shared with other children is further proof. Having discussions each week on a specified afternoon puts this procedure on the schedule and guarantees that it will get done. Using the cards to form the groups each week is quick and easy and helps ensure that children will interact with many other children over the course of the year.

The procedure just described, however, worries some teachers because it sounds terribly regimented. What if children don't want to share on Thursday? What if a child wants to share for 10 minutes rather than 2 minutes? What if they don't want to share with the people who end up in their group? These and other questions are valid concerns and must be considered, but we must also consider the alternative. In the best of all possible worlds, reading and sharing would take place daily in a less formal and regimented way. In the real world of many classrooms, however, reading and sharing get pushed aside for the more formal, scheduled activities. It should be the goal of every elementary teacher to be able to say at the end of each week, "All my children took time to read simply for the pleasure of it, had a chance to talk with others about what they were reading, and to hear what their classmates were reading." This goal can be achieved in informal and less-structured ways, and can be achieved with an organized activity such as the one described here. What matters is that reading and talking about what was read play a large role in all children's reading experience.

Contests and Book Reports—Yuck!

Before leaving the subject of voluntary reading in the intermediate grades, we must consider the value of two common practices—reading incentive programs and book reports. Many schools set up reading incentive programs in an attempt to get children to read real books. These programs take many different forms. Children are given T-shirts that proclaim, "I have read 100 books!" or whole classes are rewarded with pizza parties if they can read the most books. These reward systems are set up with the best intentions and may even motivate some children to begin reading. Unfortunately, another message can be communicated to children who are exposed to such incentive programs. The message goes something like, "Reading is one of those things I must do in order to get something that I want." Reading thus becomes the means to the end, rather than the end in itself. Many teachers (and parents) report that children only read "short, dumb" books so that they can achieve the longest list.

Book reports are another device used to motivate reading and can often have the opposite effect of what they were intended to have. When adults are asked what they remember about elementary school that made them like or dislike reading, they report that having their teachers read books aloud to the class, being allowed to select their own books, and having time to read them turned the adults on to reading. Book reports are the most commonly mentioned "turnoff." Likewise, few children enjoy doing book reports; their dislike is often transferred to the act of reading. Some children report on the same books year after year and others even admit lying about reading a book.

Children who are going to become readers must begin to view reading as its own reward. This intrinsic motivation can be nurtured only as children find books that they "just couldn't put down" and subsequently seek out other books. Incentive programs and book reports must be evaluated on the basis of how well they develop this intrinsic motivation.

Self-Selected Writing

To establish daily writing time in your class, you would follow many of the same principles described in the reading section. Children need to see writing as something adults do. Teachers also need to write both functional things such as notes, lists, and reports, as well as personal expression items such as songs, stories, and poems.

Children need to understand that writing—like reading, tennis, and piano—can be improved by instruction, by practicing specific writing strategies, and just by writing. In classrooms where children understand that reading is one of the most important ways to become a good reader, teachers find it easy to help children understand the parallels between how reading helps a person become a better reader and how writing helps improve both reading and writing. In Chapter 4, you can find strategies to use for improving the specific writing skills of students. It is also important, however, that children take time each day just to write, the same way that they take time each day just to read.

Some older children will not write because they have a long history of receiving red marks and unacceptable grades for writing. These children will only begin to write again if you assure them that just doing it is what counts. The daily writing is not graded but the teacher does check to see that something is written. (In some classrooms teachers give children a point each day for writing. These points are then added as bonus points to the final language grade. This should only be used if they "won't do it if it doesn't count for a grade.") Once again, because children do like to share what they have written, setting aside the last 15 minutes of a designated afternoon and using the index cards to put them in groups to share something they have written can be beneficial.

Although many teachers use writing folders for daily writing, we have found that it is much easier to keep up with the children's writing and to see their progress if daily writing is done in a notebook used exclusively for this purpose. Many teachers find that this notebook, if kept in the children's desks, might become a convenient source of paper for the children; a 60-sheet notebook—that should last half the year—is quickly used up if paper is torn out and used for other purposes. So, teachers often store the notebooks on a shelf for children to pick up each morning and then replace them when they are finished. Most teachers tell children to write about one page. (This is not as much as it sounds because we have children write on every other line so there is space to write additional information or to make corrections if they choose to revise some of these first drafts.) This one-page limit should not be enforced too strictly. Children should understand that they might write a little less one day and a little more another, but that over the course of the week they should average about one page each day.

The biggest problem we have encountered with daily writing is the "what to write about" problem. Just as we let them read about whatever they choose to read about, we want them to write about whatever they choose to write about. In some classrooms, however, many children were "written out" after the first month of school.

From time to time, it is helpful to sit down with children and brainstorm a list of things that the class thinks would be worth writing about. In some classrooms, the children use the first page of their notebooks to record possible topics as they occur to them.

As with reading, elements of structure here are worrisome. Some days children are just not in the mood to write. Should they have to write even when they do not want to? Should everyone write about a page each day? Once a week for 15 minutes is not really enough sharing time. Real writers find their own topics, so children should find their own topics too. Giving students varied springboards to writing and recording, such as a 2-minute brainstormed list of words, however, has definitely stimulated children who would not write otherwise. Having children review their earlier drafts may foster revision and rewriting on that same topic. Each teacher, looking at a class of intermediate-aged children who have not become writers, must decide how much structure is needed to achieve the goal of having every child write something every day.

SUMMARY

To create powerful classroom environments in which all children learn to read and write, teachers need to be concerned with models, materials, and motivation. Whether the children are 5–6 years old or 11–12 years old, all need to see reading and writing demonstrated and need to be continuously engaged in real reading and writing. This takes time; classroom teachers might begin by deciding about how much time children will spend reading and writing each day. How much time will be set aside for reading to children? How much time will be set aside for teacher-directed instructional activities?

The next question that needs to be answered is where do the books, magazines, and newspapers come from? Throughout this chapter we have suggested a variety of strategies for acquiring these materials, but ideally, classrooms would be well stocked (as would school libraries) with classroom libraries containing 500–1,000 paperback titles and several magazines for children to read.

In the remaining chapters of the book, we describe activities that explicitly teach students the strategies they need to develop the self-improving systems that all good readers and writers have. Daily encounters with reading and writing real things are the foundation that supports this strategy instruction.

CHAPTER 2

Words

Words are the building blocks of reading and writing. To read and write children must learn to recognize and spell the most commonly used words quickly and automatically. For many children, this is not an easy task. The most frequently occurring words are meaningless, abstract, connecting words (*of, and, the, is,* etc.). Children use these words in their speech but they are not aware of them as separate entities. Read these sentences with a natural speech pattern and notice how you pronounce the italicized words:

- *What* do you want?
- Can I have a piece *of* pie?
- Where are *they*?

In natural speech, *what* and *do* are slurred together and sound like "wudoo." *Of* is pronounced like "uh." *They* is tacked on to the end of *are* and sounds like "ah-thay." All children use the highly frequent words such as *what, of,* and *they* in their speech, but they are not as aware of these words as they are of the more concrete, tangible words such as *want* and *pie*. To make life more difficult, many of these high-frequency words are not spelled in a regular, predictable way. *What* should rhyme with *at, bat,* and *cat*. *Of* should be spelled u-v. *They*, which clearly rhymes with *day, may,* and *way* should be spelled the way many children do spell it—t-h-a-y.

When you consider that the most frequently occurring words are usually meaningless, abstract words that may be irregular in their spelling or pronunciation and that children use but do not even realize are separate words, it is a wonder that any child learns to recognize and spell them! To read and write fluently, however, children must learn to recognize these words instantly and spell them automatically. In this chapter, we describe how using a word wall can help children learn these critical words.

In addition to learning to read and spell the most frequent words instantly, children must learn how to figure out the spelling/pronunciation of a word they do not know. All proficient readers have the ability to look at a regular word they have never seen before and assign it a probable pronunciation. Witness your ability to pronounce these made-up words:

bame   spow   perzam   chadulition

Of course you were not "reading" because pronouncing these words did not create any meaning. But if you were in the position of most young readers who have many more words in their listening/meaning vocabularies than in their sight-reading vocabularies, you would often meet words that were familiar in speech but unfamiliar in print. The ability to figure out the pronunciation of unfamiliar-in-print words would rapidly enable you to use your huge store of familiar-in-speech words and thus create meaning.

Before we continue, how did you pronounce the made-up word *spow*? Did it rhyme with *cow* or with *snow*? Because English is not a one-sound-per-letter language, the ways to pronounce certain letter patterns differ; the number of different ways is limited, however, and with real words (unlike made-up words) your speaking vocabulary lets you know which pronunciation to assign.

Not only do readers use their phonics knowledge to enable them to read words they have not seen before, but this same knowledge also enables them to write. If the four made-up words had been dictated to you and you had to write them, you would have spelled them in a way that was reasonably close to the way we spelled them. You might have spelled the first one *baim* and the last one *chedulition*, but your "invented" spelling would have resembled our made-up spelling to a remarkable degree.

All good readers and writers develop the ability to come up with pronunciations and spelling for words they have never read or written before. Many poor readers do not. When good readers see a word they have never before seen in print, they stop momentarily and study the word—attending to print detail and looking at every letter in a left-to-right sequence. As they look at all the letters, they are not thinking of a sound for each letter because good readers know that sounds are determined by letter patterns, not by individual letters. Good readers look for letter patterns they have seen together before and then search their mental word banks looking for words with similar letter patterns. If the new word is a big word, they "chunk" it—that is, they put letters together that make familiar-sounding chunks.

Based on careful inspection of the letters and a search through their mental banks for words with the same letter patterns, good readers try out a pronunciation. If the first try does not result in a word they have heard and have stored in their mental word bank, they usually try another pronunciation. Finally, they produce a pronunciation that they recognize as sounding like a real word they know. Then they go back and reread the sentence that contained the unfamiliar-in-print word and see whether their pronunciation makes sense with the meaning they are getting from the context of surrounding words. If the pronunciation they come up with makes sense, they continue reading. If not, they look again at all the letters of the unfamiliar word and see what else would "look like this and make sense."

Imagine a young child reading this sentence:

The man was poisoned by lead.

Imagine that he pauses at the last word and then pronounces *lead* so that it rhymes with *bead*. Because that is the only similar real word he remembers hearing, his eyes then glance back and he quickly rereads the sentence. He then realizes, "This doesn't make sense." He studies all the letters of *lead* again and searches for similar letter patterns in his mental word bank. Perhaps he now accesses words such as *head* and *bread*. This gives him another possible pronunciation for this letter pattern—one that is also recognized as a previously heard word. He tries this pronunciation, quickly rereads the sentence, realizes that it now "sounds right," and continues reading.

From this scenario, we can infer the strategies that good readers use to decode an unfamiliar-in-print word successfully:

1. Recognize that this is an unfamiliar word and look at all the letters in a left-to-right sequence.
2. Search your mental bank for similar letter patterns and the sounds associated with them.
3. Produce a pronunciation that matches that of a real word you already know.
4. Reread the sentence to cross check your possible pronunciation with meaning. If meaning confirms pronunciation, continue reading. If not, try again!

Had this unfamiliar-in-print word been a big word, the reader would have had to use a fifth strategy:

5. Chunk the word by putting together letters that usually go together in the words you know.

The strategies of looking at all the letters in a left-to-right sequence, matching letter patterns with pronunciations, chunking big words, and cross checking are supported by numerous research studies (Adams, 1990) and by commonsense observations of what we—as good readers—do. Unfortunately, they are not what children are usually taught to do.

Consider some of the traditional phonics instruction given to children:

- The *e* on the end is silent and makes the vowel long.
- When a vowel is followed by *r*, it is *r* controlled.
- When two consonants are in the middle of a word and are not a digraph or a blend, divide between them.

This kind of rule-based, jargon-filled instruction is confusing to many children and does not represent what people actually do when they come to an unfamiliar word in their reading, or when they are trying to figure out how a word might be spelled. The traditional phonics rules are descriptions of how the letter–sound system works. They are not what you use when you need to pronounce or spell an unfamiliar word.

This chapter contains activities that teach children to do what good readers and writers actually do when they read or spell an unfamiliar word. (Many of these activities come from Cunningham, 2000, *Phonics They Use: Words for Reading and Writing*, which includes more detail and variation than can be described in this one chapter.) The chapter is divided into five sections. Activities in the first section are designed to help children build basic understandings about words and letter–sound patterns. These activities should play a major role in kindergarten instruction and should continue throughout first grade until children develop the essential understandings about words. Some struggling second and third graders may not have developed these critical concepts yet—particularly if they are just learning to speak English. These activities can be adapted for older beginning readers.

The second section contains activities designed to ensure that children develop an instant and automatic ability to read and write the high-frequency words. The third section focuses on the important skill of cross checking meaning with letter–sound knowledge. The fourth and fifth sections help students learn the patterns essential for decoding and spelling. Activities in the fourth section help students decode and spell regular one- and two-syllable words.

The final section provides activities that help children learn to read and spell multisyllabic words. These activities are most appropriate for students in grades 4 and up but have also been used successfully with third graders who are tired of those "baby words" and are impressed with themselves when they start to acquire a store of "really big words!"

RECOMMENDED RESOURCES

For grade-level specific descriptions of working with words activities, see *Month by Month Phonics for First Grade* (Cunningham & Hall, 1997), *Month by Month Phonics for Second Grade* (Hall & Cunningham, 1998), *Month by Month Phonics for Third Grade* (Cunningham & Hall, 1998), and *Month by Month Phonics for Upper Grades* (Cunningham & Hall, 1998).

BUILDING A FOUNDATION FOR WORD AND LETTER–SOUND LEARNING

In preceding chapters, you learned about the most important part of the foundation for word and letter–sound learning. Instruction in kindergarten and beginning first grade must simulate the early reading/writing experiences of children from literate homes. Reading and writing materials must be omnipresent. Teachers must read from a variety of books and real-world materials. Children must be encouraged to "read" the predictable books, songs, and poems that are an integral part of their day. Their fledgling efforts at pretend reading and writing must be applauded and supported. All children can and should develop a clear understanding of what reading and writing are for, as well as the "of course I can" attitude that is critical for their development as readers and writers.

Once children understand what reading and writing are for and are convinced that they too can join the literate community, they must develop some smaller—but still critical—understandings. Children must learn the conventions and jargon of print. They must develop phonemic awareness. They must begin to learn letter names and the sounds often associated with letters.

Print is what you read and write. Print includes all the funny little marks— letters, punctuation, space between words and paragraphs—that translate into familiar spoken language. In English, we read across the page in a left-to-right fashion. Because our eyes can only see a few words during each stop (called a fixation), we must actually move our eyes several times to read one line of print. When we finish that line, we make a return sweep and start all over again. If there are sentences at the top of a page, a picture in the middle, and more sentences at the bottom, we read the top first and then the bottom. We start at the front of a book and go toward the back. These arbitrary rules about how we proceed through print are called *conventions*.

Jargon refers to all the words we use to talk about reading and writing. Jargon includes terms such as *word, letter, sentence,* and *sound*. We use this jargon constantly as we try to teach children how to read:

"Look at the first word in the second sentence. How does that word begin? What letter makes that sound?"

Using some jargon is essential when talking with children about reading and writing, but children who do not come from literacy-rich backgrounds are often hopelessly confused by this jargon. Although all children speak in words, they do not know that words exist as separate entities until they are put in the presence of reading and writing. To some children, letters are what come in the mailbox, sounds are horns, bells, and slamming doors, and sentences are what you have to serve if you get caught committing a crime! These children are unable to follow our "simple" instructions because we are using words that either have no meaning to them or have an entirely different meaning.

Phonemic awareness is not just another word for phonics. It is the ability to take words apart, put them back together again, and change them. A child's level of phonemic awareness is a very good predictor of beginning reading success. Phonemic awareness develops through a series of stages in which children first become aware that language is made up of individual words, that words are made up of syllables, and that syllables are made up of phonemes. It is important to note here that it is not the "jargon" that children learn. Five-year-olds cannot tell you that three syllables are in *dinosaur* and one syllable in *Rex*. What many of them *can* do is clap out the three beats in *dinosaur* and the one beat in *Rex*. Likewise, they cannot tell you that the first phoneme in *mice* is *m-m-m . . .* , but some can tell you that you would have *ice* if you took the first sound off of *mice.*

Children develop this phonemic awareness as a result of the oral and written language they are exposed to during their preschool years. Nursery rhymes, chants, and Dr. Seuss books usually play a large role in this development. Lap reading, in which children can see the print being read to them, also seems to play an important role. Most children who have the luxury of being read to on demand will select a favorite book that they insist on having read again and again. They will ask questions about the words, such as, "Where does it say *snort*?" "Is that *zizzerzazzerzuzz*?"

Children also develop a sense of sounds and words as they try to write. In the beginning, many children let a single letter stand for an entire word. Later, they write more letters and often say the word that they want to write, dragging out its sounds to hear what letters to use. Children who are allowed and encouraged to "invent-spell" develop an early and strong sense of phonemic awareness.

ACTIVITIES FOR BUILDING THE FOUNDATION

Teachers can help children learn the conventions and jargon of print, can develop phonemic awareness, and can teach letter names and sounds in many ways. Kindergarten and first-grade teachers and children find the following ways to be effective and enjoyable.

Names and Other Concrete Words

Most kindergarten and first-grade teachers begin their year with some get-acquainted activities. As part of these get-acquainted activities, they often have a "special child" each day. In addition to learning about each child, you can focus attention on the special child's name and use that name to develop some important understandings about words and letters.

To prepare for this activity, write all the children's first names (with initials for last names if two names are the same) in permanent marker on sentence strips. Cut the strips so that long names have long strips and short names have short strips. Each day, reach into the box and draw out a name. This child becomes the "King or Queen for a day" and the child's name becomes the focus of many activities. Reserve a bulletin board and add each child's name to the board. (Some teachers like to have children bring a snapshot of themselves or take pictures of the children to add to the board as the names are added.) Following are some day-by-day examples of what you might do with the names.

Day One Close your eyes. Reach into the box, shuffle the names around, and draw one out. Crown that child king or queen for the day! Lead the other children to interview this child and find out what he or she likes to eat, play, or do after school. Does she or he have brothers? Sisters? Cats? Dogs? Mice? Many teachers record this information on a chart or compile a class book with one page of information about each child.

Now focus the children's attention on the child's name—David. Point to the word *David* on the sentence strip and develop the children's understanding of jargon by pointing out that this *word* is David's name. Tell them that it takes many *letters* to write the word *David,* and let them help you count the letters. Say the letters in *David*—D-a-v-i-d, and have the children chant them with you. Point out that the word *David* begins and ends with the same letter. Explain that the first and the last *d* look different because one is a capital *D* and the other is a small *d* (or uppercase/lowercase—whatever jargon you use).

Take another sentence strip and have children watch as you write *David.* Have them chant the spelling of the letters with you. Cut the letters apart and mix them up. Let several children come up and arrange the letters in just the right order so that they spell *David,* using the original sentence strip on which *David* is written as a model. Have the other children chant to check that the order is correct.

Give each child a large sheet of drawing paper and have them write *David* in large letters on one side of the paper using crayons. Model at the board how to write each letter as they write it. Do not worry if what they write is not perfect (or even if it does not bear much resemblance to the one you wrote). Also resist the temptation to correct what they write. Remember that children who write at home before coming to school often reverse letters or write them in funny ways. The important understanding is that names are words, that words can be written, and that it takes lots of letters to write them.

Finally, have everyone draw a picture of David on the other side of the drawing paper. Let David take all the pictures home!

Day Two   Draw another name—*Caroline.* Crown Caroline and do the same interviewing and chart making that you did for David. (Decide carefully what you will do for the first children because every child will expect equal treatment!) Focus their attention on Caroline's name. Say the letters in *Caroline* and have the children chant them with you. Help the children count the letters and decide which letter is first, last, and so on. Write *Caroline* on another sentence strip and cut it into letters. Have children arrange the letters to spell *Caroline,* using the first sentence strip name as their model. Put *Caroline* on the bulletin board under *David* and compare the two. Which has the most letters? How many more letters are in the word *Caroline* than in the word *David*? Does *Caroline* have any of the same letters as *David*? Finish the lesson by having everyone write *Caroline.* Have everyone draw Caroline pictures and let Caroline take all of them home.

Day Three   Draw the third name—*Dorinda.* Do the crowning, interviewing, and chart making. Chant the letters in Dorinda's name. Write it, cut it up, and do the letter arranging. Be sure to note the two *d*'s and to talk about first and last letters. As you put *Dorinda* on the bulletin board, compare it to both *David* and *Caroline.*

This is a perfect time to notice that both *David* and *Dorinda* begin with the same letter and the same sound. Finish the lesson by having the children write *Dorinda* and draw pictures for Dorinda to take home.

Day Four   *Mike* comes out. Do all the usual activities. When you put *Mike* on the bulletin board, help the children realize that David has lost the dubious distinction of having the shortest name. (Bo may now look down at the name card on his desk and call out that his name is even shorter. You can point out that he is right but that Mike's name is the shortest one on the bulletin board right now. What is really fascinating about this activity is how the children compare their own names to the ones on the board even before their names get there. That is exactly the kind of word/letter awareness you are trying to develop!)

When you have a one-syllable name with which many words rhyme (*Pat*, *Tran*, *Flo*, *Sue*, etc.), seize the opportunity to help the children listen for words that rhyme with that name. Say pairs of words—some of which rhyme with Mike—Mike/ball, Mike/bike, Mike/hike, Mike/cook, Mike/like. If the pairs rhyme, everyone should point at Mike and shout, "MIKE!" If not, they should shake their heads and frown.

Day Five   *Cynthia* comes out. Do the various activities and then take advantage of the fact that the names *Caroline* and *Cynthia* both begin with the letter *c* but have different sounds. Have Caroline and Cynthia stand on opposite sides of you. Write their names above them on the chalkboard. Have the children say *Caroline* and *Cynthia* several times, drawing out the first sound. Help them understand that some letters can have more than one sound and that the names *Caroline* and *Cynthia* demonstrate this fact. Tell the class that you are going to say some words, all of which begin with the letter *c*. Some of these words sound like *Caroline* at the beginning and some of them sound like *Cynthia*. Say some words and have the children say them with you—*cat*, *celery*, *candy*, *cookies*, *city*, *cereal*, *cut*. For each word, have them point to Caroline or Cynthia to show which sound they hear. Once they have decided, write each word under *Caroline* or *Cynthia*.

Day Six—Last Day   Continue to have a special child each day. For each child, do the standard interviewing, charting, chanting, letter arranging, writing, and drawing activities. Then, take advantage of the names you have to help children develop an understanding about how letters and sounds work. Following are some extra activities many teachers do with the names.

Write the letters of the alphabet across the board. Count to see how many names contain each letter. Make tally marks or a bar graph and decide which letters occur in the most names and which letters occur in the fewest names. Ask whether any letters do not appear in anyone's name in the whole class.

Pass out laminated letter cards—one letter to a card, lowercase on one side, uppercase on the other. Call out a name from the bulletin board and lead the children to chant the letters in the name. Then, let the children who have those letters come up and display the letters and lead the class in a chant, cheerleader style. "David—D-a-v-i-d—David—Yea! David!"

When you have finished all the names, you may want to do similar activities with other concrete words. Many teachers have the children learn the color words using similar activities. When studying animals, add an animal name to an animal board each day. Activities with the children's names and other concrete words can be done even when many children in the class do not know their letter names yet. Young children enjoy chanting, writing, and comparing the words. They learn letter names by associating them with the important-to-them words they are learning.

Being the Words

The Being the Words activity can be done with any predictable book that the children have read many times or with a chant, song, or poem that has been written and displayed on a chart or poster. In this activity, children are given words to make sentences. They do this by matching their word to the words in the predictable book or on the chart. Two pages of a predictable book or two lines of a poem/chant are matched, then the next two, and so on. To prepare for this activity, write all the words on sentence strips and cut them to match the size of the word. (Do not make duplicate words unless they are needed to make the sentences on the two pages of the book or two lines of the poem/chant that is going to be displayed simultaneously. Make separate cards for any words that are sometimes shown with a capital letter and sometimes with a small letter. Make separate cards for each punctuation mark needed. Laminate these cards so that you can reuse them for Being the Words and word-sorting activities.)

Begin the activity by passing out all the cards containing the words and punctuation marks. Let the children look at their words and point out the distinction between words and punctuation marks. Tell the children that they are going to *be* their words and will come up to make the sentences. Ask the children to help read the sentences with you. Point to each word as you reread the sentences and have the children look to see whether their word matches any words they see in the book. Explain that you do not need to say anything when you get to the period, but that it lets you know that the sentence is over. Have all the children who have a word or punctuation mark in this sentence come up and get in the right order to make the sentence. Help the children arrange themselves in the appropriate left-to-right order, get the period at the end of the sentence, and hold the words right-side up. When everyone is in order, have the children who are not in the sentence read the sentence as you move behind each child who is a word.

Being the Words is one of the favorite activities of most children. They ask to do it again and again. Through this activity, children learn what words are, that words make up sentences, and that punctuation signals the end of the sentence but is not read. They also practice the left-to-right order of print and realize that the order of words makes a difference in what is read. Many children also learn new words during this activity. You will observe this as you hand out the words for *Brown Bear, Brown Bear, What Do You See?* a second or third time and hear children say, for example, "Oh, boy, I'm the bear!" Your most advanced children will even learn the abstract repeated words *what, do, you, see, at,* and *me!*

Many teachers put the book and the laminated words in a center. Children delight in turning the pages of the book and laying out the words on the floor to make the sentences.

Counting Words

For this activity, all children should have 10 counters in a paper cup. (Anything that is manipulative is fine. Some teachers use edibles such as raisins, grapes, or small crackers and let the children eat their counters at the end of the lesson. This makes clean-up quick and easy!) Begin by counting some familiar objects in the room, such as windows, doors, trash cans, and so forth, having all children place one of their counters on their desks for each object.

Tell children that you can also count words by putting down a counter for each word you say. Explain that you will say a sentence in the normal way and then repeat the sentence, pausing after each word. The children should put down counters as you slowly say the words in the sentence, then count the counters and decide how many words you said. As usual, children's attention is better if you make sentences about them. (Carol has a big smile. Paul is back at school today. I saw Jawan at church.) Once the children catch on to the activity, let them say some sentences—first in the normal way, then one word at a time. Listen carefully as they say their sentences because they usually need help saying them one word at a time. Not only do children enjoy this activity and learn to separate words in speech, they are also practicing critical counting skills!

Clapping Syllables

The first way that children learn to pull apart words is into syllables. Say each student's name and have everyone clap the beats in that name as they say it with you. Help them see that Tran and Pat are one-beat names, Manuel and Patrick, two beats, and so on. Once students begin to understand, clap the beats and have all the students whose names have that number of beats stand up and say their names as they clap the beats with you.

Once children can clap syllables and can decide how many beats a given word has, help them see that one-beat words are usually shorter than three-beat words—that is, they take fewer letters to write. To do this, write some words that children cannot read on sentence strips and cut the strips into words so that short words have short strips and long words have long strips. Have some of the words begin with the same letters, but have the words be different lengths so children will need to think about word length to decide which word is which.

For the category of animals, you might write *horse* and *hippopotamus, dog* and *donkey, kid* and *kangaroo,* and *rat, rabbit,* and *rhinoceros.* Tell the children that you are going to say the animal names and that they should clap to show how many beats the word has. (Do not show them the words yet!) Say the first pair—one at a time—horse/hippopotamus. Help children decide that *horse* is a one-beat word and *hippopotamus,* which takes a lot more claps, is a five-beat word. Now, show them the two words and say, "One of these words is *horse* and the other is *hippopotamus.* Who thinks they can figure out which one is which?" Explain that because *hippopotamus* takes so many beats to say, it probably takes more letters to write.

Blending and Segmenting Games

The ability to segment words into sounds and then blend them back together is one of the most sophisticated phonemic awareness skills—and for many children one of the most difficult. Call students to line up by stretching out their names, emphasizing each letter. As each student lines up, have the class stretch out the name with you.

As a variation, say a sound and let everyone whose name contains this sound anywhere in their name line up. Be sure you have the children respond to the sound and not the letter. If you say "sss," Sam, Jessie, and Cynthia can all line up!

Display familiar pictures. Let children take turns saying the names of the pictures (one sound at a time) and call on another child to identify the picture. In the beginning, limit the pictures to five or six whose names are very different and are short—*truck, frog, cat, pony, tiger.*

Some teachers help children understand the difficult concept of segmenting and blending by having children talk like ghosts. Each child says a sentence in a slow, drawn-out moaning voice. Everyone else translates what the ghost said!

> **RECOMMENDED RESOURCES**
>
> Many sources for good, fun activities for developing phonemic awareness are available. Three of our favorites are *Phonemic Awareness: Playing with Sounds to Strengthen Beginning Reading Skills* (Fitzpatrick, 1997), *The Phonological Awareness Handbook for Kindergarten and Primary Teachers* (Ericson & Fraser-Juliebo, 1998), and *Rhymes & Reasons: Literature and Language Play for Phonological Awareness* (Opitz, 2000).

Rhyming Books

While on the subject of methods that have stood the test of time, do you remember being read *Hop on Pop; One Fish, Two Fish, Red Fish, Blue Fish;* and *There's a Wocket in My Pocket*? These books also appeal to the silly rhythm/rhyme–oriented child who is our kindergartner. From these books, children develop important understandings. You can nudge these understandings on a bit if you help the children notice that many of the words that rhyme are also spelled alike. As you reread one of these favorite books, let the children listen for the rhyming words and make lists of these. Read the words together. Add other words that are spelled alike and rhyme and make more rhymes with those. Make up "silly words" that rhyme too, and decide what they might mean. Try to illustrate them! If you can have a

RECOMMENDED RESOURCES

Two Wonderful Tongue Twister Books

The Biggest Tongue Twister Book in the World (Gyles Brandeth, 1978)

Alphabet Annie Announces an All-American Album (Susan Purviance & Marcia O'Shell, 1988)

"wocket" in your pocket, you can have a "hocket" in your pocket. What would a *hocket* be? What could you do with it?

Tongue Twisters

Children love tongue twisters and they are wonderful reminders for the sounds of beginning letters. Use children's names and let them help you create the tongue twisters. Have students say them as fast as they can and as slowly as they can. When students have said them enough times to have them memorized, write them on posters or in a class book.

Use Favorite Words with Pure Initial Sounds as Key Words

Letter sounds can be learned by rote or by association. Learning the common sound for *b* by trying to remember it or by trying to remember that the word *bears* begins with it when you cannot even read the word *bears* requires rote learning. But if you have read and reread and been the words from *Brown Bear, Brown Bear,* you can probably read the word *bear.* Once you can read the word *bear* and realize that the common sound for *b* is heard at the beginning of *bears,* you no longer only have to remember the sound. You can now associate the sound of *b* with something already known—the word *bear.* Associative learning is the easiest, quickest, and most long lasting.

Children from print-rich environments know some concrete words when they come to school. As they are taught letter sounds, they probably associate these with the words they know, thus, making the learning of these sounds easier and longer lasting. We can provide the opportunity for associative learning for children who do not know words when they come to school by capitalizing on the words they are learning from their predictable books and poem/chant charts. Names of children in the class are also concrete words that make it easy for children to remember letter–sound associations.

When teaching the first letter–sound relationships, begin with two letters that are very different in look and sound and that are made in different places of the mouth—*b* and *l,* for example. Show the children the two words *bear* and *Larry,* which serve as key words for these letters. Have the children pronounce the two key words and notice the position of their tongues and teeth as they do. Have one child stand in the front of the room and hold the word *bear.* Have Larry hold a card with his name on it. Say several concrete words—*bike, lemon, box, book, ladder, lady, boy*—that begin like *bear* or *Larry* and have the children say them after you. Have them notice where their tongues and teeth are as they say the words. Let the children point to the child holding *bear* or *Larry* to indicate how the word begins.

Begin a key-word bulletin board on which you put the letters *b* and *l* and the key words *bear* and *Larry*. Repeat the activity just described using other *b* and *l* words until most of the children begin to understand the difference in the letter sound. Then add a third letter and a key word—perhaps *m* and *mouse*. Have them listen for and repeat words beginning with all three letters—*b*, *l*, *m*. Be sure to point out that the words they already know can help them remember the sound.

The Alphabet Song and Alphabet Books

"The Alphabet Song" has been sung by generations of children. Children enjoy it and it seems to give them a sense of all the letters and a framework in which to put new letters as they learn them. Many children come to school already being able to sing "The Alphabet Song." Let them sing and teach it to everyone else. Once the children can sing the song, you may want to point to alphabet cards (usually found above the chalkboard) as they sing. Children enjoy "being the alphabet" as they line up to go somewhere. Simply pass your laminated alphabet cards—one to each child, leftovers to the teacher—and let the children sing the song slowly as each child lines up. Be sure to hand out the cards randomly so that no one gets to be the *A* and lead the line or has to be the *Z* and bring up the rear every day!

Wonderful alphabet books are available. You can read these books aloud over and over. Kindergarten children can select these books to "read" during their self-selected reading. Teacher aides or parent or grandparent volunteers can "lap read" these in the reading corner, and so on. Your class can create their own alphabet book modeled after their own favorite alphabet book.

Letter Actions

Teach children actions for the consonants. Write the letter on one side of a large index card and the action on the other. The first time you teach each letter, make a big deal of it. Get out the rhythm sticks and the marching music when you march for *M*. Go out on the playground and do jumping jacks for *J*. Play hopscotch for *H* and hop like bunnies.

Once the children have learned actions for several letters, you can do many activities in the classroom without any props. Have all the children stand by their desks and wait until you show them a letter. They should do that action until you hide the letter behind your back. When they have all stopped and you have their attention again, show them another letter and have them do that action. Continue this with as many letters as you have time to fill. Be sure to make comments such as, "Yes, I see everyone marching because *M* is our marching letter."

In another activity, you pass out the letters (for which children have learned the actions) to individual children. Each child gets up and performs the action required and calls on someone to guess which letter he or she was given. Another letter action game is Follow the Letter Leader, in which the leader picks a letter card and does that action. Everyone else follows the leader doing the same action. The leader then picks another card and the game continues.

Teachers have different favorites for letter actions and you will have your own favorites. Try to pick actions with which everyone is familiar and that are only called by one name. A list of actions we like follows this paragraph. The action for *s* is our particular favorite. You can use it to end the game. Children say it is not an action at all, but they remember that *s* is the "sitting letter."

bounce	hop	nod	vacuum
catch	jump	paint	walk
dance	kick	run	yawn
fall	laugh	sit	zip
gallop	march	talk	

Seven Signs of Emergent Literacy

Observe the children as they engage in reading, writing, and the activities described in this section and you will notice the following behaviors:

1. They pretend read favorite books and poems, songs, and chants.
2. They "write" and can read what they write even if no one else can.
3. They can "track print"—that is, show you what to read and point to the words using left-to-right and top-to-bottom conventions.
4. They know critical jargon and can point to just one word, to the first word in the sentence, to one letter, to the first letter in the word, to the longest word, and so forth.
5. They recognize some concrete words—their names and names of other children and favorite words from books, poems, and chants.
6. They have phonemic awareness—they can count words, clap syllables, blend and segment words, and recognize if words rhyme.
7. They can name many letters, tell you words that begin with common letters, and tell you common sounds for some letters.

Children develop these critical understandings as they engage in the shared reading and writing described in upcoming chapters as well as from the activities described in this chapter.

FLUENCY WITH HIGH-FREQUENCY WORDS

For as long as anyone can remember, struggling readers have had difficulty with words such as *was, saw, of, for, from, they, that, what, with, will*. Many of these words have no meaning, are not logically spelled, and look a lot like each other. One strategy we have found to be effective for teaching high-frequency words is "doing" a word wall. Doing a word wall is not the same as having a word wall. Having a word wall might mean putting all these words up somewhere in the room and telling students to use them. In our experience, struggling readers cannot use them because they do not know them and do not know which is which! Doing a word wall means (1) being selective and "stingy" about what words go up there, that is, limiting the words to those really common words that children need a lot in writing; (2) adding words gradually—five a week; (3) making the words very accessible by putting them where everyone can see them, writing them in big black letters, and using a variety of colors so that the constantly confused words (*for, from, that, them, they, this,* etc.) are distinctly different colors; (4) practicing the words by chanting and writing them because struggling readers are not usually good visual learners and cannot just look at and remember words; (5) doing a variety of review activities to provide enough practice so that the words are read and spelled instantly and automatically; and (6) making sure that word-wall words are spelled correctly in any writing the students do. Teachers who "do" word walls (rather than just have word walls) report that *all* of their children can learn these critical words.

Doing a Word Wall

Select five words each week and add them to a wall or bulletin board in the room. The selection of the words varies from classroom to classroom, but the selection principle is the same. Include words students often need in their reading and writing and words that are easily confused with other words. First-grade teachers who

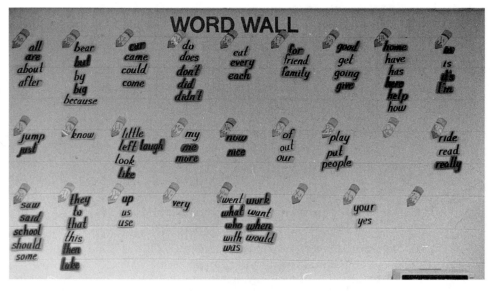

Here is a word wall from a first-grade classroom. Cutting around the shapes and putting the words on different-colored pieces of paper helps the children distinuish the easily confusable ones and maeks an interesting, eye-catching display.

use a basal usually select some high-frequency words that are taught in that basal. Others select high-frequency words from big books or other trade books that children are reading.

The word wall grows as the year goes on. The words on the word wall are written on different colored construction paper scraps with a thick black permanent marker. Words are placed on the wall alphabetically by first letter and the first words added are very different from one another. When confusing words are added, put them on different colored paper from the words they are usually confused with.

Beginning with third grade, teachers like to start their word wall by putting up words that are commonly misspelled, such as

again	could	have	pretty	was
because	does	of	said	were
come	from	people	they	where

As children write, look for high-frequency, commonly misspelled words and add these to the wall as well. Most teachers add five new words each week and do at least one daily activity in which the children find, write, and chant the spelling of the words. The activity takes longer on the day that words are added because you will want to take time to make sure that students associate meanings with the words. You will also want to point out how the words differ from words they are often confused with. The following sections describe a variety of ways to get at least one daily practice with the word-wall words.

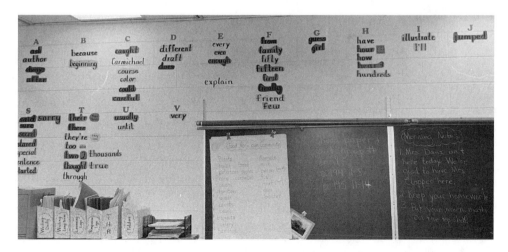

Here is a part of a third-grade word wall. Notice the clues next to the homophones: they're—they are, two—2, hour—clock sketch.

Clap, Chant, and Write

Have students number a sheet of paper from 1 to 5. Call out the five words, putting each word in a sentence. As you call out each word, have a child find and point to that word and have all the children clap and chant its spelling before writing it. When all five words have been written, point to the words and have a volunteer spell each word as students check and/or fix their own papers.

On the day that you add words, call out the five new words. During the rest of the week, however, any five words from the wall can be called out. Words that children need more practice with should be called out almost every day.

Review Rhyme with the Word Wall

Students clap, chant, and write, but they also find the word that rhymes with a word you give. Give them both a first letter and a rhyming clue, such as

Number 1 begins with a *t* and rhymes with *walk.*
Number 2 begins with an *m* and rhymes with *by.*
Number 3 begins with an *f* and rhymes with *run.*
Number 4 begins with an *l* and rhymes with *bike.*
Number 5 begins with a *g* and rhymes with *stood.*

To check the answers, you say the rhyming word and let students say the word they wrote and chant its spelling. "Number 1 rhymes with *walk,* what did you write?" Children respond, "Talk—t-a-l-k."

Review Cross Checking with the Word Wall

To review cross checking, tell students to decide which wall word makes sense and begins correctly. For each word, write the first letter of the word on the board. Then say a sentence leaving out a word that begins with that letter. Students decide which word makes sense in your sentence and write that word. Here are some examples.

1. Write *t* on the board. Say, "The first word begins with a *t* and fits in the sentence, *Paula likes to _____ on the telephone.*"
2. Write *r* on the board. Say, "Number 1 begins with an *r* and fits in the sentence, *Midge had to _____ fast to win the race.*"
3. Write *w* on the board. Say, "Number 3 begins with a *w* and fits in the sentence, *Carlos went to China _____ his father.*"

To check the answers, read the sentences again and have students tell you what word they wrote and chant its spelling.

120 HIGH-FREQUENCY WORDS OFTEN FOUND ON PRIMARY WORD WALLS

about	can't	give	little	our	the	*went
after	*car	go	*look	*out	their	were
again	children	good	*made	over	them	what
*all	come	*had	*make	people	*then	*when
*am	could	has	many	*play	there	where
*and	*day	have	me	pretty	they	who
are	*did	he	*more	*ride	they're	*why
*at	do	her	*my	said	*thing	*will
be	don't	here	*new	*saw	this	with
because	*down	him	*nice	*school	to	won't
before	*eat	his	*night	*see	too	you
*best	favorite	house	no	she	two	your
*big	for	*how	*not	sister	*up	
*black	friend	I	of	some	us	
*boy	from	*in	off	*talk	very	
brother	*fun	is	*old	teacher	want	
*but	get	*it	on	*tell	was	
*can	girl	*like	other	*that	we	

*These words help with decoding and spelling lots of rhyming words.

Be a Mind Reader

Be a Mind Reader is a favorite word-wall activity. In this game, the teacher thinks of a word on the wall and then gives five clues about that word. Choose a word and write it on a piece of scratch paper, but do not let the students see which word you have written. Have students number a paper 1 to 5 and tell them you are going to see who can read your mind and figure out which word on the board you are thinking of and have written on your scratch paper. Tell them you will give them five clues. By the fifth clue, everyone should guess your word, but if they read your mind, they might get it before the fifth clue.

For your first clue, always give the same clue: "It's one of the words on the wall." Students should write the word they think it might be next to number one. Each succeeding clue should narrow what the word might be until by the fifth clue, only one word is possible. As you give clues, students write the word that they believe is correct next to each number on their paper. If succeeding clues confirm that the word a student has written next to one number is correct, that student writes the same word next to the following number. Clues can be any features of the word you want students to notice (e.g., it has more than two letters; it has less than four letters; it has an *e;* it does not have a *t*). After the fifth clue, show students the word you wrote on scratch paper and say, "I know you all have the word next to number 5, but who has it next to number 4? 3? 2? 1? Some students will have read your mind and will be as pleased as punch with themselves! Five sample clues follow:

1. It's one of the words on the wall.
2. It has four letters.
3. It begins with *th.*
4. The vowel is an *e.*
5. It finishes the sentence, I gave my books to _____.

Reading, Writing, and Word Walls

Once you have a word wall growing in your room, you will know without a doubt that your students are using it as they read and write because you will see their eyes quickly glance to the exact spot where a word is displayed that they want to write. Even when children are reading, they sometimes glance at the word wall to help them remember a particularly troublesome word.

---

90 WORDS COMMONLY FOUND ON INTERMEDIATE WORD WALLS

about	except	probably	very
again	excited	really	want
almost	favorite	*right (wrong)	was
also	first	said	*wear (shirt)
always	friends	school	*weather (rain)
another	getting	something	*we're (we are)
anyone	have	sometimes	went
are	*hole (donut)	terrible	*were
beautiful	I'm	that's	what
because	into	*their	when
before	*it's (it is)	then	*where
*buy (sell)	*its	*there (here)	*whether
*by	*knew	they	who
can't	*know	*they're (they are)	*whole
could	laugh	thought	with
didn't	let's	*threw (caught)	*won
doesn't	myself	*through	won't
don't	*new (old)	*to	wouldn't
enough	*no (yes)	*too (Too late!)	*write
especially	off	trouble	*your
everybody	*one (1)	*two (2)	*you're (you are)
everyone	our	until	
everything	people	usually	

*Clues are attached to homophones and may include pictures and opposite words.

Word walls provide children with an immediately accessible dictionary for the most troublesome words. Because the words are added gradually, stay in the same spot forever, are alphabetical by first letter, are visually distinctive by different colors of paper, and because of the daily practice of finding, writing, and chanting these words, most children learn to read and spell almost all the words. Because you select words they need constantly in their reading and writing, their recognition of these words becomes automatic and their attention can be devoted to less-frequent words and to constructing meaning as they read and write.

CROSS CHECKING

The ability to use some letters in a word along with the sentence or story context is an important decoding strategy. We have found two ways to help children develop automatic cross-checking abilities. The first is a daily cross-checking activity we call Guess the Covered Word. The second is the way teachers respond during oral reading.

Guess the Covered Word

Many words can be figured out by thinking about what would make sense in a sentence and seeing whether the consonants in the word match what you are thinking of. You must learn to do two things simultaneously—think about what would make sense and think about letters and sounds. Struggling readers often prefer to do one or the other, but not both. Thus, they may guess something that is sensible but ignore the letter sounds they know or guess something that is close to the sounds but makes no sense in the sentence! Doing a weekly Guess the Covered Word activity helps students combine these strategies effectively.

Before class begins, write four to five sentences on the board that start with your students' names, follow a similar word pattern, and end with words that vary in their initial sounds and word length. For the first lessons use only words with single consonants.

> Rasheed likes to play **soccer.**
> Kate likes to play **softball.**
> Rob likes to play **basketball.**
> Juan likes to play **hockey.**

Cover the last word in each sentence with sticky notes, tearing or adjusting them to the length of each word.

Begin the activity by reading the first sentence and asking students to guess the covered word. Write three or four guesses on the board next to the sentence. Uncover the first letter. Erase guesses that do not begin with that letter. Have students continue offering guesses that make sense and begin with the correct letter.

Write their responses on the board. Keep the students focused on both meaning and beginning letters. When the first letter is revealed, some students guess anything that begins with that letter. For example, if the first letter is an *s*, they may guess *sand*. Respond with something like, "*Sand* does begin with an *s*, but I can't write *sand* because people don't play sand." Finally, uncover the whole word and see whether any guesses were correct. Repeat the procedure for the remaining sentences.

Once students understand how Guess the Covered Word works, include some sentences in which the covered word begins with the digraphs, *sh, ch, th,* and *wh*. Explain that the rules of this game require you to show them all the letters up to the first vowel. Then show them some sentences that contain the digraphs *sh, ch, th,* and *wh* as well as single consonants. Include examples for both sounds of *c*. Vary your sentence patterns and where in the sentence the covered word is.

Corinda likes to eat **cherries**.
Watermelon is Chad's favorite fruit.
Jessica likes strawberries on her **cereal**.
Bo likes strawberry **shortcake**.
Melinda bakes pies for **Thanksgiving**.
I don't know **which** pie I like best.

Guess the Covered Word works for teaching or reviewing blends—groups of letters in which you can hear the sounds blended together, such as *br, pl,* and *str.* As with digraphs, vary the sentence pattern and where in the sentence the covered word is.

Justin likes to swim in the **summer.**
Curtis plays baseball in the **spring.**
Skiing is Jennifer's favorite sport in the winter.
Jennifer likes to **skate** too.
Val likes to play all kinds of **sports.**

Be sure that when you uncover the beginning letters, you uncover everything up to the vowel. If you have uncovered an *s* and someone guessed the word *snow*, tell them that was good thinking for the *s*. Then have everyone say *snow* slowly and hear the *n*. "My rule is that I have to show you everything up to the vowel so if the word were *snow*, I would have to show you not just the *s* but the *n* too."

Sometimes, struggling readers get the idea that the only time you use reading strategies is during reading time! It is important to show them how cross checking can help them figure out words when they are reading all kinds of things. You might write a paragraph, such as this, related to your science topic on mammals. Cover the words in the usual way and have the whole sentence read before going back to guess without any letters and then with all the letters up to the vowel (covered words are bold).

> Mammals are warm-blooded animals. Their body **temperature** stays the same regardless of the weather. All mammals at some time in their **lives** have hair. For **whales,** they have hair only before they are born. Mammals nurse their babies and give them more **protection** than other animals. Mammals also have a larger **brain** than any other group of animals.

One more way to vary Guess the Covered Word is to cover some words in a big book. Use the same procedures of guessing without any letters and then with all the letters up to the vowel. Help children verbalize that one way to decode words is to read the whole sentence and then think what would make sense, be about the right length, and have *all* the correct letters up to the vowel.

Responding to Oral Reading

Most reading children do should be silent reading with a focus on understanding and enjoying what they read. It is also helpful and fun for children to have time to read aloud. Young children like to read aloud and as they are reading, teachers have a chance to see whether they are using their strategies and to coach them in the appropriate use.

When children read aloud, they always produce a few misreadings. It is these misreadings that allow teachers a "window into the mind" of the reader. It is in responding to these misreadings that teachers have a chance to coach children into strategic reading. Here are some suggestions for making oral reading an enjoyable and a profitable endeavor.

Have Children Read Silently Before Reading Orally   For comprehension, silent reading should precede oral reading to ensure that students do not lose track of the fact that reading is understanding and reacting to the meaning of the printed words. Young children who are just beginning to read should also read material to themselves before reading it orally. When beginning readers read, however, it is seldom silent. They do not yet know how to imagine the words in their minds; reading to themselves can be described as "mumble" or "whisper" reading.

Oral Reading Should Be from Material That Is Fairly Easy   Material that students read orally should be easy so that they make no more than three to five errors per hundred words read. If the average sentence length is seven words, this would be no more than one error every three sentences. It is very important that children do not make too many errors because their ability to cross check drops dramatically when they make so many errors that they cannot make sense of what they are reading.

Children Should Never Correct the Reader's Error   Allowing students to interrupt and correct the misreadings inhibits the reader's ability to self-correct and forces the reader to try for "word-perfect reading." The same is true when the teacher interrupts and corrects the reader. Although it might seem that striving for word-perfect reading would be a worthy goal, it is not because of the way our eyes move when we read.

When we read, our eyes move across the line of print in little jumps. The eyes then stop and look at the words. The average reader can see about 12 letters at a time—one large word, two medium words, or three small words. When your eyes stop, they can only see the letters they have stopped on. The following letters are not visible until the eyes move forward and stop once again. Once your eyes have moved forward, you cannot see the words you saw during the last stop. As we read orally, our eyes move ahead of our voice. This is how we can read with expression because the intonation and emphasis we give to a particular word can only be determined when we have seen the words that follow it. The space between where your eyes are and where your voice is, is called your eye–voice span. Fluent readers, reading easy material, have an eye–voice span of five to six words.

Good readers read with expression because their voice is trailing their eyes. When they say a particular word, their eyes are no longer on that word but, rather, several words down the line. This explains a phenomenon that all good readers use. They make little non-meaning-changing errors when they read orally. They read "can't" when the actual printed words were *cannot.* They read "car" when the actual printed word was *automobile.* Non-meaning-changing errors are a sign of good reading! They indicate that the eyes are out there ahead of the voice using the later words in the sentence to confirm the meaning, pronunciation, and expression given to the previous word. The reader who says "car" for *automobile* must have correctly recognized or decoded *automobile* or he or she could not have substituted the synonym *car.* When the reader says "car," the word *automobile* can no longer be seen because the eyes have moved on.

Good readers make small non-meaning-changing errors because their eyes are not focused on the words they are saying. If other children are allowed to follow along while the oral reader reads, they will interrupt the reader to point out these errors. If children were allowed to correct non-meaning-changing errors, they would learn to keep their eyes on the very word they are saying when reading orally! This fosters word-by-word reading. Too much oral reading, with each error corrected by other children or the teacher, results in children not developing the eye–voice span all fluent readers have. Constant interruptions by the teacher or other children also work against developing appropriate cross-checking strategies and spontaneous self-corrections.

Eliminating interruptions by other children is not easy unless you have all the children who are not reading put their fingers in their books and close them! When one child is reading, the others should not be "following along" with the words. Rather, they should be listening to the reader read and following the meaning.

Ignore Errors That Do Not Change Meaning   Of course, because you recognize small, non-meaning-changing errors as a sign of good eye–voice span, you will grit your teeth and ignore them!

When the Reader Makes a Meaning-Changing Error, Wait!   Control the urge to stop and correct the reader immediately. Rather, wait until the reader finishes the sentence or paragraph. What follows the error is often the information the reader needs to self-correct. Students who self-correct errors based on subsequent words read should be praised because they are demonstrating their use of cross checking while reading. Students who are interrupted immediately never learn to self-correct. Instead, they wait for someone else to correct them. Without self-correcting and self-monitoring, children never become good readers.

If Waiting Does Not Work, Give Sustaining Feedback   If the reader continues beyond the end of the sentence in which they made a meaning-changing error, the teacher should stop the reader by saying something like:

> "Wait a minute. That didn't make sense. You read, 'then the magician stubbled and fell.' What does that mean?"

The teacher now has reinforced a major understanding that all readers must use if they are to decode words well. The word must have the right letters and must make sense. The letters in *stubbled* are very close to the letters in *stumbled*, but *stubbled* does not make sense. The teacher should then pause and see whether the reader can find a way to fix it. If so, the teacher should say,

> "Yes, *stumbled* makes sense. Good. Continue reading."

If not, the teacher should say something like,

> "Look at the letters in the word you called *stubbled*. What word do you know that looks almost like *stubbled* but is something people often do before they fall?"

If this does not help, the teacher might just pronounce the word. Later, it may be useful to return to that page, review the misreading, and point out the *m* before the *b* or suggest a known rhyming word such as *crumbled* or *tumbled*.

DECODING AND SPELLING ONE- AND TWO-SYLLABLE WORDS

English is an alphabetic language. Once you get past the most frequent words, you will find a great deal of predictability in the letter–sound patterns. This

MOST COMMON PHONOGRAMS (SPELLING PATTERNS)

The 37 most useful phonograms, or spelling patterns, are found in hundreds of words children read and write (Wylie & Durrell, 1970):

ack	ame	at	ell	ight	ink	op	ump
ail	an	ate	est	ill	ip	ore	unk
ain	ank	aw	ice	in	it	ot	
ake	ap	ay	ick	ine	ock	uck	
ale	ash	eat	ide	ing	oke	ug	

predictability is not based on a one-letter, one-sound relationship, however; it is based on the pattern of letters that follow the vowel. The vowel and following letters have been given a variety of labels. Some teachers call them word families, others call them phonograms. Linguists refer to them as rimes. Although the terminology is not important, we prefer to call them spelling patterns because we want children to learn the patterns that constitute how words are spelled and pronounced.

Many activities can help children become sensitive to the patterns in words. We describe two of our favorites: Making Words and Reading/Writing Rhymes.

Making Words

Making Words (Cunningham & Cunningham, 1992) is an activity in which children are given some letters and use these letters to make words. To plan a Making Words lesson, we begin with the "secret" word—a word that can be made from all the letters. The word for this lesson is *winter.* Using the letters in *winter,* we choose 10–15 words that give us some easy and harder words and several sets of rhymes. We then decide on the order in which words will be made, beginning with short words and building to larger words. We write these words on index cards to use in the sorting/transferring parts of the lesson. As all the children make the words in their holders, we choose one child to come and make it in the pocket chart.

MATERIALS NEEDED FOR MAKING WORDS LESSON

Holders made from file folder cut in thirds, leaving the fold in the middle (Fold up the bottom edge about an inch to create a pocket. Crease well and staple on both ends.)

Letter cards for the students that fit in holder (Make vowels different color; put capitals on back.)

Large letter cards and pocket chart

Index cards with words to be made written on them

The children have holders and letters and are ready to begin the lesson. Big letter cards are displayed on the chart.

As the lesson begins, the letters **e, i, n, r, t,** and **w** are in the pocket chart. The children have the same letters and a holder. The teacher leads them to make words by saying:

> "Take two letters and make **in.**"
>
> "Add a letter to make the three-letter word **tin.** Some cans are made of tin. Let's all say **tin.**"
>
> "Now change just one letter and **tin** can become **ten.** You have ten fingers and ten toes. Say **ten.**"
>
> "Move the letters in **ten** around and turn your **ten** into a **net.**"
>
> "Now change just one letter and **net** can become **wet.**"
>
> "Let's make one more three-letter word **win.** Everyone say **win.**"
>
> "Now, we are going to make some four-letter words. Add one letter to **win** and you will have **twin.** My friend has a twin sister. Stretch out the word **twin** and listen to the sounds you hear yourself saying."
>
> "Take all your letters out and start over and make another four-letter word— **went.**"
>
> "Now change just one letter and **went** can become **rent.** Let's all say **rent.**"
>
> "The next word is a four-letter word but you only hear three letters. Make **tire.** See whether you can figure out what letter you don't hear but you need to spell **tire.** Let's all say **tire.**"

"Now change just one letter and **tire** can become **wire**."

"Now, let's make a five-letter word. Use five letters to spell **twine**. Twine is a heavy string we use to tie things with. Everyone say **twine**."

"Has anyone figured out the secret word? I will come around to see whether anyone has the secret word."

A child who has figured out **winter** makes it in the pocket chart and then everyone makes **winter** in their holders to finish the first part of the lesson.

Once all the words are made, we lead the students to sort for patterns. For the sorting part of the lesson, we put the words on index cards in the pocket chart. The first sort in this lesson is for beginning sounds. We pull out the word **win** and have them find the other words that begin with **w**—**wet, went, wire, winter**. Next, we take the word **tin** and have them find the other words that begin with **t**—**ten, twin, tire, twine**. Finally, we separate the **t** words into **tin, ten,** and **tire** and **twin** and **twine** and have them notice that **twin** and **twine** begin with **tw** and that if you stretch the words out, you can hear both letters.

Next we help them sort the words into rhymes:

in	net	rent	tire
tin	wet	went	wire
win			
twin			

The teacher finds a child who has correctly made the word and sends him up to make it with the big letters.

Here are the words the children made, including the secret word, which can be made with all the letters.

Here are the words at the end of the lesson. The teacher helps the students use these rhyming words to read two new words and spell two new words with the same rhyming pattern.

When the rhyming words are sorted, we remind the children that rhyming words can help them read and spell words. We then write two new rhyming words on cards and have them place these words under the rhyming words and use the rhymes to decode them:

fire   **spent**

Finally, we say two more new rhyming words and help them see how the original rhyming words help them spell the new words:

tent   **thin**

The first several lessons we do have only one vowel and make fewer words:

Letters:	a b l s t
Make:	as at lab tab sat bat bats stab last blast
Sort for:	l b
	-ab -at -ast
Transfer Words:	cab fast past rat

Letters:	o g n r s t
Make:	so no go got rot not rot rots sort song snort strong
Sort for:	g n r s
	-o -ot -ort -ong
Transfer Words:	clot sport long slot

Letters:	i g n p r s
Make:	in sin pin pig rig rip sip snip sing ring rings spring
Sort for:	s p r
	-in -ing -ig -ip
Transfer Words:	strip string twin twig

We often tie in lessons with what we are reading or with something we are studying. Here are some December lessons:

Letters:	e e n p r s t
Make:	net pet pets pest nest rest rent sent spent enter pester present (and serpent)
Sort for:	n p r
	-et -est -ent
Transfer Words:	wet west chest vent

Letters:	a e c d l n s
Make:	as an can Dan and sand land clan clean dance dances cleans candles
Sort for:	c cl -an -and
Transfer Words:	band stand bran hand

Lessons in which the last words are sports related are always motivating:

Letters:	a o o b f l l t
Make:	at bat fat all ball fall tall tool fool boat flat float football
Sort for:	-at -all -oo -oat
Transfer Words:	stall stool chat goat

Letters:	a a e b b l l s
Make:	all lab slab blab ball bell sell seal sale bale able sable baseball
Sort for:	-al -ab -ale -ell -able
Transfer Words:	cable spell flab whale

STEPS IN PLANNING A MAKING WORDS LESSON

1. Choose your "secret word," a word that can be made with all the letters. In choosing this word, consider child interest, the curriculum tie-ins you can make, and the letter–sound patterns to which you can draw children's attention through the sorting at the end.
2. Make a list of other words that can be made from these letters. (Go to www.wordplays.com and enter your secret word to see *all* the words that can be made from these letters.)
3. From all the words you could make, pick 12–15 words using these criteria:

   - Words that you can sort for the pattern you want to emphasize
   - Little words and big words to create a multilevel lesson (making little words helps your lower-achieving students; making big words challenges your highest-achieving students)
   - Words that can be made with the same letters in different places (barn/bran) so children are reminded that ordering letters is crucial when spelling words
   - A proper name or two to remind the children that we use capital letters
   - Words that most students have in their listening vocabularies

4. Write all the words on index cards and order them from smallest to biggest.
5. Once you have the two-letter words together, the three-letter words together, and so on, order them so you can emphasize letter patterns and how changing the position of the letters or changing/adding just one letter results in a different word.
6. Store the cards in an envelope. Write the words in order on the envelope, the patterns you will sort for, and the transfer words.

STEPS IN TEACHING A MAKING WORDS LESSON

    1. Place the large letter cards needed in a pocket chart or along the chalk tray.
    2. Have children pass out letters or pick up the letters needed.

3. Hold up and name the letters on the large letter cards and have the children hold up their matching small letter cards.

4. Write the numeral 2 (or 3 if no two-letter words are in this lesson) on the board. Tell them to take two letters and make the first word. Have them say the word after you stretch out the word to hear all the sounds.

5. Have a child who makes the first word correctly make the same word with the large letter cards on the chalk tray or pocket chart. Do not wait for everyone to make the word before sending a child to make it with the big letters. Encourage anyone who did not make the word correctly at first to fix the word when they see it made correctly.

6. Continue to make words, giving students clues, such as, "Change the first letter only" or "Move the same letters around and you can make a different word" or "Take all your letters out and make another word." Send a child who has made the word correctly to make the word with the large letter cards. Cue them when they are to use more letters by erasing and changing the number on the board to indicate the number of letters needed.

7. Before telling them the last word, say, "Now it's time for the secret word—the word we can make with all our letters. I am coming around to see whether one of you has made the secret word in your holder." If someone has figured it out, send that child to make the big word. If not, tell them the word and let everyone make it.

8. Once all the words have been made, take the index cards on which you wrote the words and place them one at a time (in the same order that children made them) along the chalkledge or in the pocket chart. Have children say and spell the words with you as you do this. Have the children sort these words for patterns—including beginning sounds and rhymes.

9. To encourage transfer to reading and writing, show students how rhyming words can help them decode and spell other words. Write two words on index cards and have students put these two new words with the rhyming words and use the rhyming words to decode them. Finally, say two words that rhyme and have students spell these words by deciding which words rhyme with them.

Making Big Words   When working with older students and with more than eight letters, we print the letters on strips and duplicate them. Children cut the strips into letters and use them to make words.

Letters on strip:	e e e i c d n p s t
Make:	nice need deep seep seen dent sent cent scent spend steep dense tense scene nicest insect decent descent deepest neediest inspected centipedes
Sort for:	est (ending)
	ent eep ense
	seen/scene sent/cent/scent
Transfer Words:	spent creep creepiest steepest

Letters on strip:	e e o u y l m m n n p t
Make:	ump yum plum lump lumpy melon lemon lemony employ moment monument employment unemployment
Sort for:	ment
	um ump
Related Words:	employ, employment, unemployment; lump, lumpy; lemon, lemony
Transfer Words:	bump bumpy grump grumpy

Reading/Writing Rhymes

Reading/Writing Rhymes is another activity that helps students learn to use patterns to decode and spell hundreds of words. In addition, all beginning letters are reviewed every time you do a Reading/Writing Rhymes lesson. Once all the rhyming words are generated on a chart, students write rhymes using these words and then read each other's rhymes. Because writing and reading are connected to every lesson, students learn how to use these patterns as they actually read and write.

To do a Reading/Writing Rhymes lesson, you will need a deck of cards containing all the beginning sounds. The 3 × 5 index cards are laminated and have the single-letter consonants written in blue, the blends in red, and the digraphs and other two-letter combinations in green. On one side of each card, the first letter is a capital letter. The deck contains 50 beginning letter cards that include:

Single consonants: b c d f g h j k l m n p r s t v w y z

Digraphs (two letters, one sound): sh ch wh th

Other two-letter, one-sound combinations: ph wr kn qu

Blends (beginning letters blended together, sometimes called clusters): bl br cl cr dr fl fr gl gr pl pr sc scr sk sl sm sn sp spr st str sw tr

At the beginning of the lesson, we distribute all the cards to the students. In most classrooms, each child gets two or three cards. Once all the cards are distributed, we write the spelling pattern we are working with 10–12 times on a piece of chart paper. As we write it each time, we have the children help spell it and pronounce it.

Next we invite all the children who have a card they think makes a word to come up to place their card next to one of the written spelling patterns and to pronounce the word. If the word is indeed a real word, we use the word in a sentence and write that word on the chart. If the word is not a real word, we explain why we cannot write it on the chart. We write names with capital letters and if a word is both a name and not a name, such as *will* and *Will*, we write it both ways. When all the children have come up who think they can spell words with their beginning letters and the spelling pattern, we call children up to make the words not yet there by saying something like, "I think the person with the *qu* card could come up here and add *qu* to *ill* to make a word we know." We try to include all the words that any of our children would have in their listening vocabulary, but we avoid obscure words. If the patterns we wrote to begin our chart get made into complete words, we add as many more as needed.

ill	
bill	skill
Bill	mill
fill	drill
chill	grill
Jill	pill
gill	quill
Rill	
will	
Will	
still	
spill	
Kill	
dill	

Once the chart of rhyming words is written, we work together in a shared writing format to write a couple of sentences using lots of the rhyming words. Next the students write some silly sentences. If children choose to, we let them write with a friend. We give them a limited time—9 minutes—to write. When the time is up, we gather the children together and, if they want to, let them read their silly sentences to the class.

Reading/Writing Rhymes can also be used to teach spelling patterns for words with two common patterns. We head the chart with the two patterns and distribute the beginning letter cards. Children line up who think their beginning letters make a real word. We write the word on the correct side of the chart. If both patterns make a real word (*plain, plane*), we write each word in the appropriate column and talk about the different meanings of the words. If a rhyming word is spelled with another pattern (*reign, Maine*), we write it at the bottom of the chart with an asterisk. The chart for the ain/ane long vowel spelling pattern follows.

ain	ane	
rain	cane	
brain	crane	
train	sane	
pain	pane	
plain	plane	* reign
drain	Jane	Maine
vain	vane	
chain	Shane	
gain	mane	
grain	Zane	
stain		
strain		
Spain		
sprain		

All the common vowel patterns can be taught through Reading/Writing Rhymes. We always choose the patterns that generate the most rhymes, and when there is more than one common spelling for a rhyme, we include both—or in some cases all three—spelling patterns. Children enjoy writing the silly sentences. Following is an example written by two friends working from the ain/ane chart.

> Jane went to Spain with Zane and Shane. They went on a plane then took a train. Shane tripped on a chain and fell in the lane in the rain. He had a sprain in his leg and a lot of pain and needed a cane.

STRATEGIES FOR BIG WORDS

Big words present special decoding problems. Most of the words we read are one- and two-syllable words, but polysyllabic words often carry most of the content. Decoding and spelling polysyllabic words is based on patterns, but these patterns are more sophisticated and require students to understand how words change in their spelling, pronunciation, and meaning as suffixes and prefixes are added. The *g* in *sign* seems quite illogical until you realize that *sign* is related to *signal, signature,* and other words. Finding the *compose/composition* and *compete/competition* relationship helps students understand why the second syllable of *composition* and *competition* sound alike but are spelled differently.

To decode and spell big words, children must (1) have a mental store of big words that contain the spelling patterns common to big words; (2) chunk big words into pronounceable segments by comparing the parts of new big words to the big words they already know; and (3) recognize and use common prefixes and suffixes. The activities in this section are designed to help children build a store of big words and use these big words to decode and spell other big words.

Big Word Boards

Reserve one of the bulletin boards in your room for use as a big word board. As you teach science and social studies units or read literature selections, identify 15–25 big words that are key to understanding. Write these on large index cards with a black, thick permanent marker. Do not overwhelm your students by presenting all the words at once. Rather, add three or four each day as you introduce these words. As you put the words on the board, have the students chant the spelling (cheerleader style) with you. Then have them close their eyes and chant the spelling again. Next, have them write a sentence that uses as many of the words as they can and still have a sensible sentence.

Once the words are displayed on the board, draw students' attention to these words as they occur in lectures, films, experiments, or discussions. As students write about what they are learning, encourage them to use the big words and to refer to the board for the correct spelling. Help students develop a positive attitude toward learning these big words by pointing out that every discipline has some critical big words; using these words separates the pros from the amateurs.

The following list of words appeared on a big word board while students were studying Antarctica:

Antarctica	**geologic**	**regulation**
exploration	**exploitation**	**conservation**
conservationists	**minerals**	**petroleum**
controversial	**development**	**resources**
environmentalists	**environment**	**continent**
vacationers	**policies**	**confrontation**
geologists	**inhospitable**	**international**

As you can see, the big words students need as they read and write about Antarctica are numerous. Notice also how many of the common polysyllabic patterns are illustrated by just this one set of words. Students who can read and write *exploration, exploitation, regulation, conservation*, and *confrontation* now have several known big words that end in the reliable, but totally unexplainable, letter pattern t-i-o-n, which we pronounce "shun"! The words *geologists, conservationists*, and *environmentalists* contain the suffix *ists*, which usually transforms a word from "the thing" to "the people who work on or worry about the thing." Including two important forms of the same base word—*conservation/conservationists, environment/ environmentalists, geologic/geologists*—allows students to see how the endings of words often change what part of the sentence they can be used in. If your students are not very sophisticated word users, you can greatly extend the control they have over language by pointing out how words change and by pointing out the similarities and differences in pronunciation, use, and spelling.

Modeling How to Decode Big Words

When you model, you show someone how to do something. In real life, we use modeling constantly to teach skills. We would not think of explaining how to ride a bike. Rather, we demonstrate and talk about what we are doing as the learner watches and listens to our explanation. Vocabulary introduction is a good place to model how you figure out the pronunciation of a word for students. Modeling is more than just telling them pronunciation; it is modeling the thinking that goes on when you meet up with a big word.

The word should be shown in a sentence context so that students are reminded that words must have the correct letters in the correct places and must make sense. Here is an example of how you might model for students one way to decode the word *international.* Write on the board or overhead:

The thinning of the ozone layer is an international problem.

"Today, we are going to look at a big word that is really just a little word with a prefix added to the beginning and a suffix added to the end."

Underline *nation* in the sentence you have just written.

The thinning of the ozone layer is an inter<u>nation</u>al problem.

"Who can tell me this word? Yes, that is the word *nation*. Now, let's look at the prefix that comes before *nation*."

Underline *inter*.

The thinning of the ozone layer is an <u>inter</u>national problem.

"This prefix is *inter*. You probably know *inter* from words such as *interrupt* and *internal*. Now, let's look at what follows *inter* and *nation*."

Underline *al*.

The thinning of the ozone layer is an internation<u>al</u> problem.

"You know *al* from many words, such as *unusual* and *critical*."

Write *unusual* and *critical* and underline the *al*.

unusu<u>al</u>   critic<u>al</u>

"Listen as I pronounce this part of the word."

Underline and pronounce *national*.

The thinning of the ozone layer is an inter<u>national</u> problem.

"Notice how the pronunciation of *nation* changes when we put *a-l* on it. Now let's put all the parts together and pronounce the word—*inter nation al*. Let's read the sentence and make sure *international* makes sense."

Have the sentence read and confirm that ozone thinning is indeed a problem for many nations to solve.

"You can figure out the pronunciation of many big words if you look for common prefixes, such as *inter*, common root words, such as *nation*, and common suffixes, such as *al*.

In addition to helping you figure out the pronunciation of a word, prefixes and suffixes sometimes help you know what the word means or where in a sentence we can use the word. The word *nation* names a thing. When we describe a nation, we add the suffix *al* and have *national.* The prefix *inter* often means "between or among." Something that is *international* is between many nations. The Olympics are the best example of an *international* sporting event."

This sample lesson for introducing the word *international* demonstrates how a teacher can help students see and use morphemes—meaningful parts of words— to decode polysyllabic words. Notice that the teacher points out words that students might know and that have the same parts. In addition, meaning clues provided by the morphemes are provided whenever appropriate.

A similar procedure could be used to model how you would decode a word that did not contain suffixes or prefixes. For the word *resources,* for example, the teacher would draw students' attention to the familiar first syllable *re* and then point out the known word *sources.* For *geologic,* the teacher might write and underline the *geo* in the known word *geography* and then point out the known word *logic. Policies* might be compared to *politics* and *agencies.*

Modeling is simply thinking aloud about how you might go about figuring out an unfamiliar word. It takes just a few extra minutes to point out the morphemes in *international* and to show how *policies* is like *politics* and *agencies,* but taking these extra few minutes is quickly paid back as students begin to develop some independence in figuring out those big words that carry so much of the content.

The Nifty-Thrifty-Fifty

English is the most morphologically complex language. Linguists estimate that for every word you know, you can figure out how to decode, spell, and build meaning for six or seven other words if you recognize and use the morphemic patterns in words. Activities in this section teach students how to spell a Nifty-Thrifty-Fifty store of words to decode, spell, and build meaning for thousands of other words. These 50 words include examples for all the common prefixes and suffixes as well as common spelling changes. Because these 50 words help with so many other words, we have named them the Nifty-Thrifty-Fifty.

The Nifty-Thrifty-Fifty words should be introduced gradually and students should practice chanting and writing them until their spelling and decoding become automatic. The procedures for working with these words and their important parts follow:

1. Display the words, arranged by first letter, someplace in the room. Add four or five each week. You may want to use a bulletin board or hang a banner above a bulletin board and attach the words to it. The words need to be big and bold so that they are seen easily from wherever the students are writing. Using different colors makes them more visible and attractive. Many teachers use large colored index cards or write them with different colors of thick, bold permanent markers.

THE NIFTY-THRIFTY-FIFTY

Nifty-Thrifty-Fifty Transferable Chunks

antifreeze	anti	
beautiful		ful (y-i)
classify		ify
communities	com	es (y-i)
community	com	y
composer	com	er
continuous	con	ous (drop e)
conversation	con	tion
deodorize	de	ize
different		ent
discovery	dis	y
dishonest	dis	
electricity	e	ity
employee	em	ee
encouragement	en	ment
expensive	ex	ive
forecast	fore	
forgotten		en (double t)
governor		or
happiness		ness (y-i)
hopeless		less
illegal	il	
impossible	im	ible
impression	im	sion
independence	in	ence
international	inter	al
invasion	in	sion
irresponsible	ir	ible
midnight	mid	
misunderstand	mis	
musician		ian
nonliving	non	ing (drop e)
overpower	over	
performance	per	ance
prehistoric	pre	ic
prettier		er (y-i)
rearrange	re	
replacement	re	ment
richest		est
semifinal	semi	
signature		ture
submarine	sub	
supermarkets	super	s
swimming		ing (double m)
transportation	trans	tion
underweight	under	
unfinished	un	ed
unfriendly	un	ly
unpleasant	un	ant (drop e)
valuable		able (drop e)

2. Explain to students that in English many big words are just smaller words with prefixes and suffixes added to the word. Good spellers do not memorize the spelling of every new word they come across. Rather, they notice the patterns in words and these patterns include prefixes, suffixes, and spelling changes that occur when these are added.

3. Tell students that one way to practice words is to say the letters in them aloud in a rhythmic, chanting fashion. Tell students that although this might seem silly, it really is not because the brain responds to sound and rhythm. (That is one of the reasons you can sing along with the words of a familiar song even though you could not say the words without singing the song, and also why jingles and raps are easy to remember.) Point to each word and have students chant it (cheerleader style) with you. After "cheering" for each word, help students analyze the word, talking about meaning and determining the root, prefix, suffix, and noting any spelling changes. Here is an example of the kind of word introduction students find most helpful:

> **composer**—A composer is a person who composes something. Many other words, such as *writer, reporter,* and *teacher,* are made up of a root word and the suffix *er* meaning a person or thing that does something. When *er* is added to a word that already has an *e,* the original *e* is dropped.
>
> **discovery**—A discovery is something you discover. The prefix *dis* often changes a word to an opposite form. To cover something can mean to hide it. When you discover it, it is no longer hidden. *Discovery* is the root word *cover* with the added prefix *dis* and suffix *y.* There are no spelling changes.
>
> **encouragement**—When you encourage someone, you give them encouragement. Many other words, such as *argue, argument* and, *replace, replacement,* follow this same pattern. The root word for *encourage* is *courage.* So *encouragement* is made up of the prefix *en,* the root word *courage,* and the suffix *ment.*
>
> **hopeless**—Students should easily see the root word *hope* and the suffix *less.* Other similar words are *painless* and *homeless.*
>
> **impossible**—The root word *possible* with the suffix *im.* In many words, including *impatient* and *immature,* the suffix *im* changes the word to an opposite.
>
> **musician**—A musician is a person who makes music. A beautician helps make you beautiful, and a magician makes magic. *Musician* has the root word *music* with the suffix *ian,* which sometimes indicates the person who does something. None of the spelling changes but the pronunciation changes. Have students say the words *music* and *musician, magic* and *magician* and notice how the pronunciation changes.

4. Once you have noticed the composition for each word, have helped students see other words that work in a similar way, and have cheered for each word, have students write each word. Writing the word with careful attention to each letter and the sequence of each letter helps students use another mode to practice the word. (Do not, however, assign students to copy words five times each. They just do this "mechanically" and often do not focus on the letters.) Students enjoy writing the words more and focus better on the word if you make it a riddle or game. You can do this simply by giving clues for the word you want them to write:

1. Number 1 is the opposite of discouragement.
2. Number 2 is the opposite of hopeful.
3. For number 3, write the word that tells what you are if you play the guitar.
4. For number 4, write what you are if you play the guitar but you also make up the songs you play.
5. Number 5 is the opposite of possible.
6. For number 6, write the word that has *cover* for the root word.

After writing the words, have students check their own papers once more chanting the letters aloud underlining each as they say it.

5. When you have a few minutes of "sponge" time, practice the words by chanting or writing. As you are cheering or writing each word, ask students to identify the root, prefix, and suffix and talk about how these affect the meaning of the root word. Also have them point out any spelling changes.

6. Once students can automatically, quickly, and correctly spell the words and explain to you how they are composed, it is time to help them see how these words can help them decode and spell other words. Remind students that good spellers do not memorize the spelling of each word. Rather, they use words they know and combine roots, suffixes, and prefixes to figure out how to spell lots of other words. Have the students spell words that are contained in the words and words you can make by combining parts of the words.

Have each word used in a sentence and talk about the meaning relationships when appropriate. Note spelling changes as needed. From just the eight words— *composer, discovery, encouragement, hopeless, impossible, musician, richest,* and *unfriendly*—students should be able to decode, spell, and discuss meanings for the following words:

compose	encourage	music	dispose	enrichment
pose	courage	rich	discourage	uncover
discover	hope	friend	discouragement	richly
cover	possible	friendly	enrich	hopelessly

7. Continue adding words gradually, going though the above procedures with all the words. Do not add words too quickly, and provide lots of practice with these words and the other words that can be decoded and spelled by combining parts of these words. Because this store of words provides patterns for so many other words, you want your students to "overlearn" these words so that they are called up instantly and automatically when students meet similar words in their reading or need to spell similar words while writing.

 NIFTY-THRIFTY-FIFTY TRANSFER WORDS

Here are just some of the words they should be able to decode, spell, and discuss meanings for by using parts of all 50 words:

conform	relive	declassify	powerlessly
conformity	repose	decompose	powerlessness
inform	reclassify	deform	superpower
informer	revalue	deformity	finalize
informant	recover	prearrange	finalizing
information	rediscover	resign	finalization
misinform	electrical	resignation	weighty
uninformed	displease	designation	weightier
formation	discontinue	significant	weightiest
formal	disposal	significance	weightless
transform	musical	freezer	undervalue
transformation	continual	freezing	friendlier
performer	employer	freezable	friendliest
responsibility	employment	subfreezing	friendliness
responsive	unemployment	underclass	unfriendliness
responsiveness	unemployed	overexpose	unpleasantness
honesty	employable	underexpose	historical
dishonesty	unemployable	superimpose	historically
honestly	difference	undercover	expressive
legally	consignment	forecaster	impressive
illegally	nationality	forecasting	repressive
responsibly	nationalities	forecastable	invasive
irresponsibly	internationalize	miscast	noninvasive
arranging	interdependence	antidepressant	invasiveness
rearranging	depress	overture	hopefully
placing	depression	empower	hopelessly
replacing	depressive	empowerment	predispose
misplacing	deport	powerful	predisposition
report	deportation	powerfully	deodorant
reporter	deportee	powerfulness	beautician
refinish	devalue	powerless	electrician

The Wheel

The popular game show "Wheel of Fortune" is based on the idea that having meaning and some letters allows you to figure out many words. On "Wheel of Fortune," meaning is provided by the category to which the word belongs. A variation of this game can be used to introduce big words and to teach students to use meaning and all the letters they know. Here is how to play The Wheel.

Remind students that many words can be figured out (even if we cannot decode all the parts) as long as we think about what makes sense and keep the parts that we do know in the right places. Ask students who have watched "Wheel of Fortune" to explain how it is played. Then explain how your version of The Wheel will be different:

1. Contestants guess all letters without considering if they are consonants or vowels.
2. They must have all letters filled in before they can say the word.
3. The word must fit in a sentence rather than in a category.
4. They will win paper clips instead of great prizes!
5. Vanna will not be there to turn letters!

Write a sentence on the board and draw blanks for each letter of an important word. Here is an example:

If you were to travel to Antarctica, you would be struck by its almost unbeliev-able _ _ _ _ _ _ _ _ _ _ .

Have a student begin by asking, "Is there a . . . ?" If the student guesses a correct letter, fill in that letter. Give that student one paper clip for each time that letter occurs. Let the student continue to guess letters until he or she gets a "No!" When a student asks about a letter that is not there, write the letter above the puzzle and go on to the next student.

Make sure that all letters are filled in before anyone is allowed to guess. (This really shows them the importance of spelling and attending to common spelling patterns!) Give the person who correctly guesses the word five bonus paper clips! As with other games, if someone says the answer out of turn, immediately award the bonus paper clips to the person whose turn it was. The student having the most paper clips at the end is the winner!

For our example, a student might ask whether there is an *r*? ("Sorry, no *r*!") The next student asks for an *s*. One *s* is filled in.

If you were to travel to Antarctica, you would be struck by its almost unbeliev-able _ _ s _ _ _ _ _ _ _ .

The student is given one paper clip and continues to ask questions. "Is there a *t*?" "Yes, one *t*!"

If you were to travel to Antarctica, you would be struck by its almost unbeliev-able _ _ s _ _ _ t _ _ _ .

The student asks for an *o*. Two *o*'s are filled in and the student receives two more paper clips.

> **If you were to travel to Antarctica, you would be struck by its almost unbeliev-**
> **able _ _ s o _ _ t _ o _.**

Next the student asks for an *i* and then for an *n*.

> **If you were to travel to Antarctica, you would be struck by its almost unbeliev-**
> **able _ _ s o _ _ t i o n.**

After much thought, the student asks for an *m*. Unfortunately, there is no *m*, so play passes to the next student who asks for an *e*, an *a*, a *d*, and an *l* and correctly spells out—*d e s o l a t i o n*! (The teacher points out that desolation is also the emotion felt by the previous student who came so close to winning!) Play continues with another big word introduced in a sentence context.

Students who are introduced to vocabulary by playing The Wheel pay close attention to the letter patterns in big words. They also get in the habit of making sure that the word they figure out, based on having some of the letters, fits the meaning of the sentence in which it occurs.

SUMMARY

Reading and writing are meaning-constructing activities, but they are both dependent on words. All good readers and writers have a store of high-frequency words that they read and spell instantly and automatically. Good readers and writers can also decode and spell most regular words. Most of the words we read are little words. The big words, however, are often the critical words—the ones that convey the information we need to learn. Many struggling readers have no strategies for decoding big words and have very few big words in their store of words that they can instantly recognize and effortlessly spell. The last section of this chapter focuses on helping children build a store of big words that they can automatically read and write, and on giving them strategies for figuring out new big words. Another part of the big-word story is developing meaning for big words. This meaning is best developed and retrieved when the words to be learned are all related to one topic. In Chapter 7, we describe how you can help all children increase the size of their meaning vocabularies as you help them increase their knowledge of important topics.

CHAPTER 3

Comprehension

In Chapter 1, you were reminded that the real reason we work so hard to teach children to read is so they will read! You also learned that reading lots of self-selected materials is critical to the development of good readers. Children do not become readers unless they have time, materials, models, and motivation. For some lucky children, their homes provide all these essentials. For *all* children to become literate, however, schools must not leave this responsibility to the homes. The first priority in all classrooms that contain struggling readers should be to set up an effective program of daily self-selected reading and writing.

Making sure that children are reading and writing is necessary for their growth. For many children, this essential component, although necessary, is not sufficient. Research (Dole, Duffy, Roehler, & Pearson, 1991; Johnston & Allington, 1991; Pressley, 1998) clearly demonstrates that struggling readers make more rapid progress when given explicit instruction in how to read and write.

Comprehension is the focus of this chapter. Specifically, it describes how teachers carry out lessons and how they structure activities that teach children how to "think as they read." The focus on thinking is inevitable because that's what reading really is—thinking stimulated by words on a page.

A myth about children who have difficulty with reading comprehension is that they "just can't think!" In reality, everybody thinks all the time and some struggling readers who must take care of themselves (and often younger brothers and sisters) are especially good thinkers and problem solvers. If children can "predict" that the ball game will be canceled when they see the sky darkening up and can "conclude" that the coach is mad about something when he walks in with a scowl on his face, then they can and do engage in higher-level thinking processes. The real problem is not that they cannot think, but that they do not think while they read. Why don't they think while they read?

Some children do not think while they read because they do not really know that they should! Imagine an extreme case of a child who had never been read to and had never heard people talking about what they read. Imagine that this child goes to a school in which beginning reading is taught in a "learn the letters and sounds" and "read the words aloud perfectly" way. This child would learn to read words just as you would read this nonsensical sentence:

He bocked the piffle with a gid daft.

You can read all the "words" correctly, and you can even read with expression, but you get no meaning. In your case, of course, you get no meaning because there is no meaning there to get.

For children who have limited literacy experience and who are taught to read in a rigid, phonics-first method with texts that make little sense (*Nan can fan a man*), the real danger is that they will not learn that thinking is the goal. The goal, to them, is sounding out all the words, which is what they try to do. Ask them what reading is and they are apt to look at you as if you are a complete fool and tell you that reading is saying all the words right!

The ability to decode is critical but when we overemphasize accurate word pronunciation and only provide beginning reading materials in which all the words are "decodable," we can create readers who not only misread the purpose of reading, but also do not comprehend the story. Children who are trained to concentrate their energies on word pronunciation exhibit word-by-word reading, a low self-correction rate, and a general lack of fluency. In short, their reading just does not sound good. Not just their comprehension is affected by an overemphasis on word pronunciation, but also the very act of reading is shaped such that comprehension is virtually impossible.

Some struggling readers are unaware that they should be thinking while they are reading, and many have inadequate background knowledge for understanding the books and curriculum materials in their schools. Read the next two sentences and think about the implications for your teaching:

> Current models do not allow expectancy-based processing to influence feature extraction from words. Indeed, most current models largely restrict expectancy-based processing and hypothesis-testing mechanisms to the postlexical level. (Stanovich, 1991, p. 419)

You are probably wondering why we would waste book space (and your time) on these two nonsensical sentences. In reality, these sentences are not nonsensical. They actually have meaning, and if you are a research psychologist, you can think and talk intelligently about them! For most of us, however, we can say these words, but we cannot really read them because we are unable to think as we say them. Background knowledge, which includes topically related vocabulary, is one of the major determinants of reading comprehension. In fact, research (Pearson & Fielding, 1991) tells us that the amount of prior knowledge a reader has about a topic is the best determinant of how much will be understood and remembered as it is read.

In addition to specific knowledge about the topic, knowledge about the type of text about to be read is called up as well. When a reader begins to read a story or a novel, a whole set of expectations based on other stories that have been heard or read are called up. The reader does not know who the characters are, but does expect to find characters. The reader also knows that the story is set in a particular time and place (setting) and that goals will be achieved or problems will be resolved. In short, the reader has a story structure in her or his head that allows her or him to fit what is read into an overall organization.

Imagine that you are going to read a *Consumer Guide* article on the newest car models. Again, you do not know what specific information you will learn, but you do have expectations about the type of information and how it will be related. You expect to find charts comparing the cars on different features and to find judgments about which cars appear to be the best buys.

Now imagine that you are about to read a travel magazine article about North Carolina. You have never been there and do not know anyone who has, so you do not know too many specifics. However, you do have expectations about what you will learn and about how that information will be organized. You expect to learn some facts about the history of North Carolina, along with some descriptions of historical regions and locations in the state. You also expect to find information about places tourists like to visit, such as the coast and the mountains. You would not be surprised to find a summary of the cultural and sporting events that are unique to North Carolina. Information about the climate and the best times to visit different parts of the state, as well as some information on how to get there and places to stay, would also be expected. As you begin to read, you may create a mental outline or web, which helps you understand and organize topic and subtopic information.

The different ways in which various reading materials are organized are referred to as text structures and genres. To comprehend what we are reading, we must be familiar with the way in which the information is organized. The fact that most children can understand and remember stories much better than informational text is probably because they have listened to and have read many more stories and thus know what to expect and how to organize the story information. If we want to create readers who think about what they read, we must help them become familiar with a variety of ways that authors organize ideas in their writing.

Even with a clear understanding that reading is primarily thinking, sufficient background knowledge, and a familiarity with the kind of text structure being read, you cannot think about what you read unless you can identify a majority of the words. Try to make sense of this next sentence in which all words of three of more syllables have been replaced by blanks:

The _____ _____ fresh ideas for action and _____ new _____ that will help the _____ _____ and the _____ meet the challenge of _____ adult and _____ _____ worldwide.

Now read the same sentence but put the words *conference, provided, generated, partnerships, literacy, community, association, promoting, adolescent,* and *literacy* in the blanks. To learn to think while you read, you must

1. Be able to identify almost all the words
2. Have sufficient background knowledge that you call up and try to connect to the new information
3. Be familiar with the type of text and be able to see how the author has organized the ideas
4. Have a mindset that reading is thinking and know how to apply your thinking in comprehension strategies

COMPREHENSION STRATEGIES

The different kinds of thinking that we do as we read are referred to as comprehension strategies. Because thinking is complex and happens inside your mind, little agreement exists concerning exactly what or how many strategies there are. Many teachers use a local or state curriculum guide to determine which strategies are deemed critical in their school or grade level. Teacher's manuals also provide teachers with lists and suggestions for teaching important comprehension strategies.

In considering which strategies to focus on, the teacher considers both the demands of the text that children are about to read and the needs and abilities of the children. Readers need to use some strategies on almost all texts, including

- Calling up and connecting relevant background knowledge
- Predicting what will be learned and what will happen
- Making mental pictures or "seeing it in your mind"
- Self-monitoring and self-correction
- Using fix-up strategies such as rereading, pictures, and asking for help when you cannot make sense of what you read
- Determining the most important ideas and events and seeing how they are related
- Drawing conclusions and inferences based on what is read
- Deciding "what you think": Did you like it? Did you agree? Was it funny? Could it really happen?
- Comparing and contrasting what you read to what you already know
- Summarizing what has been read

In addition to these "generic" strategies that we use regardless of what we are reading, particular texts cause us to use other strategies as well. These strategies are too numerous to list completely, but a few examples include

- Understanding figurative language and using it to build clear images
- Following the plot of a story and figuring out what happened to whom and why

- Determining character traits and deciding why certain characters behave as they do
- Extracting information from charts, graphs, maps, and other visuals
- Determining the objectivity or bias of an author

In planning a comprehension lesson, we decide which thinking strategies will help students make sense of the text they are reading today and be better—more strategic—readers when they are reading on their own. Most comprehension lessons involve some kind of modeling, demonstrating, explaining, and/or brainstorming before students begin to read and some follow-up after reading. If the text is particularly difficult, the teacher may give additional support during the reading.

Many different, engaging, and research-supported ways can be used to carry out comprehension lessons. There are three compelling reasons to use a large variety of types of comprehension lessons. First, comprehension is primarily thinking and thinking involves many complex processes, so no one type of comprehension lesson can teach all the different kinds of thinking. Second, comprehension of story text and informational text require different kinds of mental organizing. Third, children differ on all kinds of dimensions, including the types of comprehension lessons that engage their attention and help them learn how to think while reading. We organize our comprehension lessons into four categories: literate conversations, think-alouds, informational text lessons, and story text lessons. We hope you find opportunities throughout the year to use some of each type as you teach your curriculum and teach your students to think their way through all kinds of text.

LITERATE CONVERSATIONS

Asking students questions after reading may provide teachers with a quick assessment of student understanding, but traditional question and answer sessions do not offer much in the way of improving students' understanding of texts they have read. When students engage in conversations about what they have read, their understanding improves (Fall, Webb, & Cudowsky, 2000). Effective classrooms provide a balance of question and answer sessions and conversation about the texts students read (Allington & Johnston, 2001). So how do you get good conversations going in your classroom?

A good first step is to modify the questions you do ask so that you are asking more open-ended questions. Open-ended questions are those that can have multiple correct responses. For instance, after reading you might ask:

Is there anything you want to know more about?
Is there anything you are wondering about?
Does this story/book remind you of anything else you have read?
What did you think about . . . ?

Has anything like this ever happened to you?
What was happening in this part of the story/book?
Were you surprised by anything in this story/book?
Did anyone in the story remind you of someone you know?

Each of these open-ended questions allows for a range of responses, all potentially correct. Such questions serve to begin a conversation about the material read. In many respects the goal is to create the kind of conversation that adults typically engage in when discussing something they have read. Adults do not interrogate each other. They do not ask each other the types of questions that teachers typically have asked. Instead, they discuss, they converse. The goal is to share understandings and through this to gain an even better understanding of the material read.

One way to think about creating classroom conversations is provided by Keene and Zimmerman (1997). The framework they provide focuses on helping children think about three types of connections:

- Text to self (Do any of you have a pet that is creating problems like the one in the story?)
- Text to text (What other book have we read where a child was brave?)
- Text to world (Has anyone ever ridden on a subway? Tell us what it was like.)

It is just these kinds of connections that good readers make as they actively read a story or book. It is these kinds of connections we make as we discuss something we have read with someone else.

Some students find responding to open-ended questions easier than others do. Some find it easier to make connections to a story. We need to help all students develop and refine their ability to engage in literate conversations. Initially, a teacher might simply begin to model such responses after a read-aloud activity. In other words, after a read-aloud the teacher might say, "This story reminds me of *The Little Engine That Could* because the boy in the story just wouldn't give up." Of course, in this case, the children must be familiar with the book *The Little Engine That Could* before the connection can make any sense. The teacher might then discuss a personal incident of persistence and ask the children to make the same connections. Such demonstrations are designed to help all children learn to engage in literate conversations.

In some cases, especially with older students lacking experience talking about what they have read, it may help for the teacher to model and then to provide a minute or so for kids to jot their responses into a notebook. After a minute or two, the teacher can initiate the conversation by calling on kids to tell what they wrote. This "quickwrite" procedure provides a bit of thinking time for all kids as well as an interlude for those students who need a short time to generate a connection.

Although whole-class discussions are useful, increasing evidence shows that literature circles offer even greater benefits for improving comprehension. The typical literature group has three to seven members, all reading the same text on a common schedule. The texts that each group is reading may reflect a selected theme (families), genre (biography), or curricular topic (Civil War). Day and her colleagues note that the smaller groups involved in literature circles better promote discussion because smaller groups foster the following (Day, Spiegel, McLellan, & Brown, 2002):

- Greater opportunities for children to talk
- More natural context for conversation
- Ability to find texts all members of the group can and want to read
- Greater choice of books for all students
- Cooperation and collaboration
- Personal responsibility

In the next chapter you can learn more about organizing literature circles so that children can get in the habit of having literate conversations with one another.

In addition to giving students multiple opportunities to develop thoughtful literacy by engaging them in conversations guided by higher-level questions—the kind of conversations adults often hold about their own reading—teachers can initiate two other types of activities to help children engage in conversations. In Questioning the Author, the teacher and children raise questions that they would like to discuss with the author. In the Oprah Winfrey strategy, teachers and children become interviewers—like Oprah—and the people they interview are characters from books.

Questioning the Author (QTA)

When we read, we do not just understand what the author is saying; rather, we figure out what the author means. This might sound like a picky distinction, but helping struggling readers put this distinction into practice as they read makes a huge difference in their comprehension. If you have ever taught students who read a passage carefully and then tell you they cannot answer the questions because the passage "didn't say!" you have experienced the reason students need to have their reading guided by a constructivist strategy such as Questioning The Author (QTA).

The word *constructivist* is currently in danger of death from overuse, but it names a simple and powerful concept. When we read, we use the author's words to construct meaning. The meaning is more than what the author has written. Authors cannot tell us everything. They assume we know some things that we will connect to what they are telling us. They assume that we will form some opinions based on what they tell us and what we know. Our initial assertion—that reading, at its heart, is thinking—means that reading is a constructive activity. Readers construct meaning by understanding what the author is saying, figuring out what the author means, and forming opinions based on the author's meaning and what the reader already knows. This description of QTA is based on an excellent book by Isabel Beck, Margaret McKeown, Rebecca Hamilton, and Linda Kucan (1997) that gives detailed examples of QTA lessons, suggestions for planning and implementing QTA lessons, and results of QTA use in several classrooms. If our brief description intrigues you, we highly recommend you read their practical and clearly written book.

Several things distinguish QTAs from other comprehension-fostering formats. The most important differences to us are that the instruction goes on not before students read or after students read but as students are reading, and that the teacher's job is to pose queries that foster meaning construction, not to ask questions to assess if that meaning construction took place. To plan a QTA lesson, the teacher carefully reads the text and decides (1) what the important ideas are and what problems students might have figuring out these ideas; (2) how much of the text to read in each segment before stopping for discussion; and (3) what queries to pose that might help students construct meaning from the text. A clear distinction is made between queries, which lead the students to think and construct, and questions, which usually assess whether students have been able to think or construct. The teacher's job in a QTA is to pose the types of queries that can help students use what they know and figure out what the author means. Having decided on important ideas and segmented the texts, teachers plan both initiating and follow-up queries. The following example is adapted from Beck and her colleagues as students are about to read and construct meaning for a social studies passage on how Pennsylvania was formed.

The teacher and students are seated in a circle or horseshoe shape so that they can all see each other. They all have copies of the book open. For this lesson, the teacher has decided that the first segment to be read is just the first sentence. She tells the students to read the first sentence to themselves:

> The shape of the land in North America has changed over millions of years. (p. 51)

And then poses a typical initiating query:

> "What do you think the author is telling us?"

Initially, students may want to respond by just reading the sentence aloud, but the teacher responds by saying,

> "Yes, that's what the author says, but what is the author trying to tell us?"

The teacher then poses the follow-up query designed to help them connect information learned in previous chapters.

> "What have we already learned about the different kinds of shapes land can have that we need to connect here?"

The second segment contained many sentences and ended the paragraph. It is important to note that the segment division is not determined by paragraphs but by ideas. (Sometimes you want to make sure students are constructing meaning from a single sentence, and sometimes you may want them to read several paragraphs.) The teacher segments the text so that students stop at points where they need to construct important meanings. This segment developed the concept of glaciers, and after students had read this segment to themselves, the teacher initiated the query:

"What is the author telling us about snow and ice and glaciers?"

The QTA continued with the teacher telling the students how much to read and posing both initiating and follow-up queries until students had worked together to construct meaning for this difficult and complex text.

Children often think that authors are infallible! In doing QTAs with children, teachers point out that authors are not perfect! Sometimes they do not write clearly. Sometimes they assume we know lots of things that we do not know, and they leave out important facts. Children who engage in regular QTAs learn that when you are reading, you try to figure out what the author means—not just remember what the author says. They are then on the path to constructing meaning and active reading.

The "Oprah Winfrey" Strategy

This is another technique that fosters involvement. To use it, several children must be reading the same book. You play the role of Oprah (initially) and interview them about their lives and roles. For instance, after reading *Anastasia at Your Service* (Lois Lowry), assign students the roles of Anastasia, Mrs. Bellingham, and her granddaughter, Daphne. (We could also add Mr. and Mrs. Krupnik, Sam, and perhaps the surgeon or the maid.) Now, just like Oprah, invite the students to appear on your "show." Arrange chairs alongside your desk, facing the rest of the class. Seat the "guests," with Anastasia next to your desk, and welcome them.

Begin with broad questions: "Tell me a bit about yourself, Anastasia." "What seemed to be the problem?" Then move to other characters for verification: "Do you agree with her, Daphne?" "What else would you add, Mrs. Bellingham?" You might even turn to the audience for questions, especially if some members have not read the book. Basically, like Oprah, you let your guests tell their stories. Ideally, readers transform themselves into the characters, taking on mannerisms and speech patterns that seem appropriate. You may want to model this transformation yourself by letting a student take Oprah's role while you become Mrs. Bellingham or another character. This activity can be brief (3–5 minutes is all most guests get on talk shows!) and takes little time to set up after the initial exposure. The activity provokes thought about the characters and their motives, attitudes, and personalities. In short, it is a wonderfully innovative way to foster thinking and involvement while reading.

LITERATE CONVERSATIONS

Literate conversations mimic the conversations real readers in the real world have about real books they really want to talk about! The key to good literate conversations is to help the children learn to ask and think about the questions real readers ask each other and friends who have read the book. Real readers do not interrogate each other about books. They do not ask, "Who were the main characters?" or "What year did the conflict break out?" Rather, they ask and converse about the big ideas—and particularly their reactions to and feelings about what they have read. To promote literate conversations in your room:

1. Conduct your discussions with your readers as conversations—not interrogations. Ask them higher-level questions that require reactions and responses—questions to which you don't know the answer because there isn't one right answer.
2. Model for your students the types of connections readers make—text to self, text to text, and text to world. Your comments and questions should regularly focus them on these connections so they get in the habit of making these connections when reading on their own.
3. Arrange for students to have literate conversations in small groups. Literature circles is one format for organizing small group conversations.
4. For variety, use Questioning the Author and the Oprah Winfrey strategy to increase the number of people with whom your students can have conversations.

THINK-ALOUDS

Think-alouds are a way of modeling or "making public" the thinking that goes on inside your head as you read. To explain think-alouds to young children, we tell them that two voices are really speaking as we read. The voice you can usually hear is your voice reading the words but inside your brain is another voice telling you what it thinks about the material you are reading. We use think-alouds to demonstrate for children how we think as we read.

Thinking as we read takes many different forms. We make connections—to ourselves, to other things we have read, and to the world. Teachers use sentence starters to think aloud about the connections they are making:

"This reminds me of . . ."
"I remember something like this happened to me when . . ."
"I read another book where the character . . ."
"This is like in our school when . . ."
"Our country doesn't have that holiday, but we have . . ."

We predict and anticipate what will happen next:

> "I wonder if . . . "
> "I wonder who . . . "
> "I think I know what is coming next . . . "
> "He will be in trouble if . . . "
> "I think we will learn how . . . "

We summarize what has happened so far and draw conclusions not stated by the author:

> "The most important thing I've learned so far is . . . "
> "It didn't say why she did that, but I bet . . . "
> "I know he must be feeling . . . "
> "So far in our story . . . "
> "So far I have learned that . . . "

We question what is happening and monitor our own comprehension:

> "I wonder what it means when . . . "
> "I don't understand . . . "
> "It didn't make sense when . . . "
> "I'm going to reread that because it didn't make sense that . . . "

We imagine and infer and enter into the world the author is describing:

> "Even though it isn't in the picture, I can see the . . . "
> "Mmm, I can almost taste the . . . "
> "That sent chills down my spine when it said . . . "
> "For a minute I thought I could smell . . . "
> "I could hear the . . . "
> "I can imagine what it is like to . . . "
> "I can picture the . . . "

We make evaluations and form opinions and decide how we think and feel about things:

> "My favorite part in this chapter was . . . "
> "I really liked how the author . . . "
> "What I don't like about this part is . . . "
> "It was really interesting to learn that . . . "
> "I am going to try this out when I . . . "
> "I wish I could . . . "
> "If I were her, I would . . . "

RECOMMENDED RESOURCES

Two wonderful sources just full of examples to teach children to think and share their thinking are *Strategies That Work* (Harvey & Goudvis, 2000) and *Mosaic of Thought* (Keene & Zimmerman, 1997).

Teachers use think-alouds in a variety of ways but the most efficient and effective use of time is probably to read and think-aloud the first quarter or third of a selection the children are about to read. In addition to hearing you think your way through the text, children get introduced to the selection, including characters, setting, type of writing, and important vocabulary. After listening to you think-aloud your way through the first part of the text, children collaborate in small groups, finish reading the selection, and share the thinking voices inside their brains.

The following example of a think-aloud is based on the first part of *Missing: One Stuffed Rabbit* by Maryann Cocca-Leffler (1999). The think-aloud begins with the cover of the book. The teacher reads aloud the title, *Missing: One Stuffed Rabbit,* and looks at the picture saying something like what follows:

> "This is an intriguing illustration on the cover of the book. A girl is reading from a notebook labeled Coco and she looks very unhappy. The two children listening look surprised and upset. Because the title of the book is *Missing: One Stuffed Rabbit,* I bet the unhappy and surprised looks have something to do with the lost rabbit. I wonder who lost the rabbit and who the rabbit is and what the notebook has to do with it?"

The teacher turns the page and thinks aloud about the picture on the first two pages:

> "I see a teacher holding a stuffed rabbit and reaching into a fishbowl to pull out a slip of paper. The children in the class are all watching her. They all look happy and excited. In the other picture is the stuffed rabbit and the notebook labeled Coco. I bet Coco is the name of the stuffed rabbit."

The teacher then reads aloud the text on these two pages, which explains that Coco is indeed the stuffed rabbit and that the teacher is pulling the name of one student who will get to take Coco home for the weekend. She pulls out a slip of paper and the lucky winner is Janine!

> "I bet Janine is the girl in the front in the glasses. She is also the unhappy-looking girl on the cover, reading from Coco's notebook."

The teacher turns the page and thinks aloud first about the pictures.

> "There's Janine looking very happy and hugging Coco and his notebook."

The teacher reads the text aloud and we discover that the notebook is Coco's diary. Each student gets to take Coco home overnight and write Coco's thoughts about the adventure in his diary.

> "I used to have a diary when I was younger. I wrote in it every night."

The next two pages have some of the diary entries written by children who have already taken Coco home and helped him write about his adventures. We learn that Coco fell off the monkey bars while playing with Danny, went to Matthew's soccer game and cheered when Matthew got a goal, and went to the skating rink with Christina. The teacher makes these comments:

> "I love how the author showed the diary pages. I can tell different children wrote them because you can see the different handwriting. I can't wait to see what Janine does with Coco and what she writes in the diary."

The pictures and text on the next two pages show Janine and Coco being picked up by Janine's mom and heading home. The following pages show Janine and Coco having a good time together. Janine reads Coco a bedtime story and rides him on the back of her bike. After reading these four pages, the teacher comments:

> "They seem to be having such a good time. But I am worried. I remember how unhappy Janine looked on the cover, and the title of the book says a stuffed rabbit is missing. I hope Janine is not going to let Coco get lost!"

The next four pages show the family shopping at the mall and, sure enough, as they are having lunch, Janine realizes that she cannot find Coco! She thought she put him in one of the bags, but he is not there. Coco is missing!

> "I can just imagine how Janine must be feeling. She looks like she is going to cry, and I feel like crying too! How could she have lost him? Will she find him? What will the other kids—and the teacher!—say if she doesn't find him?

At this point in the book, the teacher stops reading and thinking aloud and turns to the children, asking them what they think will happen. They share some ideas and the looks on their faces show how concerned they are. The teacher quickly reviews the pages read and reminds the children that she shared her thinking with them about the pictures and the words. Next the teacher forms small groups of three or four students and tells them that it is now their turn to read and share their thinking. She chooses one group to model for the others what they will do, and, with the teacher's help, this group shares their thinking about the pictures and words on the next two-page spread. The teacher tells them that when they read, little voices inside their heads tell them what their brains are thinking. When we do think-alouds, we let that little voice talk out loud so that we can hear what all our different brains are thinking.

The groups form and begin reading. The teacher circulates to the various groups and helps them to take turns and to verbalize their thinking. She also writes down some of the most interesting thoughts to share with the whole group when they reconvene after reading to react to the story and "debrief" their thinking.

Many teachers, when they first hear about think-alouds, are afraid to do them because they do not know exactly what they are supposed to think! We hope that our example shows you that your brain is thinking as you read, and if you tune into that thinking and learn how to communicate your thinking to children, think-alouds are not difficult to do. It is important to read the selection and plan what you are going to say as you think aloud. Many teachers find it helpful to attach sticky notes with reminders to the appropriate pages. We try to use as many different ways of expressing our thinking as we can and try to have it match as closely as we can the thinking actually engendered by the text.

Although we normally invite participation, it is important not to let the children "chime in" as you are thinking. If you use the procedure of beginning the selection with your think-aloud and finishing the selection with the children sharing their think-alouds, they are usually willing to let you have your turn! Some teachers tell the children that they are to pretend to be invisible while the teacher is reading and thinking. They get to hear the teacher thinking, but they are invisible and should not let the teacher know they are there! You want to signal the children when you are reading and when you are thinking. Many teachers look at the book when they are reading and then look away from the book—perhaps up toward the ceiling—when they are thinking. Other teachers use a different voice to signal their thinking. They read in their "reading voice" and think in their "thinking voice."

THINK-ALOUDS

The goal of comprehension instruction is that children learn how to think as they read on their own. Think-alouds help children see what good comprehenders do. If you do your think-aloud based on the first part of the selection they are going to read, you give them a "jumpstart" into the selection. To do think-alouds,

1. Choose a selection that truly causes you to think.
2. Decide how much of that selection you will read aloud.
3. Look at the pictures and read the selection before you do the think-aloud. Look for places where you actually use different thinking strategies—connect, predict, conclude, self-monitor, image, infer, evaluate. Think about how you will explain your thinking to your children. Mark these places with sticky notes and cryptic comments if this helps you remember.
4. Do the think-aloud as the "invisible" children watch and listen. Comment on pictures first; then read the text, stopping at appropriate places, and comment.
5. Provide a structure for your children to get in tune with and share their thinking as they finish the selection or read another selection.

INFORMATIONAL TEXT LESSONS

Most readers are much better at comprehending stories than at comprehending informational text. Elementary children need a better balance between information and story text in their reading instruction. Because many children have difficulty with informational text, they approach reading informational text with less confidence and enthusiasm. Children who engage in KWL lessons and who learn how to construct a variety of graphic organizers become better and more enthusiastic readers of informational text.

KWL

One of the most flexible and popular ways of guiding students' thinking is KWL (Ogle, 1986; Carr & Ogle, 1987). The letters stand for what we **k**now, what we **w**ant to find out, and what we have **l**earned. This strategy works especially well with informational text. Imagine that the teacher is planning to have the class read about Washington, D.C. The teacher might begin the lesson by finding Washington, D.C., on a map and asking which students have been there. A chart such as the following would then be started:

Washington, D.C.		
What we know	**What we want to find out**	**What we learned**

The students brainstorm what they know about Washington, D.C., and the teacher writes their responses in the first column. When the children have brainstormed all their prior knowledge, the chart might look like this:

Washington, D.C.		
What we know	**What we want to find out**	**What we learned**
Capitol White House president lives there lots of drugs azaleas in spring cold in winter near Virginia near Maryland		

Next, the teacher would direct the students' attention to the second column and ask them what they would like to find out about Washington, D.C. Their questions would be listed in the second column:

Washington, D.C.		
What we know	**What we want to find out**	**What we learned**
Capitol	How old is it?	
White House	How big is the White House?	
president lives there	What else is in D.C.?	
lots of drugs	Where is the FBI?	
azaleas in spring	What kind of government	
cold in winter	does D.C. have?	
near Virginia	Why do so many people	
near Maryland	visit D.C.?	
	How many people live there?	
	What do the people do who	
	aren't in the government?	

Once the questions are listed, students read to find out which questions were answered and to find other interesting "tidbits" they think are important. After reading, the teacher begins by seeing which questions were answered, then leads the students to add other interesting facts. This information is recorded in the third column. All members of the class are encouraged to contribute to this group task, and no one looks back at the book until all initial responses are shared. Disputed or unclear information is marked with question marks.

When all the initial recalls are recorded, children go back to the text to clarify, prove, or fill in gaps. The teacher encourages the children to read the relevant part aloud and helps them explain their thinking. When the information on the chart is complete and accurate, the teacher points out how much was learned and how efficiently the chart helped to record it. Inevitably, some questions are not answered in the reading. A natural follow-up to this lesson is to help the children use additional resources to locate the answers to these questions.

Graphic Organizers

Another popular format for a guided reading lesson involves having the students construct or fill in a graphic organizer. Webs are the most commonly used graphic organizer at the elementary level. They are wonderful ways of helping readers organize information when their reading gives lots of topic and subtopic information. Imagine that your class is going to read an informational selection about birds. You might begin a web to help them organize the information they will be learning:

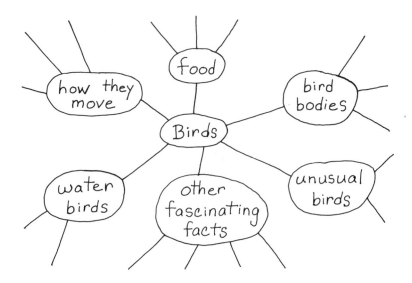

As you set up each spoke of the web, you can discuss with the children what they might expect to find out: "What are some ways you already know that birds move? What do you already know that birds eat? What body parts do birds have?" Children then read to find out more about birds. After reading, the children reconvene and complete the web.

Webs are an efficient graphic organizer for topic and subtopic information, but many other ways to show types of relationships exist. A feature matrix helps children organize information about several members of a category when they are reading. Imagine that the children are reading a selection that compares and contrasts many different types of birds. This information would be better organized in a feature matrix than in a web. Here is what that feature matrix skeleton might look like:

Birds						
	fly	**swim**	**build nests**	**lay eggs**	**have feathers**	**molt**
robins						
whippoorwills						
penguins						
ostriches						

Before reading, the teacher and the children talk about the birds listed and about the categories. Children make predictions based on what they know about which birds fly, swim, build nests, and so forth. The teacher then points out the four blank lines and tells the children that, in addition to robins, whippoorwills, penguins, and ostriches, four other birds will be described. The children read to decide which features apply to the four birds listed on the matrix and to the four other birds they will add after reading. Once the children have read the selection, the teacher leads them to fill in a yes/no or a +/– for each feature.

Feature matrices are infinitely adaptable. *Semantic Feature Analysis: Classroom Applications* (Pittelman, Heinlich, Berglund, & French, 1991) is full of wonderful variations. One suggestion adapted from this book (p. 40) that we particularly like includes having kindergartners classify fruit using happy and sad faces, like this:

Fruits							
	round	has peel	bumpy peel	orange	red	eat peel	smooth peel	eat seeds
orange	☺	☺	☺	☺	☹			
apple								
banana								

We also like their suggestion that some things do not break down into neat yes/no classifications. They suggest that feature matrices can become much more useful if you consider using an A/S/N (Always/Sometimes/Never) classification scheme.

Data charts are another way of helping children organize information that compares and contrasts members of the same category. Rather than indicate whether something has a feature, children fill in particular facts. Here is a data chart used in a science classroom:

Planets in Our Solar System			
Name	**Size (1 = biggest)**	**Distance from sun**	**Earth days in year**
Earth	6	92,960,000 mi.	365
Mars			
	1		
		3,660,000,000 mi.	
			60,188

To begin this chart, you might partially fill in the chart for the students, talking as you write about what is needed in each column:

"Earth is the sixth largest planet. Its mean distance from the sun is 92,960,000 miles. The year is the number of days it takes a planet to orbit the sun, and the earth year is 365 days."

Now you point to the second row and have students explain what they will try to put in each column about Mars. For the third row, help them notice that because you put a 1 in the size column, this planet has to be the biggest planet. The fourth row must be completed for the planet that is 3,660,000,000 miles from the sun. The planet that takes 60,188 earth days to orbit the sun goes in the fifth row. The remaining four rows are filled in with the remaining four planets.

Webs, feature matrices, and data charts are the most popular graphic organizers used in elementary classrooms, but they are not the only possibilities. Here are two other types of graphic organizers:

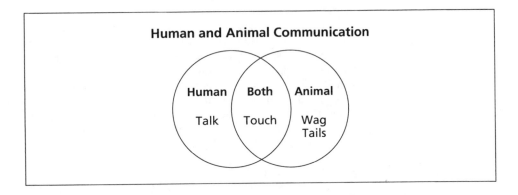

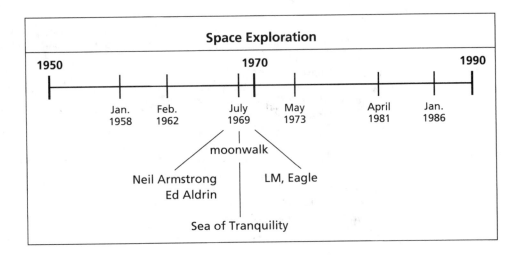

If the relationships depicted by these graphic organizers are obvious to you, they demonstrate how clearly graphic organizers communicate and how well they help students see important relationships in the information they are reading. In the

INFORMATIONAL TEXT LESSONS

KWL

KWLs help children connect what they know to new information. They are particularly helpful to children as ways to guide their reading with science and social studies texts.

1. Before beginning the chart, lead a general discussion of children's experiences with the topic. By letting children discuss these experiences (e.g., "My uncle lives in Washington"; "We're going to go to Washington some summer"), you avoid having to put these "experiences" in the known column.
2. After the discussion of experiences, ask children what they know about the topic and list these in the K (known) column. If children disagree about a fact, put it in the W (want) column with a question mark. ("Washington is in Virginia." "No, it's not!" Record this exchange as, Is Washington in Virginia?)
3. When you have all the known facts recorded, show them what they will read and ask them to come up with questions they think that text will answer. If their questions are too specific, help make them broader.
4. After reading, begin with the questions first and add answers to the L (learned) column. Then add other important facts.
5. If they are going to continue reading about the topic for another day, ask them whether what they have read so far has helped them think of more questions that the remaining part might answer. Add these to the W column.

GRAPHIC ORGANIZERS

Graphic organizers help children organize and summarize information. They are often used as the prewriting activity for focused-writing lessons.

1. Look at the text and decide how the information can best be organized. If the text structure is topic/subtopic/details, you probably want a web or data chart. If the text compares two or more things, a feature matrix, data chart, or Venn diagram works well. Time lines help children focus on sequence.
2. Let the children see you construct the graphic organizer skeleton. Use this time to discuss the words you are putting there because these are apt to be key vocabulary from the selection.
3. Have students read to find information to add to the organizer.
4. Complete the organizer together.
5. You may want to do a focused-writing lesson in which you help children use the information from the organizer to write summaries or reports.
6. When children understand and can complete the various organizers, have them preview text and decide what kind of graphic organizer works best, and have them help you construct the skeleton.

Venn diagram, which we and children like to call a "double bubble," children compare and contrast how animals and humans communicate. The time line is an excellent device to use when order or sequence is important, for instance, in history, historical fiction, and biography. Students fill in the important space exploration events that occurred on each date and a few details about each. A variation is to give students a time line of events and have them fill in the dates.

In one fifth-grade classroom that we visited, the teacher had created a permanent time line that ran across the whole front of the room. The dates on the time line ranged from 1000 B.C. to 2000 A.D. Several important historical dates were recorded on the time line at the beginning of the year when the students arrived. Then the era of students' births was marked. Across the year, dates that arose in novels, textbooks, and discussions were placed on the time line.

STORY TEXT LESSONS

Children understand stories better than informational text, but they still need instruction in story comprehension. Story maps, the Beach Ball, and "doing" the book are three activities that help children understand story structure and develop independent story comprehension strategies.

Story Maps

Story maps are a popular and effective device to guide students' thinking when they are about to read a story. There are many different ways of creating story maps, but all help children follow the story by drawing their attention to the elements that all good stories share. Stories have characters and happen in a particular place and time, which we call the setting. In most stories, the characters have some goal they want to achieve or some problem that they need to resolve. The

Story Map
Main Characters:
Setting (Time and Place):
Problem or Goals:
Event 1:
Event 2:
Event 3:
Event 4:
Event 5:
Solution:
Story Theme or Moral:

events in the story lead to some kind of solution or resolution. Sometimes stories have implicit morals or themes from which we hope children learn. The story map on page 89 is based on a model created by Isabel Beck (Macon, Bewell, & Vogt, 1991). Here is the story map filled in for *The Three Little Pigs:*

Story Map

Main Characters: Mother Pig, three little pigs, Big Bad Wolf

Setting (Time and Place): Woods, make-believe time and place

Problem or Goal: Pigs wanted to be independent and have own house.

   Event 1: Mother Pig sends three little pigs out to build their own houses.

   Event 2: First little pig gets some straw and builds a straw house. Big Bad Wolf blows the straw house down.

   Event 3: Second little pig gets some sticks and builds a stick house. Big Bad Wolf blows the stick house down.

   Event 4: Third little pig gets some bricks and builds a brick house. Big Bad Wolf cannot blow the brick house down.

   Event 5: Big Bad Wolf runs off into woods (or gets scalded coming down the chimney, depending on how violent the version of the story is).

Solution: Pigs live happily ever after in strong brick house.

Story Theme or Moral: Hard work pays off in the end!

When using story maps to develop a sense of story structure, the teacher must work through several of them with the children first. For readers who are having trouble comprehending, it is not enough to distribute story maps for them to complete. After reading a story, display the story map on an overhead projector. As you complete the map, think aloud so the thought processes you use are audible to children. Teacher think-alouds provide the expert model many struggling readers need to develop the thinking strategies that underlie good comprehension.

Once children understand the elements and how to fill them in, they can complete story maps in small groups and then independently. It is important to have children read the whole story before completing the map and to help children see that the map is a device that helps them determine and remember important elements in a story.

The Beach Ball is not a story map activity, but using this format helps children develop all the important concepts and can lead to the development of written story maps. The beach ball has a question written in black permanent marker on each colored stripe of the ball:

Who are the main characters?
What is the setting?
What happened in the beginning?
What happened in the middle?
How did it end?
What was your favorite part?

After reading a story, the teacher and children form a large circle. The teacher begins by tossing the ball to one of the students. The first student to catch the ball can answer any question on the ball. The teacher then tosses the ball to another student. The next student can add to the answer given by the first student or answer another question. The ball continues to be thrown to various students until all the questions have been thoroughly answered. Some questions, such as, *What happened in the story?* and *What was your favorite part?* have many different answers.

The beach ball is a favorite comprehension follow-up for children in all the classrooms in which it is used, including intermediate-aged children. In classrooms in which the teacher regularly uses the beach ball to follow up story reading, children begin, as they read, to anticipate the answers they will give to the questions on various stripes. These children have developed a clear sense of story structure, and their comprehension (and memory) increases as they organize what they are reading and thinking around those colored beach ball stripes.

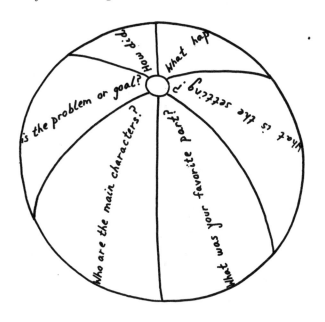

Doing the Book

Children who "do" the book become more active readers. Characters, setting, events, dialogue, conclusions, mood, and motivation become important, and children pay more attention to them when they have to interpret and recreate the drama. Doing the book greatly increases story comprehension. Doing the book can take a variety of forms, from performing a play, to acting out stories, to concentrating on recreating a single scene of a play.

Do a Play   Children of all ages enjoy being in a play and some wonderful stories for children are already written in play format. Recasting a story as a play can also be a powerful reading/writing activity, especially if the children create the script and stage directions from the original story. Not only do children write, they also must read carefully to transform ideas into action.

Most basal readers have at least one or two plays. Children's magazines, including *My Weekly Reader* and *Sprint* (Scholastic), often contain plays for children to do. *Take Part Starters, Grades 2–3* and *Take Part Plays, Grades 3–6* (Sundance) are play versions of favorite tales and stories, including *The Clever Little Tailor, Robin Hood, Treasure Island,* and many others. Curriculum Associates publishes some plays, including fables, fairy tales, and others, in the Primary Reader's Theatre series. Rigby produces a set of PM readers called Traditional Tales and Plays. These include familiar tales—*Robin Hood, The City Mouse and the Country Mouse, The Three Billy Goats Gruff,* and more—at different reading levels. The first part of each book tells the tale and the last pages of each book contain a play version of that tale—ready to be read and done.

When having struggling readers do a play, remember that doing repeated readings is a powerful way to help children develop oral reading fluency and an understanding of characters. It helps their reading more if they do not memorize lines but, rather, read and reread their parts until they can read them fluently.

Some teachers do not do plays because there are not enough parts for everyone, or they do not know what to do with the children who are not in the play while the players are preparing. Most children enjoy preparing to do the play and then watching each other do it. If you have a play that requires seven actors and you have 24 children in your class, divide your class into three groups of eight, putting a director and seven actors in each group. Let all three groups prepare and practice the play simultaneously. Then let each "cast" put on the play for the others.

If you have children do plays, remember that the purpose of this activity is for them to become more active readers, to visualize characters, to do some repeated readings, and to transfer their enjoyment from being in the play to reading. "Doing it" is what matters, not how professionally it is done. Props, costumes, and scenery should be nonexistent or very simple. Take the "process attitude" that the play helps develop important reading processes, not a "product attitude," and you will develop a new appreciation for plays.

Some teachers find that letting children make a simple mask to hide behind (using a paper plate and popsicle stick) can help diminish shyness and stage fright.

This is especially true for ESL children, who are less self-conscious about their language ability when they have something to hide behind!

Act Out a Story   Acting out a story is another way to help children think actively and to visualize as they read. The best stories for acting out are the ones that you can visualize as plays. Everyone should have a part, as they did in the plays. Many teachers write down on little slips of paper the characters' names along with a number to designate acting cast:

First Little Pig 1	**First Little Pig 2**	**First Little Pig 3**
Second Little Pig 1	**Second Little Pig 2**	**Second Little Pig 3**
Third Little Pig 1	**Third Little Pig 2**	**Third Little Pig 3**
Mama Pig 1	**Mama Pig 2**	**Mama Pig 3**
Wolf 1	**Wolf 2**	**Wolf 3**
Man with sticks 1	**Man with sticks 2**	**Man with sticks 3**
Man with straw 1	**Man with straw 2**	**Man with straw 3**
Man with bricks 1	**Man with bricks 2**	**Man with bricks 3**
Director 1	**Director 2**	**Director 3**

The teacher then explains to the students that three groups will be acting out the story and that they will all have parts. She explains what the parts are and that she will pass out the slips after the story is read to determine what parts they will have. She encourages them to think about what all the characters do and feel because they might end up with any of the parts.

After the story is read and discussed, the teacher hands a slip of paper to each child randomly. (This procedure of letting chance determine who gets starring roles and who gets bit parts is readily accepted by the children and easier on the teacher, who will not have to try to decide who should and could do what. Sometimes, the most unlikely children are cast into starring roles and astonish everyone—including themselves!) The children then form three groups and whoever gets the director slip in each group helps them act out the story. The teacher circulates among the groups, giving help and encouragement as needed. After 10–15 minutes of practice, each group performs their act while the other groups watch. Just as they enjoy doing a play, children generally enjoy acting out a story. Teachers who keep their focus on the "process" children go through as they read and act out stories enjoy this activity and do not worry too much about the product. Acting out stories is designed to turn the children into avid readers, not accomplished actors.

Make a Scene!   Whereas full-blown plays may seem a bit daunting for children and teachers (and take time), a variation on this theme is often easier for children and can be quickly incorporated into many lessons. Rather than acting out a full play, have the children recreate a single scene. Scenes can be done by individuals, pairs, or small groups. They simply require the readers to select a scene, transform it into a script (not necessarily written out), briefly rehearse it, and then present it—no props, no costumes, just reenactment! The scene can be as short as a single exchange between characters, or can even be a single sentence delivered in the appropriate voice. Children who can literally become Richard Best from *The Beast in Ms. Rooney's Room* (Pat Reilly Giff) or the sassy little brother in *Island of the Blue Dolphins* (Scott O'Dell) demonstrate an understanding of the story and the characters.

STORY TEXT LESSONS

The goal of comprehension instruction is that children learn how to independently do the strategies as they read on their own. How to follow story structure and how to summarize stories are two important comprehension strategies. Story maps, the Beach Ball, and "doing" the book activities all help children develop story structure and learn to summarize and conclude.

STORY MAPS
1. Decide on a story map skeleton that will work best for your children.
2. Talk about the slots on the map and make sure they understand their purpose for reading.
3. Have them read in whatever format you choose.
4. Have them complete the story map as a class or in small groups.

THE BEACH BALL
1. Decide on the questions and write them with permanent marker on a beach ball.
2. Talk about the questions on the stripes and make sure children understand their purpose for reading.
3. Have them read in whatever format you choose.
4. Toss the beach ball and answer the questions.

DOING THE BOOK
1. Include plays in your reading repertoire. Have children read and do plays, and have older children turn stories into plays by writing scripts for them.
2. Have children do some impromptu acting out of stories—no scripts, props, or costumes needed. Children should read the story several times, parts should be chosen, and children should "do their thing." To include more children, have several casts performing the same story.
3. Have children act out scenes from longer stories. Let small groups pick different scenes; then have each group perform in order of scenes. All the groups not in a particular scene become the audience for that scene.

SUMMARY

Comprehension is the reason for reading! We read to enjoy, to be entertained, to learn new information, to figure out how to do things, and to help us make decisions. Comprehension requires word identification and a certain level of prior knowledge. But comprehension is primarily thinking directed by text. Children can learn to think as they read. Engaging children in a variety of literate conversations, modeling our thinking through think-alouds, and teaching children the particular strategies needed for informational and story text allow all children to develop thoughtful literacy. All students need many opportunities to summarize and synthesize what they are reading. Answering comprehension questions may measure comprehension; it does not teach it.

CHAPTER 4

Writing

Imagine coming upon someone sitting, pen in hand or with fingertips poised over a keyboard, staring at a blank page or blank screen. You ask, "What are you doing?" The person often responds, "I'm *thinking!*" Continue to observe and you see the person move into the writing phase eventually, but this writing is not continuous. It is marked with constant pauses. If you are rude enough to interrupt during one of these pauses to ask, "What are you doing?" the writer will probably once more respond, "I'm *thinking!*"

Eventually, the writer finishes the writing or, rather, the first draft of the writing. The writer may put the writing away for a while or may ask someone, "Take a look at this and tell me what you think." Later, the writer returns to the writing to revise and edit it. Words are changed and paragraphs are added, moved, or deleted. Again, the writer pauses from time to time during this postwriting phase. If you ask what the writer is doing during this phase, you will get the familiar response, "I'm *thinking!*"

We offer this common scenario as proof that the essence of writing is thinking and that even the most naïve writer knows this basic truth. Because writing is thinking and because learning requires thinking, students who write as they are learning will think more and, thus, will learn more.

In addition to the fact that writing is thinking, writing is hard! It is complex, involving thinking about many things at the same time. Writers must contend with some difficult questions:

What do I want to say?
How can I say it so that people will believe it?
How can I say it so that people will want to read it?

In addition to these big issues are a host of smaller, but still important, issues:

How can I begin my writing in a way that sets up my ideas and grabs the reader's attention?

Which words best communicate these feelings and thoughts?
What examples can I use?
Do I need to clarify here or include more detailed information?
How can I end it?
Now, I have to think of a good title!

And if these grand and not-so-grand issues are not enough, writers also have a number of small details to worry about. Sometimes these details are taken care of during the postwriting phase, but often writers think about them as they write. Some examples include

I wonder whether this sentence should begin a new paragraph?
Do I capitalize the word *state* when it refers to North Carolina?
How do you spell *Beijing*?
Does the comma go inside or outside the quotation marks?

We have not depicted this juggling act and sampling of the balls writers have to keep in the air as they perform the difficult act of writing to discourage you. They are included to convince you that students need instruction, guidance, support, encouragement, and acceptance if they are going to be willing and able participants in writing. Unfortunately, writing instruction in schools has often focused primarily on the editing skills of handwriting, spelling, mechanics, and grammar. Schools once used language books, handwriting books, and spelling books as the base for the writing curriculum. In these schools, children rarely had the opportunity to think, compose, or write. Instead, they spent most of their time concentrating on the skills.

Recently, many schools have moved away from commercial programs and have set out to create their own writing curriculum in which the emphasis is on writing. In addition, most recently published basal reader programs have added writing components. In most schools, children write more now than they did a few years ago, but whether writing is actually being taught—especially thoughtful writing—is still a concern. Also of concern is whether the writing children are doing is broad and representative of the various types of writing necessary in school and outside school. Do children spend substantially more time composing stories than they do reports? Do schools actually teach how to search out, gather, and organize information for reports? Are children learning to revise? Are children learning to edit?

This chapter cannot provide full answers to all these questions, but a broad view of writing and a clear view of how to develop struggling readers' writing ability is presented. Children who are struggling to become literate are the very children who need the most opportunities to write and the best writing instruction across the elementary grades. This chapter is focused on these children.

In Chapter 2, we emphasized the importance of daily self-selected writing. The opportunity to write daily is especially critical for children who come from homes where they have few opportunities to see adults write or to actually write themselves. Writing every day helps develop thoughtful readers as well as thoughtful writers. The single most important thing you can do to help students become better writers is to provide them with time to write, materials with which to write, and instruction that demonstrates to them the process and the importance of writing. Once the children are writing on a regular basis, specific instructional activities can be used to develop their writing abilities. This chapter describes five effective ways to guide children's writing and thinking.

SHARED AND GROUP WRITING

Shared reading is a process in which the teacher and the children read together. Shared writing is a process in which the teacher and children write together. Generally, the teacher leads the children to share ideas and then records the ideas as the children watch. Shared writing—like individual writing—can be used to write a wide variety of things. Regie Routman (1991), in her wonderfully practical, readable book *Invitations,* includes this list of some possibilities (p. 60):

- Wall stories and big books
- Stories, essays, and poems
- Original story endings
- Retellings of stories
- Class journal entries
- Class observations of pets, plants, and science experiments
- Shared experiences such as field trips and special visitors
- Class rules and charts
- Weekly newsletter to parents
- News of the day
- Curriculum-related writing
- Reports
- Informational books
- Evaluations of books and activities

Language Experience Approach

Shared writing is similar to language experience in that the teacher writes as the children watch, but it has one important feature that differs. One cardinal principle of language experience has always been that the teacher should write down exactly what the child says. Van Allen and Allen (1966), Stauffer (1980), and others who promoted language experience as an approach to beginning reading and writing, argued that children must learn that what they say can be written down and then read back. This important learning can occur only if the child's exact words are recorded. The problem for teachers arises when a child's spoken dialect differs from standard written English.

Teachers find it difficult to record sentences such as

I ain't got no sisters.
I done broke my foot.

Most teachers, when working with individual children, however, write down the sentences just as they are spoken because they realize that the child will read the sentence the way it was spoken. If the sentence,

I ain't got no sisters.

is changed to the standard,

I don't have any sisters.

then the child, remembering what was said, will read the word *don't* as the spoken "ain't," the word *have* as "got," and the word *any* as "no." Likewise, if the child's spoken sentence,

I done broke my foot.

is changed to the standard,

I broke my foot.

then the child, remembering what was said, will "read" the word *done* while looking at *broke,* the word *broke* while looking at *my,* the word *my* while looking at *foot,* and then run out of written words before finishing the spoken sentence. If language experience is being used to help an individual child understand what reading and writing are and to show the child that what he or she says can be written down and read, then the child's exact words must be used. To do anything else would hopelessly confuse the child about the very things you are trying to clarify by using individual language experience.

Shared Writing

The situation changes, however, when you are working with a class or a small group of children. The group invariably includes children who use a variety of different language structures. Recording sentences when you are working with children whose language usage differs from standard English can lead to confusion

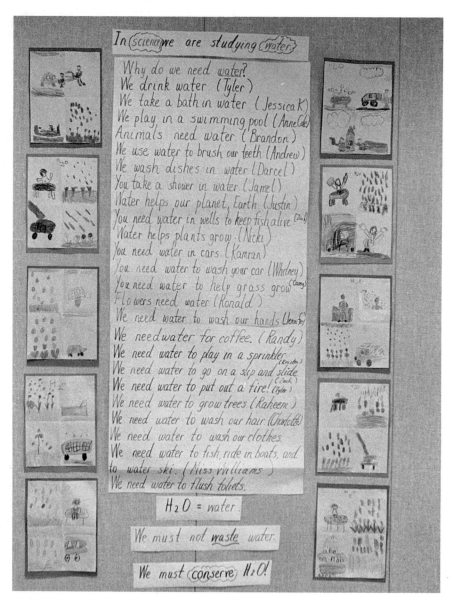

Here is a shared writing chart that was created in one primary classroom as the children studied water.

and sometimes ridicule from children whose spoken language is closer to standard written English. In addition, the charts, letters, books, and so forth that you create during shared writing are apt to be displayed in the classroom or sent home to parents. Explaining to parents why nonstandard usage is being written down can be difficult; some teachers have even been accused of "not knowing how to write good English."

Shared writing differs from language experience because the teacher and the children all "share" the construction of the writing. In creating a daily entry for the class journal, the teacher asks the children what important things they think should be included. She listens to all suggestions and accepts whatever kind of spoken dialect children use. After listening to the suggestions, she records them using standard written English and imposing some kind of order and cohesion. She then reads aloud the sentences she has written. Because the teacher listens to the suggestions of many children and then records the gist, but not the exact words of any child, the problem of recording and reading nonstandard usage does not occur.

Likewise, shared writing provides the opportunity to rework awkward constructions that students may verbalize. Most teachers would not write down verbatim sentences such as

We was going there then but then we didn't until the next day.
Well, a lizard is one of those, ah, reptile things, I think.

By collaboratively reworking these sentences aloud with students, the teacher models the shift from oral to written language and the editing process that all writers must learn.

Both shared writing and individual language experience are valuable tools to use with children whose reading and writing experiences have been limited at home and at school. In individually dictated language experience situations, children's exact words should be written down. To do otherwise is to defeat the purpose of individual language experience. When working with a group to create something for public consumption, however, shared writing, in which all the children share ideas and the teacher writes a composite, seems to be the best alternative.

Group Writing

A natural offshoot of shared writing is group writing. Group writing works especially well with descriptive and other informational writing genres. Children who have been regularly engaged in coming up with ideas and in helping the teacher create a readable, cohesive piece that represents all their ideas know how people can work together to share writing. When you want students to write communally, you can use a variety of ways to organize.

The easiest way to have children work together is occasionally to give them a writing task and tell them that because sometimes two heads are better than one, they can work with a friend. Let the friends negotiate whether one person will write the first draft or whether they will take turns. Usually, one child writes and shares what has been written and the other creates, listens, and offers editorial comment. Encourage the partners to brainstorm ideas first and then to talk about the best way to put these ideas in writing. Normally, children who are allowed to choose a friend to write with have little difficulty deciding who will do what.

You might also assign students to work together in groups of three in which one person records the ideas of the entire group. This communal writing seems to work best when everyone contributes ideas that one or more students jot down and another student produces a first draft and reads it to the group. All group members can then suggest ways to make the writing better or more clear. Finally, the third member of the group can complete the editing and revise the first draft into the final draft.

For a lengthy piece, students can divide up the sections. They first plan which parts each person writes and set some guidelines about the content and the writing style. Each person then writes his or her part and everyone in the group responds to it. The group works together to produce a draft to which they all contribute.

WRITER'S WORKSHOP

Writer's Workshop (Graves, 1995; Calkins, 1994) is the term most commonly used to describe the process of children choosing their own topics, writing, revising, editing, and publishing. In Writer's Workshop, we try to simulate as closely as possible an atmosphere in which real writers write and to help children see themselves as real authors.

Writer's Workshop usually begins with a minilesson during which the teacher writes. Next, the children write. As the children write, the teacher helps those who have chosen a piece to revise and edit. Writer's Workshop usually concludes with an Author's Chair in which children read their writing and get responses from the other "writers" in the room. The following section is an example of how one teacher conducts her Writer's Workshop.

The Minilesson in Which the Teacher Writes and Edits

Writer's Workshop in this classroom begins in the same manner every day. The teacher sits down next to the overhead and the children gather on the floor around her. They are eager to see what she will write about today! The teacher holds her overhead pen and thinks aloud.

"A lot of ideas are in my mind this Monday morning. I could write about how cold it was at our house when the power went off and how it stayed off almost all day on Saturday." (Some children nod and look like they want to tell about similar situations at their houses over the weekend. Other children look puzzled. You can tell by looking at them that they had no electrical problems that weekend and are curious about what happened.)

"I could write about the visitor we are going to have this afternoon and the animals he will probably bring with him." (The children appear delighted at the prospect of someone coming who might bring animals. "What kind of animals?" they wonder.)

"I could write about the book I finished last night. I could write about the accident I saw on the way to school this morning. I could write about running into Jamie at the grocery store on Friday afternoon and seeing her baby brother. So many things have happened since we left here on Friday afternoon that I could write about and share with you. It is so hard to decide!"

After sitting there in a "thinking posture" for a few more seconds, the teacher decides and begins to write. She puts her name in the left-hand corner of the paper and writes the title in the center of the first line:

A Saturday without Electristee

As she writes *electristee,* she says the word slowly, stretching out the sounds so the children can tell that she is trying to figure out how to spell it. The teacher continues writing. From time to time she stops as if to think what to say next. She invent-spells some words and looks up at the classroom word wall to find out how to spell others. She leaves out one punctuation mark, an important word or two, and a capital letter. The children watch her carefully and you can tell from their shaking heads and pointing fingers that they notice many things that need fixing. When the teacher finishes writing, she says, "Now, when I finish writing, I always reread my writing to see whether I said what I wanted to say." She then reads the paragraph aloud, filling in one word she left out and changing a few capitals, but otherwise not finding several things that need fixing.

Next, the teacher reminds the children that this is a good "draft"—not perfect but good. She can read it and it makes sense:

"If I wasn't going to publish this, it would be just fine the way it is. If I wanted to read it when it was my turn in the Author's Chair, I would be able to read it to you. But what do I need to do if I decide to make this into a book or decide to put it on our writer's board or in our class newspaper?"

(The children respond in chorus.) "Choose a friend to help you edit it."

"That's right, and I choose Ramona."

The teacher hands Ramona a different color marker, and Ramona proudly takes her place at the overhead projector. The teacher then points to a chart in the room and leads Ramona and the class to read each item that needs to be checked.

Editing checklist and date each item was added to the list:

1. Name and date (9/3)
2. Title in center (9/17)
3. Sentences make sense (9/24)
4. Possible misspelled words (10/17)
5. Ending punctuation.?! (11/25)
6. Capitals in right places (1/14)
7. Stays on topic (2/14)

Ramona, with help from the class, pretends to be the friend and edits the piece. She looks for the name and date; she does not find the date, so she writes it in. She then writes a 1 on the bottom of the page to show that she checked for number 1. The class agrees that there is a title and that it is in the center and so Ramona writes a 2 beside the 1. Ramona then reads all the sentences and finds that two of them do not make sense because a word is missing. The teacher states what words she meant to include and Ramona draws a ⌃ and inserts them. She then writes a 3 to show that she checked for number 3.

Children who want Ramona to circle some words that "need checking" raise their hands. (This includes one word that is spelled correctly, which is fine because the editing friend is only supposed to help you find the ones you need to ask someone about or need to check in the dictionary if you can.) When the potentially misspelled words are circled, Ramona writes a 4 at the bottom. The sentences are read again and a period is put at the end of one of them. Ramona and the class decide to change another period to an exclamation point. Ramona writes a 5 at the bottom. Next, the class makes suggestions about a word that needs a capital letter. Ramona changes this and writes a 6 at the bottom. Finally, Ramona asks what the topic was and whether everyone thinks that the teacher's writing stayed on this topic. They agree that all the sentences were about not having electricity on Saturday, and Ramona writes a 7 at the bottom. The teacher thanks Ramona and the class for all of their help and tells them that they have made her piece much easier for other people to read. She then reminds the children of the steps she went through in writing the piece.

First, she had to decide about what to write and then she had to think about what to say. She wrote the first draft as best she could, used the word wall when needed and "figured out" how some words might be spelled. When she had finished the piece, she reread it to see whether it made sense and made a few more changes. The teacher then reminded the children that they did not need to choose a friend to help them edit every piece. The children knew that editors—friends and teachers—were needed when a piece was going to be made into a book or published in the class newspaper. If they were going to publish a piece, they should

> ### WHY MODELING AND DEMONSTRATION ARE CRITICAL FOR STRUGGLING READERS
>
> Many teachers who have tried to get struggling readers involved in the writing process express frustration with the limited abilities and the unwillingness of the children to write and edit. We believe that teacher demonstration of the steps in the writing process is the critical factor in establishing a successful Writer's Workshop with struggling readers. Children who watch the teacher think aloud about what topics to write on and about what to say are much less apt to complain, "I ain't got nothing to write about." Children who watch the teacher invent-spell some words and leave out some words, punctuation, capitalization, and so on have more than just our word for the fact that first drafts are never perfect. Children who watch the teacher organize (and reorganize) information while composing develop a better "feel" for organizing their own work. Children who use a gradually added-onto checklist to help edit a piece written by the teacher learn how a first draft can be improved if it is going to be published.

choose a friend who would read the piece for the seven editing items they had learned so far.

The teacher drew their attention to the dates next to each item on their editing checklist and asked whether they remembered what these dates meant. The children responded that the date was the first day that they had added this item to the checklist. The children were clearly proud that at the beginning of October they were only checking for three things. Now they had learned seven things to check for. They also wanted to know when they could add the eighth thing. The teacher reminded them of the juggling analogy she told them about in the beginning. A juggler learns to juggle by first juggling one or two items and then gradually adds one more when ready. She pointed out that they had only been checking to see whether a piece stayed on the topic for a few weeks, and that they would have to get very good at this before adding item number 8.

The Children Write

After this minilesson (which takes longer to describe than it actually takes to do!), the children begin working on their writing. Some children get their writing notebooks and begin a new piece. Other children continue working on the piece that they started yesterday. The children are encouraged to write about anything they choose to write about, but the teacher's musing about what she might write about and her piece itself clearly remind the children of things they want to write about. Several children whose homes had also been without electricity on Saturday write about what it was like at their house. Although the teacher did not write about meeting Jamie and her baby brother at the grocery store, Jamie was stimulated to describe this encounter.

Conferencing, Revising, Editing, and Publishing

Early in the year, we set three major writing goals we want to accomplish. First, we want children to get in the habit of writing each day and coming up with their own topics based on what they want to tell. Second, we want them to learn to use the word displays in the room for spelling words and to learn how to stretch out big words that they need to write what they really want to tell. Third, we want them to realize that they can take several days to write a piece if they have a lot to tell and that they need to read what they have already written to be able to add on to their piece. Many children need our individual help and encouragement, but with that help and encouragement they can all learn how to use their writing time productively.

Once these goals are accomplished and most children are writing relatively willingly each day, the teacher can use his or her time and energy conferencing with individuals or small groups of children, helping them learn how to revise and edit their pieces. Teachers carry out the editing, revising, and publishing conferences in a variety of ways depending on the age of the children, how well the children write, how many children they have, and whether they have assistance. Some general guidelines and suggestions can make the revising/editing/publishing process go more smoothly.

Do Not Even Try to Publish Every Piece   Much of the progress children make in writing comes from the daily process of sitting down and writing, particularly after watching the teacher model writing each day. Publishing is the icing on the cake. Children are very proud of their published "books" and feel like real authors when others read and respond to their writing. In most classrooms, once children have established the daily writing habit, the teacher establishes a rule that they can publish a piece when they have three to five good first drafts. The piece they choose goes through the revising, editing, and publishing process with help from friends and the teacher.

Once the children have chosen a piece to publish and have the teacher's okay that they do indeed have the required number of good first drafts and can proceed with publishing, they spend their writing time each day revising, editing, and publishing until the "book" (or other form of publishing) is complete. Then they go back to first-draft writing, working to produce another group of good first drafts from which they can pick another piece to publish. In general, we like children to spend approximately the same percentage of their time in first-draft writing as they spend in revising, editing, and publishing. This varies from child to child, but many children take 6 or 7 days to write four first drafts and approximately the same number of days turning one of those drafts into a published piece.

Revising Should Be Complete before Editing Is Begun   Revising is changing the meaning—adding information, taking out extraneous information, choosing a better word for something. You can help children revise in a variety of ways. Some teachers call all the children together who are ready to publish. (Three to five children is a good number.) Each child reads his chosen piece to the small group and the group makes suggestions for revision. The teacher or a child in the group writes down the suggestions for each child; children then go off individually to make any changes they choose to make. Little changes, such as a word changed, added, or deleted, can be made right on the first draft. Larger changes are written on a separate sheet of paper, and the teacher shows the children how to mark the place where they will insert this addition.

Revision is not an easy skill to learn, and although we want to teach children to revise and make sure they know how to revise, we should not expect a great deal of revision, particularly not from first and second graders. The goal of revising should be that children understand that meaning comes first; that authors often add, delete, or change things to make their writing more interesting, clear, or dramatic; and that you make whatever meaning changes you want to make before you edit.

Teach Children to Edit with a Friend   We do not begin revising, editing, and publishing with children until we have some kind of editor's checklist to help children edit their writing. Children need practice using such a checklist each day. Regardless of the number of items on the checklist, the teacher should model daily how to use it before publishing begins. When children have revised their piece to their satisfaction, the next step is for them to pick a friend and ask that friend to be their editor and help them edit for the items on the checklist. Children do not have much trouble doing this when they have watched the teacher pick one of the children every day to come up and lead the editing of her piece for the items on the checklist. The editing is done right on the first draft (inserts included, if any) with a green (or red or purple or pink!) pen—just as the teacher's piece is edited with a different colored marker.

Children, of course, are at different stages of understanding about writing and editing, and some children are much better editors than others. Peer editing for the checklist items is not perfect, and teachers often find things that should have been changed that were not (and things that were changed that should not have been!). But all the children become much better editors as the year goes on, and they get in the habit of trying to edit before they publish and not leaving all the work for the teacher.

The Teacher and Child Do a Final Edit   Once the piece is revised, and has been edited with a friend for the checklist, the writer and the teacher have an individual conference in which they fix anything that needs fixing. Our goal in publishing is that children can experience the pride of being authors and having others read and enjoy their writing. This cannot happen if the final piece is not readable. So before the child goes to the publishing phase, we sit down with that

The teacher is helping one boy edit a piece of writing.

This boy is using the class-created editing checklist to edit his own piece before taking it to the teacher/editor.

child and do a final edit. We fix the spelling of words, add punctuation and capitalization, clarify sentences that do not make sense, delete sentences that are totally off the topic, and do whatever else is necessary to help the child produce a "masterpiece" of writing!

We generally do this with a different colored pen right on the first draft. This is easier than you might think because we have children write all their first drafts skipping every other line, leaving blank lines so that editing can occur. (Of course, some children cannot write on every other line, but most can and they all get better at it as the year goes on.) If something must be inserted that cannot be clearly written between the lines of text, we write it on a separate piece of paper and mark the insertion point. We read each edited piece with each child, making sure they can read anything inserted and stopping to notice where they need to add punctuation, fix spelling, and make other changes.

Give Additional Support to Your Most Struggling Writers   In almost every class, once we begin publishing, a few children's writing is really not "editable."(Like love, this is hard to describe, but you will recognize it when you see it!) We generally do not begin publishing until almost all the children are writing something "readable," but "almost all" leaves out a few children. These children's pieces are collections of letters with only a few recognizable words and very few spaces to help you decipher the letters from the words! You might think these children just are not ready to publish and should continue to produce first drafts, but the message that most children would get from being left out of the publishing process is, just as they thought, they cannot write! Once you begin publishing, you need to include everyone in the process. Some children will be able to publish more pieces than others. Some authors are more prolific than others! The goal is not for everyone to have the same number, and, in fact, we do not count and try not to let the children count. The goal is, however, for everyone to feel like a real writer because they have some published pieces.

When we begin publishing, we work with the most avid writers first. When most of them have a piece published and are on their second round of first drafts, we gather together the children who have not yet published anything. We help them choose a piece they want to publish and give them the option of reading or telling what they want to say. We let the others in the group make suggestions for revision, and we make notes of what each child wants to write and the revision suggestions.

Then we sit down individually with each child and help him or her construct their piece. We have them tell us again what they want to say. As they tell, we write their sentences by hand, later to be typed on the computer. Once their sentences are handwritten, we read them with the children several times to make sure they know what they have said. We then cut the sentences apart and have them illustrate each and put them all together into their book! They are now—like everyone else—real published authors, and they approach their second round of first-draft writing with renewed vigor—confident that they too can write!

It is important to note here that we would not be giving this kind of support to the majority of our children. If more than a few children need this support, you are not ready to pull away to hold individual and group conferences during their writing time. But when most are ready and only a few lag behind, the solution just suggested works smoothly in most classrooms and provides a big boost for your most struggling writers.

Keep the Publishing Process Simple   Although publishing can be done in a lot of different ways, you do not want to spend too much of your or your children's time in publishing. In many schools, groups of volunteers create skeleton books for children to publish in. They cut half sheets of paper and staple or bind them with a brightly colored cover into books of varying numbers of pages. Children write (or type on the computer and cut and tape) their sentences on the pages and add illustrations. In other classrooms, the pieces are typed on the computer (by the child or an assistant/volunteer), illustrated (with drawings, photos, or clip art), and displayed on the writing bulletin board. A variety of computer programs are available that make the publishing process a much less onerous one and help children produce professional-looking products. In many classrooms, children publish their pieces on the web to share with a larger audience.

This girl has had her piece edited and is now copying and illustrating it to put on the writing board.

Here are some of the books published in one classroom. Parent volunteers assembled the blank books with a Dedication page at the beginning and an About the Author page at the end. Children copy their revised/edited piece into these books and then illustrate them. These child-authored books are popular reading choices during self-selected reading.

Sharing in the Author's Chair and Beyond

In addition to demonstrations by the teacher, opportunities for the children to share and publish their own writing are critical. In the classroom just described, the writing part of each day ends with some of the children sitting in the Author's Chair and reading something to the class. Sometimes they read a "published" piece. More often, they read from a first draft that they have just written. After each child has read, he or she calls on class members to tell something that they liked about the piece. The author can also ask for questions and can elicit suggestions to make the piece better. During Author's Chair, the focus is exclusively on the message that the author is trying to convey. Here again, the role of the teacher model is extremely important. Useful comments include

> I love the way you described . . .
> I wondered why the character . . .
> Your ending really surprised me because . . .
> The way you began your story was . . .
> I could just imagine . . .
> I thought this was a true story until . . .

This child is sharing a first draft as he reads in the Author's Chair.

If the children hear the teacher responding to their message, they respond similarly.

It is important that students' writing be valued; the best evidence of this is found in classrooms where their compositions are routinely displayed. When wall space, bulletin boards, and clotheslines display compositions, children realize that they have an audience beyond the teacher. In many schools, there is an author's night scheduled each semester. Parents are invited to read and comment on the compositions students have created and selected for display. These compositions are arranged on tables and racks in classrooms, in hallways, and are posted about the rooms as well. Each composition has a comment sheet alongside it; parents and other children may read it or react to it (of course, parents first locate their child's work). This event allows parents to see how children develop throughout the elementary years and how their child is developing in particular. Often, it helps upper-grade teachers see how far children have come and helps primary-grade teachers see the development of previous students several years later.

Allocating Time for Writer's Workshop

Many teachers find it difficult to decide how much time and effort should be allotted to first drafts and to revising, editing, and publishing. Although the actual amounts may vary with the ability and age of the children, elementary children should usually spend more time writing their first drafts than they spend publishing them. In any case, the extremes should be avoided. Not every first draft should be taken through the revise, edit, publish cycle because this would greatly diminish the amount of time children would have for producing first drafts. On the other hand, children who never take a first draft through this cycle may learn that the first draft is a final draft! A balance is required if children are going to learn that first-draft writing is not expected to be perfect, while at the same time learn how to take a first draft and transform it from "sloppy copy" to the "polished and published" product.

The critical factor is the time allocated for writing and how that time is organized. For older children, two or three 1-hour periods each week may be better than daily 30-minute periods, even though the total amount of time allocated is similar. Good writing takes time and writing longer pieces takes time. If we routinely schedule relatively short periods for writing, we should expect relatively brief pieces of writing. If we want children to involve themselves in their writing, to research topics, to organize and reorganize, and to share and respond, we need to allocate longer periods than have traditionally been available in elementary schools. Of course, we should have substantial flexibility and should plan frequent writing opportunities—many of which can be brief. But we also need to plan extended writing periods, especially as children move into the intermediate grades.

Finally, when considering time, we must remember that good writing often takes more than 1 day to compose. Children who think they should begin a new piece every day and magically finish it in whatever time is allocated produce short, shallow pieces. During process writing, children learn that some pieces take many days to complete. The teacher models this during the minilesson that introduces Writer's Workshop. On some days, the teacher does not finish the piece in the allotted time. "Stay tuned tomorrow," says the teacher as he puts the just-begun piece away. When tomorrow comes, the teacher models another important writing strategy—rereading what you wrote yesterday so you can figure out where you were and continue. The most effective teachers practice what they preach. If you want your students to be willing to lay aside a piece until tomorrow and to know how to reread to get back into that piece, make sure some of your pieces require you to do the same.

FOCUSED WRITING

During Writer's Workshop, children choose their own topics as well as the type of writing they want to do. They come to think of themselves as writers and develop writing fluency and confidence. We do, however, need to teach children how to write specific forms. In addition to stories, children need to learn how to write short reports, business and friendly letters, and essays. Many children enjoy writing poetry, and many types of poetry do not have to rhyme. In many states, children are tested on their ability to do specific writing—narrative, descriptive, persuasive, and so on—at specific grade levels. Demonstration is once again the most effective teaching strategy for teaching children specific forms. The following section is a sample focused-writing lesson in which children learn to write a friendly letter.

Modeling and Demonstration

The teacher of this class has a good friend who is teaching in a faraway state. The two teachers talk regularly on the phone and have both been concerned about giving their students "real" reasons to write. One of them remembers having a pen pal whom he never met but with whom he corresponded for years. The two teachers decide that, although this is a rather old-fashioned idea, their children may still enjoy having their own pen pals. The class is indeed excited about the idea; this is their first letter-writing experience. The teacher wants them to learn the correct form for a letter while at the same time making sure the emphasis is kept on the message to be communicated.

The lesson begins with the teacher asking the children what they would like to know about their pen pals. He records these questions on large index cards.

How old is he/she?
What is school like there?
Do they have a gym?
Do they have a lot of homework?
Do they have a soccer team?
Does he/she play soccer?
Does he/she play baseball? football? other sports?
Is it cold all the time?
Does everybody ski?
What does he/she like to eat?
Do they have video games?
Do they have a mall?

It is clear that the children would like to know many things about their new pen pals. The teacher then helps them organize their questions by beginning a web like the following:

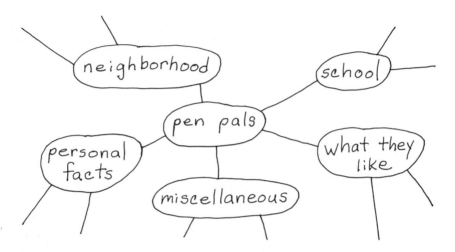

The children help decide where their questions should go and then come up with more questions that also are written on index cards and put in the correct places.

On the following day, the teacher and the children review the web, and the teacher points out that the things they would like to know about their pen pals are probably also the things their pen pals are wondering about them. He explains that they cannot possibly include all this information in the first letter, but that they will be writing back and forth all year. As the year goes on, they will share and learn about these things and many things they have not even thought of yet.

The teacher then goes to the overhead and leads the children through the process of writing the first letter. He explains that the letter will be read not only by their pen pals, but also, probably, by many other people, so each letter must be as correct and readable as possible. Today's task is to begin a good first draft that they can edit and recopy or type later. The teacher then explains and models for the children how and where they put the inside address, date, and greeting. The children watch as he does each step at the overhead. They then do the same on their papers.

Once these formalities are covered, the teacher leads them to look at the web and decide what to write about in the first paragraph. The class decides they should write about their personal facts. The teacher agrees and has them put their pencils down to watch as he writes a paragraph that communicates some personal facts about himself.

Editing as You Go

After writing this first paragraph, the teacher reads it aloud, changing a word and adding another word, to model for the children that when we write, we read and change as we go along. He points out the paragraph indentation and that his paragraph has four sentences. The teacher then instructs the children to write their first paragraph, telling some personal facts about themselves. He reminds them that we always write first drafts on every other line so that we have space to add or change things later.

The Children Write

The children begin to write their paragraphs. As they write, they glance at the web on the board and at the teacher's letter on the overhead. Even though these children are not very sophisticated writers, the demonstration they have observed along with the displayed web and letter clearly provide the support they need to write the first draft of a paragraph.

When most students have finished their paragraph, the teacher reminds them that good writers stop occasionally and read what they have written before moving on. He then waits another minute while each child reads what they have written. He is encouraged to see them making a few changes/additions they have noticed in their own rereading.

The process of the teacher writing a paragraph, reading it aloud, making changes and additions, and then giving the children time to write their own paragraph continues that day and the next as the teacher and the children construct paragraphs with information from the categories on the web. After each paragraph, the children are reminded to reread and make any changes or additions they think are needed. The teacher is encouraged to notice that when they get to the fifth paragraph, many children are automatically rereading and changing without being reminded to do so. Finally, the teacher suggests possible closings and shows the children where to put the closing. As they watch, he writes a closing on his letter; then they write one on theirs. This completes the first draft of the letters.

Revising to Publish

The next day, the teacher helps them polish their letters. He puts them into sharing groups of four children and has each child read her or his letter to the others. Just as they do for Author's Chair, this sharing is totally focused on the message. Listeners tell the author something they liked, and the author asks them whether anything is not clear or whether they have suggestions for making it better. When everyone in the group has had a chance to share, they make whatever additions and revisions they choose. Children can be seen crossing things out and inserting additional information. As they do this, it becomes apparent why writing the first draft on every other line is useful.

A Final Edit

Now that the letters are revised and the children are satisfied with their message, it is time to do a final edit. During Writer's Workshop, the children are accustomed to choosing a friend to help them edit a draft that they are going to publish, so they just tailor this process to letters. They refer to the editing checklist displayed in the classroom and decide that the editing items are still valid, but that they need to change number 1 to correspond with letter editing. Number 1 had been "Name and date." They decide that for letters, number 1 should be "Address, date, greeting, closing." The children then pair up with a friend and read for each item on the checklist together. When they have finished helping each other edit, they share their drafts with the teacher during final editing.

Publishing the Letter

On the following day, they choose some stationery from a motley collection (contributed by parents or purchased from bargain bins) and copy the letters in their most legible handwriting. Finally, the teacher demonstrates how to put the address and the return address on the envelopes. (Even though he intends to mail them all to the pen pals' school in one big envelope, he wants children to learn how to address envelopes and knows the pen pals will feel they are getting a real letter when it comes sealed in a real envelope.) The letters are mailed, and the writers eagerly await their replies. Next week, in a faraway city, this process begins again as the teacher's friend takes her class through the same steps of learning to write letters so they can write back.

The procedure just described is not difficult to carry out, but it does take time. Most classes would spend at least five 45-minute sessions going through brainstorming, webbing, modeling, first drafting, revising, and editing. When you get the letters sent off, you may think, "Never again!" But keep in mind that the first time you do anything is always the hardest—for you and the children. A month later, when the children have received their letters and are ready to write again, the process will be much easier and will go much more quickly. After three or four letters, most children know how to organize information and can write an interesting and correctly formed letter with a minimum of help. By the end of the year, they will be expert letter writers and will have gained a lot of general writing skills in the process.

Other Examples of Focused-Writing Lessons

The procedure just described for learning to write friendly letters can be used for any writing format you want children to learn. Imagine, for example, that you think they would enjoy writing cinquain poetry. Cinquains can be created in many different ways. Perhaps the easiest way for elementary children is the form shown here:

> Teachers
> Smiling, worrying
> Smart, busy, perky
> They love their children.
> Teachers

As you see, the first and last lines are the same word—the subject of the poem. On line 2, you write two *-ing* words. On line 3, you write three adjectives. On line 4, you write a four-word sentence or phrase.

To teach children how to write cinquains, draw lines to show the form of the cinquain. Duplicate this on paper for the children and on an overhead for your use:

Decide on a subject for the cinquain. (They make very impressive Mother's Day cards, but do expand the concept of mother to include a grandmother, an aunt, or whoever the primary female caretaker is!) Let children watch you write the noun on the first and last lines. Have them write the same noun on their first and last lines.

Next, have them brainstorm words that end in *-ing* and tell what mothers do, and list these on the board:

| working | talking | driving | cooking | baking |
| thinking | worrying | fussing | cleaning | singing |

Choose two of these *-ing* words and write them on your second line. Tell children to write two *-ing* words on their second line. Tell them that they can choose from the brainstormed list or can come up with any two on their own.

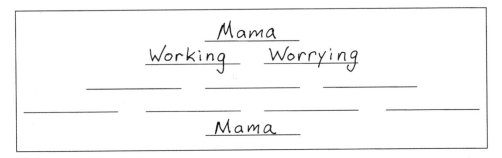

Next, brainstorm descriptive words for line 3 and write these on the board:

busy	pretty	sweet	soft	perky
smart	organized	lonely	worried	careful
tall	short	Black	proud	perfect

Write three descriptive words on your third line. You may want to use one or two words that are not on the brainstormed list to be sure your children understand that the list is just to give them ideas, not to limit their ideas.

> Mama
> Working   Worrying
> Busy   Black   Beautiful
> _____   _____   _____   _____
> Mama

For the fourth line have children brainstorm four-word phrases or sentences:

She works too hard.
She loves you best.
My mama is best.
I love her best.
She makes me laugh.

Always in the kitchen.
Some kids have two!

Write one of these or write another four-line phrase or sentence on your fourth line and have the children write one on theirs.

```
                        Mama
            Working    Worrying
     Busy       Black      Beautiful
  I       love       her       best
            Mama
```

The cinquains are now complete. Let several children read theirs aloud. They will be amazed to discover that, although the topic was the same and they all worked from the same brainstormed list, each poem is different. Once children have one cinquain written, let them make up another one on the same topic. You may then want them to choose one to use as the text on a Mother's Day card. If so, have them share, revise, and edit in the usual manner.

To get reluctant writers involved, oral histories or personal memoirs are wonderful long-term writing projects because they tell about families or themselves (familiar topics). To begin, you want to locate an oral history to share with the class or invite a member of the community (the principal?) to be your subject for a class oral history project. Interview the subject, tape record the interview, take notes, and have the children take notes also. After the interview, create a group summary using your notes, the children's notes, and the tape if a dispute arises. Memoirs abound in children's literature. Elizabeth Fitzgerald Howard's *Aunt Flossie's Hats (and Crabcakes Later)* and Cynthia Rylant's *When the Relatives Came* are two wonderful examples of this genre. Again, after reading and discussing these published memoirs, teachers may create their own, or perhaps create a class memoir based on a collective experience. Now children can begin to plan their own memoirs.

Focused Writing Using Paragraph Frames

Another way to teach children specific writing forms is through the use of paragraph frames. These frames are especially helpful in teaching children to use connecting and transition words that show the relationships among various text structures. Cudd and Roberts (1989) suggest that teachers begin by demonstrating for children how to write a particular type of paragraph. Their example for a first lesson suggests using a sequence relationship because much of what children write has a sequential relationship and because children find this an easy one to

---

LOTS OF DIFFERENT THINGS WE WRITE

A variety of writing genres range from very informal (e.g., grocery lists) to very formal (e.g., term papers). The following list provides a starting point for thinking about the many different types of writing tasks that we might offer students. Too often we have only offered students a narrow range of writing opportunities limited both by frequency and variety.

Description	Article	List	Play
Directions	Report	Comparison	Editorial
Invitation	Summary	Advertisement	Obituary
Story	History	Interview	Memo
Diary	Journal	Letter	Poem
Captions	Headline	Song	Notes

---

compose. We have adapted the steps they suggest going through for the demonstration lesson in the following list:

1. As the children watch, write a simple paragraph about a topic that lends itself to sequential ordering. Use clue words such as *first, next, then, later, finally.*
2. Copy the sentences on sentence strips and mix them up.
3. Reread the original paragraph and discuss the sequence and the sequence words with the children.
4. Have children arrange the mixed-up sentences in the correct order and read the paragraph.
5. Have students copy the paragraph and illustrate it to show the sequence of events.

Once children understand how a sequential paragraph is written, the teacher can present them with a sequence frame, such as the following:

Mother box turtles prepare for their babies in a very interesting way. First,

_____

_____

_____. Next, _____

_____

Finally, _____.

After this, _____.

Source: "Using Writing to Enhance Content Area Learning in the Primary Grades," by E. T. Cudd and L. L. Roberts, 1989, *The Reading Teacher, 42*(6), 395.

Using a shared writing technique, the teacher and the children compose the sentences to fill in the frame. Each child then copies this completed paragraph and illustrates it. Once children have seen the filling in of the frame modeled to them, they are ready to move toward independently writing their own sequentially ordered paragraphs. At this stage, the teacher provides the frame and the students fill in the appropriate events. The final move to independence occurs when students are able to use sequence words and create their own sequentially ordered paragraphs.

Cudd and Roberts provide many examples of the different types of structures children might learn to write using paragraph frames.

Mother box turtles prepare for their babies in a very interesting way. First, she looks for a safe place to burry her eggs. Next, she digs a hole so it will be moist for her eggs. Finally, she lays her eggs, burrys the hole, and then tamps it down. After this, the mother turtle leaves her babies on their own.

Source: "Using Writing to Enhance Content Area Learning in the Primary Grades," by E. T. Cudd and L. L. Roberts, 1989, *The Reading Teacher, 42*(6), 395.

Although these frames have been suggested for use by beginning writers, we have had a great deal of success using them with older children who have difficulty writing or who "hate to write." Learning how to use transition words and connecting words allows them to write something that sounds sophisticated. In addition, many older children who have had a history of failure in reading and writing are interested in learning about real things—things in real life. They can be lured into reading and writing by exploring informational books with lots of pictures on a topic that interests them, and can make a book of their own to display what they have learned. They can also write their own informational text on topics they know a lot about. (One boy in a rural school wrote about how his family made maple syrup; another wrote about how to smoke fish to preserve them.) Using the frames to help them structure their writing allows them to produce a much better product that they can be proud of. In addition, reading comprehension is enhanced as students become more familiar with different text structures.

Bats are unusual animals for several reasons.

First, _____ .

Second, _____ .

Third, _____ .

Finally, _____ .

As you can see, bats are unique in the animal world.

Illustrate with a picture of what you consider to be the most unusual thing about the bat.

Source: "Using Writing to Enhance Content Area Learning in the Primary Grades," by E. T. Cudd and L. L. Roberts, 1989, *The Reading Teacher, 42*(6), 395.

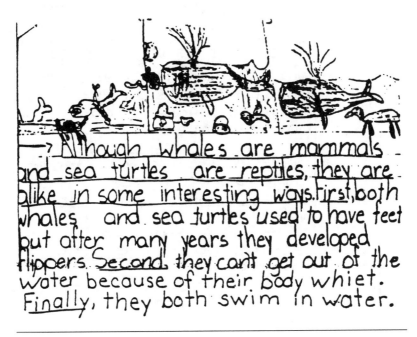

Source: "Using Writing to Enhance Content Area Learning in the Primary Grades," by E. T. Cudd and L. L. Roberts, 1989, *The Reading Teacher, 42*(6), 402.

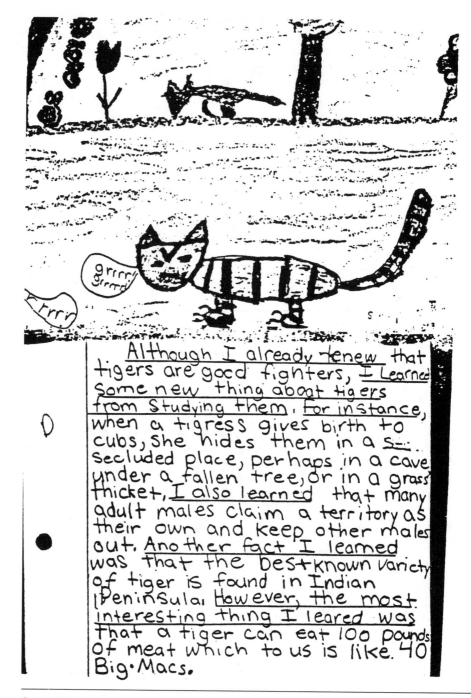

Although I already knew that tigers are good fighters, I learned some new thing about tigers from studying them. For instance, when a tigress gives birth to cubs, she hides them in a se- secluded place, perhaps in a cave, under a fallen tree, or in a grass thicket. I also learned that many adult males claim a territory as their own and keep other males out. Another fact I learned was that the best known variety of tiger is found in Indian Peninsula. However, the most interesting thing I leared was that a tiger can eat 100 pounds of meat which to us is like 40 Big·Macs.

Source: "Using Writing to Enhance Content Area Learning in the Primary Grades," by E. T. Cudd and L. L. Roberts, 1989, *The Reading Teacher, 42*(6), 399.

FOCUSED WRITING BEFORE, DURING, AND AFTER READING

Children who write become better readers. One of the most powerful connections you can make is through reading and writing (Spivey, 1997). Children who read something, knowing that they will write something, are more likely to read with a clear sense of purpose. Children who use information from their reading to write produce better writing because they have more to say. Research has shown a clear benefit from connecting reading and writing (Shanahan, 1988). It has also shown that a writing program that includes instruction in specific informational text structures improves both writing and reading comprehension (Raphael, Kirschner, & Englert, 1988). In this section, we describe a variety of structures for focused writing that connect reading and writing.

Graphic Organizers

Chapter 3 described a variety of ways to guide children's reading so they can learn how to think about different types of reading. One type of guided-reading lesson involved having students construct or fill in various types of graphic organizers. The webs, charts, diagrams, time lines, and so on that you and the children constructed to organize the information learned from reading are marvelous springboards for writing. Here is a character web about Amanda.

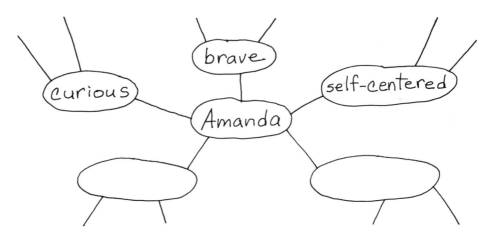

Once the web is complete, you can have the children use the information in the web to create a character summary for Amanda. To demonstrate how you do this, choose one of the adjectives that best describes her and let the children listen and watch as you create a paragraph on the board or on chart paper. When teachers think aloud as they model writing in front of the class, they provide powerful lessons about the writing process. After children watch you write and listen

> *Amanda is a very curious little girl! She always wants to know everything about Miss Morgan. One day she followed her home to find out where she lives and what her house looks like. She is also positive that Miss Morgan will marry Mr. Thompson who teaches next door. Miss Morgan isn't sure what she thinks about that! Who knows what Amanda will try and find out next!*

Here is a paragraph describing Amanda as a curious person. The children watched as the teacher wrote this paragraph. Using this paragraph as a model but using their own ideas, each child then chose the adjective he or she thought best described Amanda and wrote a descriptive paragraph.

to you think aloud about how best to combine your ideas, point out to them the features of your paragraph that you want them to use:

- The paragraph is indented.
- All sentences begin with capital letters and end with a period.
- The name *Amanda* is always capitalized.
- The first sentence tells the most important idea—that Amanda is curious.
- The other sentences are details that show how curious she is.

Now each child should write a paragraph about Amanda, choosing any one of the remaining adjectives on the web (or an adjective that is not on the web that they think best describes her). Their paragraphs will all be different but should follow the form demonstrated in your paragraph.

This type of guided writing, in which children use the information they obtain from reading and record it on some type of graphic organizer, and who then follow a model they watch the teacher create, is extremely effective for struggling readers. Almost all children will produce interesting, cohesive, well-written paragraphs and be proud of what they produce. With enough lessons such as this one, all children can learn how to construct paragraphs. This ability to create well-formed paragraphs is the basis for all different types of writing.

Almost any information recorded in graphic organizer fashion can be used for reading/writing lessons. In the previous chapter, you saw a web that children can use to organize the information read in an article about birds.

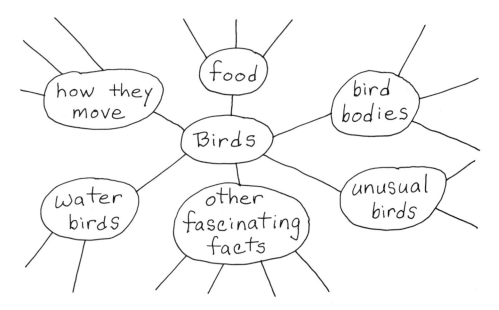

You also saw how information about birds could be recorded in a feature matrix.

Once these graphic organizers are completed, you can use them to have the children write about birds. Based on the web, the teacher would model how to write a descriptive paragraph about the different foods birds eat. Each child would then choose another one of the subtopics—bird bodies, ways birds move, and so forth—and would write a descriptive paragraph about that topic. Based on the information about particular birds from the feature matrix, the teacher would model how to write a paragraph about one of the birds and then let each child choose one of the other birds and write and illustrate a descriptive paragraph about it. After each child writes about one of the birds, the children might work in groups to revise, edit, and produce a book about birds.

Birds						
	fly	swim	build nests	lay eggs	have feathers	molt
robins						
whippoorwills						
penguins						
ostriches						

Lessons in which graphic organizers are constructed and then used based on reading as a basis for writing are particularly important and effective for children whose first language is not English. Watching the teacher use the information from the graphic organizer to write something, and then use the model they have watched the teacher write to construct their own piece of writing, is an extremely powerful way for these children to increase their control of the English language. If your class contains many children whose English is limited, lessons such as these should occur on an almost daily basis in your classroom.

Research

Another way to connect reading and writing is to have children do research to find the answers to questions. Many struggling readers find research to be an impossible task, but it can be structured so that they succeed. They gain a great sense of control and power when they can find and report information. The easiest, most manageable research format for struggling readers and writers is QUAD (*questions, answers,* and *details*) (Cudd, 1989). Children first decide on a topic that they want to research and then fill in the topic on the top of their QUAD sheet. Next, they come up with some questions to which they hope to find the answers. They take this QUAD sheet with them to the library and record answers and details in the appropriate spaces. Finally, they add the references they used at the bottom.

Name A   W

Topic: Kangaroos		
Questions	Answers	Details
1. Do kangaroos hibernate?	no	groundhogs, dormice, and bears do
2. What kinds of food do they eat?	plants	grass, grain, leaves, and twigs
3. How far can they jump?	30 feet 1 jump	
4. Do kangaroos live in one part of Australia	no	they also live in South America
5. How many different kinds of kangaroos are there?	50 or more.	grey kangaroo, red kangaroo, and tree kangaroo
References: Childrens' Britannica	Kangaroos	Book of Knowledge

Source: "Research and Report Writing in the Elementary Grades," by E. T. Cudd, 1989, *The Reading Teacher, 43*(3), 268.

Children can work in pairs or small groups to research the answers to their questions. They can then share the results of their investigations with each other by reading the information right off the sheets. As children become more able researchers, you can help them take the information recorded on the QUAD sheets and turn it into a research report.

Response Logs

Many teachers find that an easy and natural way to connect reading and writing is to have students keep a literature response log. Children are encouraged to take some time after reading each day and record their thoughts, feelings, and predictions. From time to time, the children can be asked to share the responses they have written. This is often a good basis for promoting a discussion of divergent responses to the same story. However, Sudduth (1990) reported that many of her third graders did not really know what to record in their literature logs. This was especially true of those children who were finding learning to read difficult. She outlined the step-by-step instruction that she took them through:

- At first, have the students read the same book. They can read this silently, with a partner, listen to a tape recording, or listen to a teacher read aloud.

- Have specific stopping points in the reading and help the children verbalize what they are thinking and feeling.
- On chart paper or the overhead, record some of the students' responses and have them copy the ones they agree with into their logs. Use "frames" such as:

> I was surprised when _____.
> Since _____ and _____ happened, I predict that _____ will happen next.
> The story reminds me of the time _____.

- As students understand the various open-ended ways in which they can respond to literature, move them toward independence. Continue the discussions but don't write down what they say. Rather, have them write their own personal entries following the discussions. Have the class brainstorm a list of log topics and frames, and display these so that students can refer to them when they need a "starter."
- Have students choose the book they want to read and do their own response logs. Divide the time available for self-selected reading into reading time and log-writing time, perhaps 20 minutes to read and 10 minutes to write. Once children are reading individual books, provide a time each week when they can share what they have written in a small group format.

Writing before Reading

In most classrooms, writing occurs after reading and is used to help readers clarify and solidify what is learned and to help them respond to what they have read. The reasons for having children write before they read are equally compelling. You learned in Chapter 3 that reading is primarily thinking and that, though all children can think, they sometimes do not think while they read. You learned about a variety of useful guided-reading formats for getting children thinking before, during, and after reading. Writing before reading is another way to get children thinking.

This writing can be a "quickwrite" such as "2-minute fast facts." Imagine that your children are going to read an informational selection about reptiles. Make sure everyone has some paper and a pencil ready, set your timer for 2 minutes, and have the children list as many facts as they can about reptiles. Stress that they should get as much down as they can in 2 minutes—in abbreviated list form, not worrying about spelling, complete sentences, and so forth. When the timer sounds at the end of 2 minutes, have students draw a line to show where they finished and have them number the facts they came up with before reading.

Next, have the students read or listen to the informational article about reptiles. Do not let them write anything while they are reading/listening, but make sure that they know they have 3 minutes to add to their list after reading. When students have finished reading, set your timer for 3 minutes and let them add to their list of reptile facts. Once the timer sounds, have the students compare lists in small groups. Each group might first list the facts most members knew before reading and second those facts most members learned from the article. Each group could then write these before- and after-fact lists on a chart and share with the class.

This very simple procedure is used most effectively when the students are going to read a topic about which they already have some prior knowledge. While making the 2-minute prereading list, they realize that they already know a lot and activate their prior knowledge to prepare them to think about the material they are going to read. They are always amazed at how much more they can list after reading. Children who use writing to tally up what they knew before and after reading soon learn that a lot can be learned from reading.

Sometimes you want students to do more extended writing before reading to sensitize them to the process of how authors create images, build suspense, flesh out characters, and so on. Writing before reading can be an especially powerful activity when used with children who have difficulty "getting into" a selection. These children typically begin reading with little or no attempt at bringing up relevant prior background knowledge, do not generate predictions or questions as they read, and passively enter the reading activity and focus on getting it over with, rather than getting involved with it. These children do better on factual questions than on responding to character motives. They can remember names of the characters but find it difficult to answer questions such as, Who does Russell remind you of? (They often respond, "I don't know" or, "It didn't say" or, "No one"). These children find imagery difficult and do not have good mental images of what the characters look like or how they might be dressed unless the story is illustrated or is explicit on these matters. These children have not discovered what reading is all about.

Imagine that you want students to think about how authors use words to create a certain mood. You find a story in which a child is lost out in the woods at night. The fear that the child feels becomes tangible through the images that the author creates. You decide to use a writing activity in which the children write about a time that they, or someone they knew, were lost. First talk with the children about being lost and about the fears they experience. Then talk about how authors make things seem real by giving specific details and by using powerful words. Next, let them write about a real or imagined experience of being lost and have them try to make the terror become real for the reader. After writing, let them share what they have written and notice how they used specific details, powerful words, and images.

As you show them the story you have selected for them to read, tell them that this author had the same writing task that they had. She wanted to tell about a lost child and made it so real that the readers felt like they too were lost. Have them read and compare the language and images used by this writer to the ones that they used in their stories. After they have finished reading the story, discuss specific examples of the language used and the images created by the author. Put some of the sentences on the board or on chart paper. If they are excited by the story and the way that the author created the images of fear, they may want to revise their own stories using some of the "tricks" that were used by the author of the story they just read.

Writing During Reading

In the last chapter, sticky notes were suggested as a way to help students notice and mark interesting, important, or confusing spots in the text. The cryptic notes students write on sticky notes involves them in writing—and, more importantly, in thinking—as they are in the act of reading. Clearly, readers make better writers and writers make better readers. You want your students' writing to be enriched (both in information and style) by their reading, and you want them to read with the sharp eye of a writer. When you engage the children in a writing activity

---

RECOMMENDED RESOURCES

Some Excellent Writing Software

Here is a sampling of some of the best programs we have seen. Given the pace of development, by the time our book is published, these will probably all be replaced by better and newer programs. We include this list more for the purpose of illustrating the kind of writing support computers can offer students than for specific recommendations of software. Find the newest software that perform these (and yet unimagined) functions:

Print Shop (Broderbound) allows children to produce cards, invitations, posters, and so on with "professional quality" layout and graphics.

Language Experience Primary Series (Teachers Support Software) allows teachers and tutors to record stories and print out word lists, charts, and so forth. This software allows children to choose their words to make new sentences and to illustrate what they have written. Synthesized speech is available.

Pow! Zap! Ker-Plunk! (Queue) is a comic-book maker. This program includes clip art, speech bubbles, and comic-book backgrounds that enable children to produce books, cards, mobiles, and puppets.

Story Builder (American School Publishers), Story Maker (Scholastic), Once Upon a Time (Compu-Teach), Monsters and Make-Believe (Queue), Snoopy Writer (American School Publishers) all help children learn how to form sentences, paragraphs, and stories, and provide graphic support.

Story Starters: Social Studies and Story Starters: Science (Pelican) are programs that include clip art and background related to science and social studies topics. Students can use the art and background to produce professional-looking books about U.S. history as well as animals, plants, weather, the solar system, and other science topics.

Thinking Networks for Reading and Writing (Think Network) help children learn about topics and then how to use skeleton map outlines to create text that can be structured in a variety of ways.

Children's Writing & Publishing Center (The Learning Company) is a simple desktop publishing program that allows children to create newsletters, stories, reports, and so on. It includes 150 pictures and the ability to import graphics from other sources.

before, during, or after reading, you increase their facility with and affinity for both reading and writing.

SUMMARY

Perhaps you have wondered about the role of skills in writing instruction as you have been reading this chapter. Questions such as, What about grammar, mechanics, and spelling? and Don't they need to learn these disciplines? are often asked by teachers of struggling readers. One look at their first drafts often convince us that some kind of skills instruction is needed.

The concern that teachers have about teaching these skills is legitimate. Children need to learn not only how to express their ideas and feelings, but also how to express them clearly and in ways that others can read. Decades of research (Langer & Allington, 1992), however, have made it clear that, if the goal of your skills instruction is improved writing, instruction must take place in the context of real writing. Children who put *were* and *was* in the correct blanks on worksheets and who demonstrate the ability to capitalize proper nouns on a test do not necessarily apply these skills to their own writing. In fact, we have far more children who know how to spell and punctuate than how to write thoughtfully and precisely. There is no shortcut to good writing. Children who find writing difficult can learn how to write well when they watch teachers demonstrate and think aloud about the writing and editing process day after day. They will learn how to take a first draft and polish it when they are given the time and the peer, teacher, or computer support to do so. They will learn to care about how well their writing communicates their ideas and how easily others can read it when it is regularly displayed and when teachers focus more on the clarity and quality of the message than on the penmanship and spelling.

Although we believe that engaging struggling readers in lots of self-selected writing is the most important component of a strong literacy program, we do not believe that "just writing" is enough. In this chapter, we have outlined five instructional formats teachers can use for teaching skills in the context of writing. Teachers who engage children in shared and group writing, who conduct Writer's Workshops, who do focused lessons in which children learn how to write specific forms, who connect reading and writing experiences, and who take advantage of whatever computers they have to support children's writing, will produce good writers—in every sense of the word *good*!

Teachers who engage children in lots of writing do not ignore the skills. Rather, they observe children's writing and decide which particular skills children are ready to learn. Skills that are needed by many children are taught in a writing minilesson. Skills teaching also takes place on an individual basis when teachers are helping children edit and publish their pieces. In the next chapter, we describe how teachers provide spelling instruction along with decoding instruction.

CHAPTER 5

Multilevel Instruction

Perhaps the biggest challenge every teacher faces is providing instruction that moves all children along in their literacy development—when the children all start at different places and learn at different rates. Children differ—and they differ on any dimension you can think of. The average height of 7-year-olds is about 4 feet. Many 7-year-olds are 3½ feet tall; many others are 4½ feet tall; a few are only 3 feet tall; and a few are as tall as 5 feet. The average height of children has increased in the last century, presumably due to better nutrition and other health factors. Today's tall children are much taller than the tall children of a century ago. Today's short children are taller too, but they are still short compared to the average. Parents and doctors who monitor the health of children do not try to get all children to be average height (even though we know that short people—especially short boys—are disadvantaged in many arenas). Parents and doctors do expect children to grow, and they monitor and document this growth to make sure it is happening. The growth does not happen in equal monthly increments, however. Most children who are 4 feet tall when they turn 7 years of age will be 3 inches taller when they turn 8 years old, but they do not grow a quarter of an inch each month. Some months they grow very little. Other months they "shoot up."

What does this height example have to do with literacy? Simply put, children will always vary in their reading levels. Some children will read at grade level, some a little above or below grade level, and a few will read way above or way below grade level. The goal of having all children read at grade level is not a reasonable goal (and getting the above-level children back down to being just average readers would take massive amounts of truly terrible experiences!). What is reasonable is the expectation that all children grow in their reading ability. With good instruction, we can also expect all children to read better.

The average readers in a school with a good balanced literacy program read better than average readers in schools with similar populations but less effective instruction. Struggling readers in a school with a good balanced literacy program read better than struggling readers in a school with less effective instruction even though they may not read as well as average readers. Just as with height, we need to measure children's beginning reading point and periodically monitor and document their progress. We need to demonstrate that all children, whether struggling, average, or accelerated, are growing in the level of material they can read and understand. This growth, like increases in height, often does not occur at the same rate. Children reach plateaus in their development for a few months and then spurt forward. With good instruction, most children can make 10 months of progress in reading across 10 months of instruction, but they often do not demonstrate one-tenth of that growth each month.

If this information seems so obvious to you that it is not worth the paper it is printed on, consider some regulations and legislation being passed and implemented in school districts across the country. Many states have legislated that all children come to school ready to learn. Still more states have decreed that children must be at least average in reading and math to be promoted to the next grade. We think some remedial mathematics needs to be provided to help lawmakers understand why getting everyone to at least average is a mathematical impossibility!

Children differ on all kinds of variables, including their current reading level and how rapidly and how far they can rise above that level. With good instruction, all children can read at higher levels, and the progress of all children can be accelerated. But our classrooms will always contain a variety of literacy levels. What kind of instruction can teachers reasonably be expected to provide to help all children, regardless of beginning point, make progress? We have been working on and worrying about this issue for the better part of the past 15 years. We do not have all the answers, but we do know a lot more than we did 15 years

---

THOSE WHO DO NOT LEARN FROM HISTORY ARE DOOMED TO REPEAT IT!

Providing instruction for children at all different levels is not a new challenge! Schools across the decades have tried a variety of solutions, none of which have shown good long-term results. In the early days of U.S. schooling, children were promoted to the next level based on end-of-year tests. Some children never did get promoted, and seeing a 6-foot-tall 12-year-old sitting in a tiny desk at the back of a room filled with 6- and 7-year-old children was a common sight.

Reading groups based on reading level was a common phenomenon in most elementary classrooms for much of our recent history. Data indicate that children who were placed in the "low" group almost never moved up to a higher group and that very few of these children ever reached grade level in reading. Some schools have tracked children by reading levels, putting all the low readers in one class, average readers in another class, and above-average readers in another class. This tracking was abandoned in the 1970s because of its failure to accelerate the reading progress of the low-track students.

Retention, leveled-reading groups, and tracking are all failed solutions of the past, but are once again being implemented in the hope that they work this time around. We see no reason to believe they will!

ago. We call instruction with a wide range of learning possibilities *multilevel instruction*. In this chapter, we provide many examples of ways in which teachers make their literacy instruction multilevel.

MULTILEVEL SELF-SELECTED READING, WRITING, AND WORDS

A balanced reading program is like a balanced diet. Just as a variety of different foods are essential for the development of healthy bodies, many components are necessary for the development of able, avid, thoughtful readers and writers. These components have all been described in the first four chapters of this book. Perhaps the most critical component of a balanced reading program is engaging all children in self-selected reading and writing. Simultaneously, children need to learn to read and spell high-frequency words automatically and to use word patterns to decode and spell thousands of words. While doing self-selected reading and writing and while building their word fluency, children need to engage in a variety of comprehension lessons so that they learn how to think their way through all different kinds of text, and in focused writing lessons so that they learn how to write different kinds of texts for different purposes.

The lessons and activities described in the first four chapters of this book comprise what we see as a balanced reading program. Some activities in this balanced reading program—self-selected reading and writing—are by their nature multilevel. Others—word instruction and comprehension lessons—are much more difficult to make multilevel. In the remainder of the section, we describe how to maximize the multilevel possibilities of self-selected reading, writing, and word instruction. The bulk of this chapter is devoted to the difficult task of making guided reading multilevel.

Self-Selected Reading

Self-selected reading is that part of a balanced literacy program in which children get to choose what they want to read and which parts of their reading they want to respond to. Opportunities are provided for children to share and respond to what is read. Teachers hold conferences with children about their books. The goals of self-selected reading follow:

- To introduce children to all types of literature through the teacher read-aloud
- To encourage children's reading interests
- To provide instructional-level reading
- To build intrinsic motivation for reading

Self-selected reading is multilevel because children choose what they want to read. They choose from a wide variety of easily accessible materials in a variety of genres and with a wide range of reading levels. During weekly conferences, teachers support children's choices and help children choose books for the next week that they can read and will enjoy. If you follow the guidelines and suggestions set out in Chapter 1, you can create a truly multilevel self-selected reading component.

Writing

Writing should include both self-selected writing, in which children choose their topics, and focused writing, in which children learn how to write particular forms and on particular topics. During the writing component, teachers model all the things writers do. Children write many first drafts and choose from these drafts pieces they want to revise, edit, and publish. Children share their writing with others and get feedback and help from their peers. While the children write, the teacher conferences with individual children, helping them revise, edit, and publish and providing instruction for each child on just the right level. The goals of the writing component are:

- To have children view writing as a way of telling about things
- To develop fluent writing for all children
- To teach children to apply grammar and mechanics in their own writing
- To teach particular writing forms
- To allow students to learn to read through writing

Writing is the most multilevel block. All of us—children and adults alike—can only write on our own level. (Perhaps that is why most of us find writing hard!) When we allow children to choose their own topics, accept whatever level of first-draft writing each child can accomplish, and allow them to work on their pieces as many days as needed, all children can succeed in writing. As teachers conference with children, they have the opportunity to truly individualize their teaching. Looking at the writing of the child usually reveals both what the child needs to move forward and what the child is ready to understand. The writing conference provides the "teachable moment" in which both advanced and struggling writers can be nudged forward in their literacy development.

Words

As you read in Chapter 2, a wide variety of activities can help us meet our word goals:

- To learn to read and spell high-frequency words
- To learn how to decode and spell unknown words using patterns from known words
- To use phonics and spelling patterns automatically and fluently while reading and writing

Word activities are multilevel in a variety of ways. A few examples relate to the activities described in Chapter 2. When we focus on the names of children, other concrete words, and the daily word-wall practice, some children who have learned to read the words begin to learn to spell them. Other children who require lots of practice with words begin to learn to read them. When we read and make alphabet books to help children learn letter names and sounds, children who did not know many letter names and sounds begin to learn them. Children who already knew a lot of letters and sounds often learn to read all the words in the books we read and make!

During Guess the Covered Word activities, the words are always read in the context of a sentence or paragraph. Children learn how to use word length, all the beginning letters, and known words to make a really good guess about an unknown word. In every Guess the Covered Word lesson, beginning sounds are reviewed for children who need more practice with beginning sounds. Advanced readers often learn to read all the words in the sentences used in Guess the Covered Word activities—greatly increasing the number of words they can read.

Each Making Words lesson begins with short easy words and progresses to longer, more complex words. Children who still need to develop phonemic awareness can do this as they "stretch out" words while making them and as they decide which words rhyme while sorting them. Each lesson includes sorting words into patterns and using those patterns to read and spell new words.

During Reading/Writing Rhymes lessons, children blend together the beginning letters and the rhyme to produce the word. This blending is an important component of phonemic awareness. Beginning sounds are reviewed every time the deck of beginning letter cards is distributed. Homophones are taught by writing *plain* and *plane* in both columns of the *ain/ane* chart and their different meanings are explained. Of course, when children write silly sentences using the rhyming words, they are incorporating these words into writing at their own level.

Word activities are not as "inherently" multilevel as self-selected reading and writing are. But by carefully orchestrating each activity, we have found many ways to broaden the range of understanding and applications included in each. The word activities described in Chapter 2 provide lots of review for struggling readers and some challenges for advanced readers.

PROVIDING MULTILEVEL GUIDED READING

Historically, guided reading (sometimes called directed reading) was instruction provided by the teacher to help children improve their oral reading fluency and silent reading comprehension as they read different kinds of texts. Today, some people use the term *guided reading* in a narrower sense, to refer only to the guidance the teacher gives to a small group of readers as they read material at their level. We, however, use the term in its broader sense. For us, guided reading occurs when a teacher guides some students—whether whole group, small group, or individual—through an activity designed to help them apply their word identification and comprehension strategies. Chapter 3 described a variety of activities that help children learn to think as they read. In all these activities—literate conversations, think-alouds, story maps, the Beach Ball, doing the book, KWLs, and graphic organizers—the teacher guides the thinking of the children so that they become better comprehenders.

To do a guided reading activity, you need children who need instruction (plentiful in all classrooms!), a comprehension strategy to focus on and a way to draw children's attention to that strategy, and something for the children to read. The "something for the children to read" is the problem! Remember that your children all read at different levels. Nothing you find for your children to read will be just right for everyone. What is just right for half your children will be too hard for some, too easy for some, and much too hard and much too easy for a few! What does a hard-working, smart, well-intentioned teacher do in this situation? How do you provide guided reading instruction when your children all read at different levels?

Remember the solutions of the past: retaining children until they got to grade level, putting children in reading groups according to level, and tracking children to different classrooms according to reading level. None of these produced the desired goal of getting all children on grade level. How do you do guided reading instruction with a class full of children reading at different levels? We do not have a perfect solution, but we do have a lot of doable options for you to try.

Refine and Commit to Your Self-Selected Reading, Writing, and Word Components

We described in the previous section how self-selected reading and writing are inherently multilevel and how word activities can be "tweaked" so that they became more multilevel. In a school that has a balanced reading program, substantial amounts of time each week are devoted to these multilevel components. Guided reading lessons are only one component of this balanced reading program. Although we know the reading levels of all our children and we try to vary the materials and formats we use for guided reading, all children are not on the "just right" reading level every day during guided reading. However, they are on the right level during self-selected reading and writing, and they benefit from different activities designed to teach them to decode and spell words. Guided reading instruction is just one part of a balanced reading program. Much of the challenge for our advanced readers and success for our struggling readers is achieved through the other three components.

> **DOING SELF-SELECTED READING, WRITING, AND WORD ACTIVITIES AT CENTERS**
>
> To make time to work with many small leveled groups during guided reading, some teachers set up their classrooms so children do their self-selected reading, writing, and word activities in centers. To determine how successful this is in moving all children forward, we have to assess what the struggling readers and the advanced readers are doing in those centers. Most children who read and write above grade level happily read, write, and do word activities in the centers. Unfortunately, they rarely work up to the level they are capable of working on. Struggling students, on the other hand, rarely do much reading and writing in centers and often cannot complete the word activities.
>
> When the teacher is available to conference with individual children, while the rest of the class engages in self-selected reading and writing, the teacher can monitor and provide instruction that is right for each child's level. Clever teachers notice when advanced readers are always reading books that are too easy for them and entice them into reading wonderful books that are closer to their level. Likewise, clever teachers spend extra time conferencing with struggling readers and helping them choose books they can actually read and get started reading. Individual conferences are also critical for making writing multilevel. Looking at a child's writing can tell you just what that child needs to learn to move forward, and you can provide that instruction as it is needed. The teacher is essential to making word activities multilevel by leading children through a lesson that is planned to include review and challenges. Center activities can provide needed practice, but only a teacher can stretch instruction to fit all the children.

Use a Variety of Materials at Different Levels for Guided Reading Lessons

Once your multilevel self-selected reading, writing, and word components are in place, you can consider materials for guided reading lessons. You want to use the widest variety of materials you can find, making sure to include materials each week that suit the average reading level of your students as well as materials that are easier than the average level. To do this, you need to know the reading levels of all your students. (This too is a complicated topic, and we tackle it next in Chapter 6, "Assessment.")

Teachers are most successful with guided reading when they use a variety of materials:

- Grade-level basal readers (if they have them)
- Appealing selections from easier basal readers (often from old basals, taken apart and reassembled into "skinny books")
- Class sets of real books
- Books from sets of leveled readers

- Big books, including informational big books correlated with science and social studies
- Selections from *Weekly Reader, Time,* or *Scholastic News* magazines
- Plays and poetry typed and duplicated or written on large charts
- Selections from science and social studies sources, particularly graphs, maps, charts, and other visuals
- Reader's theater selections duplicated from a source (including many sites on the Web) or written by the students
- Laminated selections from various sources relating to unit studies and used year after year

We teach a wide variety of comprehension lessons during guided reading to help children learn how to think about all different kinds of text. Multilevel guided reading instruction cannot be done with any single adopted reading text or a few class sets of books or a box of leveled readers. When a diversity of reading materials at different reading levels is used, guided reading becomes more enjoyable and multilevel.

Use a Variety of Guided Reading Formats to Provide Support for All Readers

Reading level is not a static entity like height. Interest, prior knowledge, type and amount of instruction, type of support and rereading all matter to what children can successfully read. Of course, you are limited in how readable you can make a particular text for a particular child, regardless of these other variables. A child whose reading level is at the end of first grade will not be able to read a selection written at the fifth-grade level—even if that selection is on a high-interest, high-prior-knowledge topic like dinosaurs; even if that child gets good prereading instruction; even if a partner helps the child with some words; and even if he or she is reading it for the second time. Four grade levels is just too far a leap! But most children whose measured reading level is at the end of first grade could read and understand that same selection on dinosaurs with all the same conditions if that selection were written at a late second-grade or early third-grade level.

Conversely, a student whose measured reading level is at the fifth grade but who has little knowledge of or interest in dinosaurs and minimal prereading instruction might read this fifth-grade-level text on dinosaurs by himself on the first reading but not understand much of what he read. Many grade-level readers develop reading problems in the intermediate grades when they are faced with boring text and little instructional support. Considering whether a child is reading at his or her level during guided reading requires more than just looking at the reading level of the child and the reading level of the text. We must consider factors within the child, such as interest and prior knowledge, as well as the type and amount of instruction and support we can provide.

FORMATS FOR GUIDED READING

Formats are the various ways children read during guided reading. This section describes some formats we use to make guided reading as multilevel as possible for a wide range of children.

Shared Reading of a Big Book

Shared reading is a term used to describe the process in which the teacher and the children read together. Typically, a book is read and reread several times. On the first reading, the teacher does most of the reading. As the children become more familiar with the book, they join in and "share" the reading.

For beginning readers, the best kind of books to use in shared reading are predictable books. Predictable books are books in which repeated patterns, refrains, pictures, and rhymes allow children to pretend read a book that has been read to them several times. Pretend reading is a stage most children go through with a favorite book that some patient adult has read and reread to them. Perhaps you remember pretend reading with popular predictable books such as *Goodnight Moon, Are You My Mother?,* and *Brown Bear, Brown Bear, What Do You See?* Shared reading of predictable books allows all children to move successfully into the acquisition of literacy, to develop some reading and print concepts, to learn some words, and, most importantly, to develop confidence in their ability to learn to read.

Shared reading can also be used as the format to solve a common problem encountered by teachers of older children. Many children who are otherwise good readers have trouble reading science and social studies textbooks. These books often have a table of contents, illustrations with captions, diagrams with labels, maps, charts, a glossary, and an index. Many children do not know what to do when they encounter these foreign elements in their books, so they skip over them. Informational books have different structure and special features that stories don't have. Children must slow down their reading rate and pay attention to more than just the text to comprehend informational books.

Guiding children's thinking about the special features of informational books is difficult when everyone is looking at their own individual copy of the book. All teachers have carried out lessons in which the following sample of oral instruction pertains:

> "All turn to page 28. Look at the diagram in the top, left corner of the page. What do you see in the diagram? Look at the top arrow. Where is that arrow pointing? Follow your eyes around the arrows and see how the cycle works."

This step-by-step direction sounds simple enough, but careful observation of the students demonstrates that many eyes are not focused on the diagram and still fewer eyes are following the arrows. Moreover, even those children who are

RECOMMENDED RESOURCES

Informational Big Books

Many wonderful and engaging informational big books are being published today. Textbook publishers often provide some big books along with their more pupil editions of science and social studies texts. National Geographic, Modern Curriculum Press, and Shortland Publications have a large variety of informational big books. Some magazines, including *Weekly Reader* and *Scholastic,* supply "big magazine" versions with a class subscription.

focused on the diagram may not be thinking about how this diagram graphically portrays the water cycle. (A few children may not even be on the right page!)

Informational big books allow us to focus our students' attention on what we are teaching them. The teacher and students can use a pointer, highlighting tape, or other attention getters to make sure everyone's eyes are in the right place! Most teachers know that students need to be taught how to use the special features of informational text and that learning to read and use these features greatly increases student confidence and comprehension of informational text. Because of the difficulty of accomplishing this when students have their own individual copies of textbooks, many teachers have quietly "given up." Shared reading of informational big books is a format that is encouraging many teachers to give informational book instruction another try!

How Shared Reading Is Multilevel

A good shared reading lesson has something for everyone! As we read predictable books, most beginners learn basic concepts, such as how to track print and what reading actually is, while advanced readers learn many—if not all—of the words. After several rereadings of a predictable big book, and some accompanying comprehension and word activities, all children feel that they really can read. A few children are just reproducing the memorized text; many other children are reading some words and filling in the rest from memory; and our most advanced readers are usually learning most of the words. As we continue to do shared reading with predictable books, more and more children move from the pretend reading stage to the real reading stage.

TIPS FOR READING INFORMATION

1. Preview the text to see what it is all about and what special features it has.
2. Use the table of contents and index if you are looking for something specific.
3. See whether the text has a glossary with meanings for the important big words.
4. Make a KWL chart in your brain or on paper and think about what you already know and what you want to learn.
5. When you begin to read, read the title first to see what the text is all about.
6. Read the pictures and all the quicktext (labels, captions, etc.) next.
7. Study the maps, charts, graphs, and diagrams and try to figure out what they tell you.
8. Read the text and see what it tells you that you did not learn from the visuals.
9. Stop and add things you are learning to the KWL chart in your brain or on paper.

When we use informational books for shared reading with older students, a multitude of things can be learned. The main purpose of using these books is to teach the important comprehension strategies needed for informational text. Every reader, whether struggling or advanced, can learn how to preview informational text; how to get the maximum information from pictures, maps, charts, graphs, diagrams, and accompanying quicktext; and how to use the table of contents, index, and glossary. We choose informational big books that connect to our science and social studies units, allowing every child to learn new science and social studies content and vocabulary. Of course, advanced readers learn the most—probably being able to read and have meanings for all the new words in the informational big book!

Multilevel instruction does not mean that everyone learns the same things or the same amount. Rather, multilevel activities always include a multitude of things to be learned. Multilevel activities are structured so that everyone can engage in them, learn something from them, and thus feel successful. When students experience success in an activity, they engage in that activity more energetically the next time, triggering an upward spiral: success→motivation→ engagement→learning→success.

Echo and Choral Reading

Echo and choral reading are formats we commonly use for reading plays and poetry. In echo reading, the teacher reads first and then children read it back, becoming the echo. As children echo read, they try to match the teacher's expression and phrasing. Choral reading is reading together in chorus. Children are often assigned parts, which they practice several times. Teachers often combine echo reading and choral reading. They first do an echo reading of a selection and then assign parts for choral reading.

Children seem particularly to enjoy echo and choral reading when we read plays. We first read the whole play in an echo reading format, using different voices for the different characters. Next, we assign parts to different groups and do a choral reading. We often reread the plays the following day in a play school group format in which the children read their parts in small groups.

In addition to plays and poetry, we do echo and choral reading with short easy text that has only one sentence on a page. Children especially enjoy echo and choral reading when the text has different voices. *Brown Bear, Brown Bear, What Do You See?* (Bill Martin, Jr., 1970), *I Went Walking* (Sue Williams, 1990), and *Hattie and the Fox* (Mem Fox, 1988) are favorites for echo and choral reading.

How Echo and Choral Reading Are Multilevel

Echo and choral reading are multilevel in much the same way that shared reading is. There are multiple things to be learned. Everyone learns how to read expressively. All children learn some new words and concepts. Advanced readers, who already know many of the simpler words and concepts, learn the biggest words and the most complex ideas! The repeated readings allow everyone to engage and to feel successful. Echo and choral reading help build reading fluency. They are an important part of a balanced reading program for elementary children of any age—and are particularly helpful if your class contains a lot of English language learners.

ERT . . . (Everybody Read To . . .)

The practice of taking turns reading orally, commonly known as round robin reading, has been criticized and condemned for decades. Still, round robin reading persists in many classrooms. When teachers continue to do something despite numerous and almost unanimous criticism, they must have a reason! Perhaps the reason teachers still close their door and do round robin reading is that sometimes they want to guide the whole class or a small group through the reading of a selection, making sure that the students are attending to certain critical concepts and that everyone is getting important information. By having the selection read orally and asking questions to make sure everyone is paying attention, the teacher feels assured that everyone is involved in some way in reading the selection.

Round robin reading is not a multilevel activity in which everyone feels successful, nor can multiple things be learned! ERT . . . , that is, Everybody Read To . . . , is a way of guiding the whole class (or a small group) through reading a selection. We use ERT (which rhymes with *hurt*) when we want students to do an initial reading on their own but also want to keep them together to provide guidance and support. Here is how we use the ERT format.

When we do ERT, we lead students through the text, setting purposes for each page or two-page spread. Some purposes are literal and some are inferential. We cue students to the type of question by asking students to *find out*, when the answer is directly stated on the page, or to *figure out*, when the answer is not directly stated but can be figured out based on what is written (the clues!). Students are asked to read to find out or figure out a variety of things. When they have found them or figured them out, they raise their hand but continue reading until they finish the page. When most hands are raised, we call on one child to tell the answer and another child to read the part where the answer was found or the clues that helped in figuring out the answer.

When children do the reading to find or figure out answers to our questions, that reading is done silently or in a "whisper voice" if children still need to hear themselves reading. We usually include one or two "two-handers" in each lesson, a purpose that has two questions. Students love these because they get to raise one hand and then the other and usually need to hold the book open with their elbows, providing a bit of a balancing challenge, a chance to stretch their muscles, and a comical image!

ERT can be used with both story and informational text. In the following sample ERT lesson, both literal and inferential purposes are set for students reading a social studies selection on Mount Vesuvius.

"Everybody read these two pages to figure out why Pompeii was a good place to live and what Vesuvius was compared to." (Students read and raise first one hand and then the other hand for this two-hander. The teacher reminds those whose hands are raised to finish reading the section and then calls on one student.)

"Who figured out why Pompeii was a good place to live? Jack, can you tell us?" (Jack gives an appropriate answer and the teacher calls on a different student to read some of the clues.)

"Who can read some of the clues that helped Jack figure out why Pompeii was a good place to live?" (The student selected reads some clues from the text. The teacher asks the second part of the question and calls on another student to answer.)

"Who figured out what Vesuvius was compared to?" (The student chosen to answer gives an appropriate response, and the teacher asks for another volunteer to read some of the clues.)

"Who can read some of the clues you could use to figure out what Vesuvius was compared to?" (The selected student reads several clues, and the teacher sets a literal purpose for the next page.)

"On this page, I want everyone to read to find out whether the people knew what was going to happen." (Students read and many hands are raised. The teacher calls on a student.)

"Josh, did the people know what was going to happen?" (Josh answers that the people did not know, and the teacher calls on another student to read the part where Josh found the answer. That student proudly reads.) "The people did not know what was going to happen."

How ERT Is Multilevel

An activity is multilevel if readers at all different levels can feel successful in the activity and if multiple things can be learned. ERT is a very multilevel format when you strictly follow a few rules. First, make sure that you include about equal numbers of inferential (figure out) purposes and literal (find out) purposes. Make your Find-outs very literal. In the Vesuvius example, everyone was asked to "find out whether the people knew what was going to happen" and in the text can be found the sentence, *The people did not know what was going to happen.* By including literal purposes, struggling readers soon discover that, although they may not be able to read the entire text, they can find the answers to many of the questions. They are happy to raise their hand and proud to give the correct answer! Remember that kids who do not try are kids who are convinced they cannot do it. When they experience obvious success, they try harder. As they listen and try to read the pages, they (and the teacher) usually discover that they can read more than they thought they could.

In addition to including some very literal questions, many teachers have students repeat the purpose before they read. As students respond that they are reading "to find out whether the people knew what was going to happen," they are attending to these words by the very act of speaking them. The probability that struggling readers will recognize those very same words as they turn their attention to reading the page greatly increased.

In ERT, the person who gives the answer to a question is never the same person who reads the part where the answer was found or who reads the clues used to figure it out. This ensures the participation of many students in the lesson and is also important to the participation of the struggling readers. Many struggling readers can read enough to find out and figure out some answers, but their oral reading would be choppy or hesitant. Many older struggling readers would never volunteer to answer a question if they thought they would be called on to read aloud. The teacher makes it clear after a few ERT lessons that the child who gives the answer is *never* the child who reads aloud (even if that child wants to read aloud). Struggling readers quickly figure out that it is "safe" to answer questions, and they begin to participate in the activity (instead of just sitting there waiting for it to end!).

In addition to allowing all participants to feel successful, a multilevel activity must have multiple things to be learned. ERT lessons always have multiple things to be learned. The most obvious and important thing you can learn from participating in ERT lessons is that not everything you need to think about as you read is directly stated, in so many words, right on the page. Most teachers have experienced students responding to a question that requires them to make inferences by saying, "It didn't tell us that." Some students—even good students—expect the text to tell them everything directly. In reality, most comprehension requires inference. In ERT lessons, students learn that they can find the answers to some questions, but that they have to figure out the answers to others. As they listen to their friends answer inferential questions and read clues, they learn how to connect what they read in the text to what they already know to understand what they are reading.

Many teachers experience so much success with ERT that they are tempted to use it every day. Resist the temptation! ERT is fun for the students if used judiciously, but any format becomes boring if you do it every day. Many teachers use ERT as the format for reading the first chapter in a book or the first part of a selection. The first part of any selection is hardest to read because it is where major characters are introduced and major concepts built. Once readers are successfully launched into a selection, consider using other formats, such as partner reading, play school groups, or coaching groups to provide students the support they need to continue experiencing success and learning from the selection.

Partner Reading (Two Heads Are Better than One!)

Imagine that you and your best friend both have the same task to accomplish. Perhaps you need to learn PowerPoint to create a presentation for your graduate class. Would you be likely to get together to work on it? Would doing it together be more fun than doing it alone? Would you be able to do it better and perhaps faster together than alone (provided you did not get sidetracked by other mutual interests!)? In real life, when we have something to accomplish and someone we like has the same task, we often arrange to do it together, believing the old saying that two heads are better than one.

The partner reading format allows children to learn to read better and faster, and for many children doing it with a friend is just more fun! Just as you and your friend have to stay "on track" as you work, you need to structure your partner reading format so that partners spend most of their time focused on what you want them to focus on. We have worked with teachers for many years to help them make partner reading a fun, productive, successful multilevel format. We would like to share our most important "do's" for successful partner reading.

1. *Do think about who you will partner up with whom—and who you won't!* Children whose families have been feuding for generations probably will not make good partners. The best reader in the class is probably not the best partner for the worst reader. If boys are at the stage where they "can't stand girls," same-gender partnerships are probably best. Think about your struggling readers first and who would be the best partners for them. Ask yourself "Who will be patient and not just tell them all the words?" "Who will be insightful and able to coach them and get them to talk about their reading?" In most classrooms, there are a couple of very nurturing children who would love to help some of their struggling classmates. These are the children to try out as partners for your most struggling readers.

2. *Do make sure your partners* know *their purpose for reading.* We all work more purposefully when we know exactly what we are trying to accomplish. The purpose for reading is what students are trying to learn and what they should be ready to contribute to the after-reading activity. If the Beach Ball activity is going to be done after reading, the partners should be reading and talking about their answers to the questions on the beach ball. If they are going to add things to the KWL chart, they should be reading to find things to add. Remember that guided reading lessons are intended to teach children how to think about text—the comprehension skills and strategies. Having a clear comprehension-oriented purpose for reading helps children become good thinkers and comprehenders.

3. *Do set a time limit for reading.* Before children begin reading, tell them exactly how much time they have to read. Make it a reasonable amount of time, but don't give them more time than most of them will need. Most behavior problems during partner reading happen when children have time to fool around. Don't give them the same amount of time each day because some selections are longer, and rereading selections can be done in less time. But set a time limit. Write it on the board and/or set a timer. When the time is up, tell them you are sorry if they didn't finish, but you need them to join the group, or tell them they may finish and then join the group. The course of action you choose doesn't matter, but be consistent and enforce your time limits. You will be amazed how much more they can read and how much better they behave when the "clock is ticking."

4. *Do make sure they have something to do if they finish before the time is up.* Always give students a "filler"—what they should do if they finish early. Relate this filler as closely as you can to the purpose for reading. If they are reading to answer the questions on the beach ball and finish early, tell them they should take turns asking each other the questions on the beach ball and come up with "awesome" answers. If they are reading to find information to add to the KWL chart and finish early, tell them they should begin to write down the information. If the after-reading activity is doing the book and they have a few minutes, tell them to decide which character they would like to be and to practice what they will say and how they will act.

Having fillers is absolutely essential for successful partner reading because some partners will rush through the reading and then create problems because they are "all done!" Children are not in such a rush to finish first when they have to think and prepare for another task. (Do not turn the filler into a class requirement that must be turned in or completed in a specified amount of time, or you are right back in the same old bind: "They don't all finish at the same time." Also, it is probably not a good idea to use the word *filler* when speaking to the children, but it is important for you to remember that is what it is!)

5. *Do teach your students how you want them to read with their partners.* Roleplay and model for them what partners do, how partners help each other, how partners correct each other nicely, and how to ask good questions. Here are some of the different ways we teach partners to read depending on their age and the purpose for reading that day:

> *Take Turns.* One partner reads the first page and the other partner reads the second page and so on. This is the most common way of partner reading— but not necessarily the most productive.

> *Read and Point.* One partner points to the words on one page while the other partner reads, then they switch reader/pointer roles on the next page. This is particularly helpful in the beginning when print tracking is a big issue with some children. You will be surprised at how quickly some children pick up print tracking when a nurturing, helpful partner is pointing to their words and making sure the other partner points to the words correctly when it is his or her turn. We do not recommend this practice once children become more fluent, however, because it slows down children's reading and can take their focus away from the meaning.

> *Ask Questions.* Both children read each page, silently if they can or chorally if they need help. They then ask each other a "good question" about what they have read.

Say Something. Say Something is also a good partner working strategy. The simple notion is that after you read a page, you "say something." If you do not have anything to say, you may have been concentrating too much on the words and not enough on the meaning. You may need to reread the page, thinking about what you might say about it. Some teachers have partners take turns—one partner reads a page and the other partner says something, then they reverse roles. On other days, partners read the page together or silently and then each says something.

Echo Reading. Once children know how to echo read, they will enjoy echo reading some selections. Give the child who is the echo in each partnership something to designate his or her status, or have the children read the selection twice switching their reading and echo reading roles. For struggling readers, make sure they are the echo on the first reading.

Choral Whispering. Choral whispering is a variation of choral reading. Children whisper with their partner. Children use a "whisper" voice so that their voices do not distract partners seated nearby.

ERT. . . . Children love doing ERT with each other. It is particularly effective as a rereading strategy when they know what the selection is about and need a good purpose for rereading. Even children who are not very fluent readers can usually find the answer to a question and pose a good question for their partner when they have already read the selection and this is a rereading.

6. *Do use partner reading time to assist and monitor your children's reading.* Many teachers who are accustomed to doing reading instruction in small groups worry that when they use a variety of multilevel formats they will not have time to listen to individual children read and will not know who is getting it and who isn't. Partner reading is a wonderful opportunity for teachers to circulate around and both assist and monitor the reading of individual children. Many teachers tell the children that they will be coming around to most of the partnerships to listen to the reading and discussion that is going on.

> "When I join your partnership, I may interrupt and ask each of you to read a little aloud for me so that I can hear how well you are growing in your reading ability. I may ask you to retell or summarize what you have read so far. I will write some notes here on my clipboard so that I have a record of how well you are reading and how you are all becoming such good thinkers about your reading. If I don't get around to all the partners today, I will make a note of that too and make sure I get to listen to you read and tell about your reading next time we read in partners."

Many teachers use the partner reading format 1 or 2 days each week. They use their time while partners are reading to monitor and coach individual children on word and comprehension strategies.

Play School Groups

Play school groups are like partnerships, except they have three to five children instead of two. One child in the play school group is teacher and we vary who is the teacher, depending on what type of activity the groups are doing. The guidelines for successful partner reading also apply to play school groups. We form heterogeneous groups and think about who to assign to each group. Children in play school groups always know what their purpose is, how long they have to play, and what to do if they finish before the time is up. The teacher circulates to see how individual children are doing.

Play school groups can do many of the types of activities that partnerships can do. They can ask questions, say something, echo and choral read selections, and do ERT. Because they are composed of more children, play school groups are the format to use for doing the book activities. Small-group discussions can also be carried out in play school groups. After completing a graphic organizer or KWL chart several times as a whole-class activity, the activity is turned over to play school groups. The children contribute ideas and one child does the writing on the chart. Finally, all charts are compared and displayed.

Play school groups always have a teacher. One problem is making sure all the children have a chance to be teacher. Everyone does not necessarily get to be teacher the same number of times, but the same "bossy girls" cannot be teacher every time! To get around this, consider which play school formats do not require a super reader.

Imagine that the class has read a story and completed an appropriate activity with it the preceding day. Today they are going to decide what the characters are saying and doing on each page in preparation for pantomiming the book. Divide your struggling readers, one among each group, and assign them the role "teacher." The rest of the group take turns reading the pages. Because you read it yesterday, and the struggling readers are not reading aloud, the other children should be able to fluently read their page aloud. The "teacher" tells everyone whose turn it is and then asks everyone, "Who was talking and how would they act?"

Struggling readers can also be teacher when the play school group is using the choral reading format. For echo reading, on the other hand, one of your best readers needs to be teacher. Likewise, when groups do ERT, they need a good reader to formulate the purposes for reading each page.

Play school groups are one of the children's favorite formats for reading and rereading selections. With some clever thinking, you can allow all your children to be teacher on various days. As the children read, you can circulate and coach the children as they need help with words or with the thinking required to fulfill their purpose for reading. In addition to the teacher coaching, some teachers appoint a student word coach in each group. This child—and only this child—is allowed to help other children figure out words. The word coach and the teacher are two different people, so you have more opportunities to let the children who are not the best readers be teacher.

RECOMMENDED RESOURCES

For many more ideas about and examples of all the multilevel formats
described in this section, see *Guided Reading
the Four Blocks Way* (Cunningham, Hall, &
Cunningham, 2000).

How Partner Reading and Play School Groups Are Multilevel

Working together on something is a natural arrangement in real life. Children are used to helping each
other and teaching each other all kinds of things. Most
children learn how to ride a bike and how to play a
new game from their friends. When you use partner
reading and play school groups, you increase the number of teachers in your
classroom.

Book Club Groups

In book club groups, as in literature circles, the children in the different groups
do not read the same books. Children have some choice about the books they read,
and they meet in groups to read and discuss the books. To do a book club group,
we select four books related by author, topic, genre, or theme. In our book club
groups we have used four biographies, four mysteries, four Dr. Seuss books, four
books about sea animals, and four books about friends. When selecting four books,
we always include one book that is fairly easy and one that is more challenging.

Book club groups usually meet for several days or weeks to read the book.
On the first day, children preview all four books and indicate to us their first, second, and third choice of which book they would most like to read. We promise
everyone that they will get one of their choices, but we caution them that everyone will not get their first choice.

To form groups, we first look at the choices of our struggling readers. If they
choose the easy book for any of their choices, we assign them to that book. (Obviously, we do not tell anyone about an "easy" book). If a struggling reader does not
choose the easy book for any of his or her choices, we usually assign that child to
the first choice of book, assuming the first choice is not the challenging book! Next,
we look at the choices of our advanced readers. We assign them to the challenging
book if it is one of their choices. We then assign the other children, giving as many
first choices as possible and making good groups that can work well together.

When everyone is assigned, the group reading the easy book contains some
struggling readers and some average readers who chose that book as their first
choice. The group reading the challenging book likewise contains some advanced
readers and some average readers who chose that book as their first choice. The
groups reading the average-difficulty books contain mostly average readers with
a few struggling and advanced readers who didn't choose the book closer to their
level.

The book clubs meet for as many days as you decide they need to complete
the book. The comprehension purpose/focus is the same for all the groups. Groups
share daily with the other children what they have learned so far. The next section is one example of how a book club group might work.

A Book Club Group Example

The teacher decides that all the children will read and do plays and chooses four plays from the Rigby *Tales and Plays* collection in which each book contains the tale told both in story format and in play format. The books chosen are *Goldilocks and the Three Bears* and *Town Mouse and Country Mouse* (average difficulty), *The Three Billy Goats Gruff* (easier), and *Robin Hood and the Silver Trophy* (challenging). The teacher decides to spend 4 days with the children—previewing and choosing on the first day, reading the story and play in their groups for 2 days, and reading the plays in small groups and for the other groups on the final day.

Day 1 The teacher begins these book club groups by sharing the book covers and explaining that the books contain both a story and a play! The teacher explains that today they get to look at all the books and decide on their first, second, and third choices for which one they would most like to read. Eight books of each title have been placed in four gathering places in different corners of the room. The children circulate to the different corners and have 6 minutes to look at and talk about each book. When all the children have looked at all four books, they write down their first, second, and third choices and give these to the teacher. After school, the teacher looks at their choices and assigns children to groups, considering both their reading levels and their choices.

Day 2 The teacher gathers the children together and tells them that today they will spend most of their time reading the tale told in story form. Each group has 22 minutes to read the tale, and then they will gather back together and do the Beach Ball activity. The teacher quickly reviews with the children the questions on each stripe of the beach ball and the rules for Beach Ball activities. The teacher then distributes the appropriate books to members of the different groups and assigns the groups a place to meet. The teacher tells the children that their group can decide how to read the story but that they must stop after every two pages and discuss their answers to the questions on the beach ball. As the children read, the teacher circulates and makes sure every group knows what to do. The teacher spends more time with the group reading *The Three Billy Goats Gruff*, coaching them on word and comprehension strategies.

After reading the selection, they gather together again. The teacher has each group come to a circle inside the big circle, and that group answers the questions on the beach ball as the others watch and listen. The children are very interested in all four stories and pay good attention as each group shares ideas from their particular story.

Day 3 The activity for the third day is reading the play. Today the teacher tells the students to read the play in two-page segments. They first read each segment in an echo reading format and then read it again with different children reading different parts. The teacher appoints a child to be teacher in each group. This child teacher is the voice that all the other children will echo. The groups are instructed to take turns reading so different people read different parts. The teacher again circulates as the children read, coaching them to read with appropriate expression and settling a few disputes about who reads which part on which page.

After reading the plays in small groups, the teacher gathers the children together again, once more placing each group, in turn, in the inner circle. The teacher takes the role of narrator for each group and reads the narrator parts. Then the teacher lets all the children chorally read all the other parts. The children delight in listening to the choral reading of all the groups.

Day 4   Today, the children gather in their small groups once again and read the play with one person reading each part. The teacher has assigned each child a part. The child who is the narrator in each group is also given the role of director. The children read their part and then do whatever acting is required. The teacher encourages all the groups and "rehearses" the billy goats and the troll so that they read and act with expression. After about 20 minutes of practice, the class reassembles. The members of each group read and act out their play for the other groups. Each group gets a round of applause with the loudest applause given to the big billy goat.

Literature Circles

Literature circles are similar to book club groups in that children choose books and meet in small groups to discuss them. In literature circles, children usually have different roles and can choose the role they want. These roles determine their purpose for reading. The roles can be divided up in a variety of ways. Some teachers designate the roles as character sketcher, author authority, plot person, conflict connector, and solution suggester. The student who likes drawing can become the character sketcher and sketch the characters in the story their group is reading. Another child in each group who knows a lot about the author can become the author authority. The plot person makes sure that everyone in the group understands what has happened in the story so far. To carry out this task, the plot person must keep track of who (somebody), what they wanted (to happen), what happened (but), and how the problem was solved (so). The conflict connector helps the group understand the conflict that exists (character versus character, character versus nature, character versus society, etc.) in the book and how the characters in the book work through the conflict. These roles help the children discuss the books they are reading and share what is happening in the stories with the whole class.

Another way of assigning roles is to give students a role sheet and model how to use it. The following is an example of the role sheets one teacher used:

> *Discussion Director:* Your job is to develop a list of questions that your group might want to discuss about today's reading. Try to determine what is important about today's text. Focus your questions on big ideas.

RECOMMENDED RESOURCES

You can find many more roles and their descriptions and many practical ideas for literature circles in *Literature Circles* by Harvey Daniels (1996) and *Literature Circle Role Sheets* by Christine Boardman Moan (1998).

Passage Master: Your job is to locate a few special sections of the reading that the group should look back on. You should help your group notice the most interesting, funny, puzzling, or important parts.

Vocabulary Enricher: Your job is to be on the lookout for a few especially important words that your group needs to remember or understand. You should look for new, interesting, strange, important, or puzzling words.

Connector: Your job is to find connections between the material you are reading and yourself and other students. Also, look for connections to the world and to other books we have read.

Illustrator: Your job is to draw some kind of picture related to the reading. It can be a sketch, diagram, flow chart, or stick figure scene.

How Book Clubs and Literature Circles Are Multilevel

Book club groups and literature circles are two of our favorite—and most multilevel—ways to organize guided reading. By choosing books tied together in some way, we can establish a comprehension purpose and focus for everyone to work on. Including two books at the average reading level of the class, one book that is easier, and one that is more challenging allows us to come closer to matching the reading levels of most of our students. The support children get from their group and the support the teacher is able to give while circulating to the different groups (spending more time with the group reading the easy book) means that all children can have a successful reading experience.

Most teachers find that their children participate eagerly in these groups and that the books they do not get to read are the most popular selections during self-selected reading time for the next several weeks. It is not unusual for children to read all three books their group did not read. Their knowledge of the concepts and vocabulary in each book is greatly increased by the daily sharing of books that follows the small-group reading. Because they have read one of the books, including plays, biographies, mysteries, and informational books about animals, they know how that type of book is written and how to read that genre. Even struggling readers often can successfully read a book that was a little beyond their level just a few weeks ago!

Coaching Groups

On some days, the teacher meets with a small group and coaches them to use their word and comprehension strategies. The selection of children in the coaching group changes from time to time, but, although average and some advanced readers are selected each time we do a coaching group, struggling readers are included more often than advanced readers. Including some better readers guarantees that members of the coaching group and others do not view the coaching group as the "dumb readers." Including better readers also ensures that the group has some good reading models and allows everyone to learn to be a word coach.

We explain coaching groups to the children by making analogies to sports teams. Children understand that you practice various soccer moves, and then in game format the coach watches you play, stopping you from time to time to coach you to use the skills you have practiced. Before long, children learn how to coach and begin to use their coaching skills when reading with partners or in play school groups. Once they understand how to coach, we let them play the role of word coach. We choose reading material that is at the reading level of most of the children included in this group. The children read parts of the selection to themselves first. Then someone reads aloud so that we can demonstrate what a word coach does.

Coaching Steps

Before the children start to read, we remind them of the strategies they can use to figure out an unfamiliar word. We post a chart of steps that we review before children begin each reading lesson.

> **How to Figure Out a Hard Word**
> 1. Put your finger on the word and say all the letters.
> 2. Use the letters and the picture clues.
> 3. Look for a rhyme you know.
> 4. Keep your finger on the word and finish the sentence and pretend it's the covered word.

Here is how we coach each step and why each step is important.

1. *Put your finger on the word and say all the letters.* When children come to a word they do not know, we have them put their finger on the word and name all the letters. It is very important that the children name the letters. Naming the letters is not the same as pronouncing individual sounds to sounding out the word. English is not a sound-it-out-letter-by-letter language, and the worst readers are the ones who try this phonetic approach. We want them to name all the letters because having them do so is the only way we know for sure that they have indeed looked at them and seen them all in the right order. We also want them to name the letters because strong evidence supports the idea that retrieval from the brain's memory store is auditory. Just looking at an arrangement of letters and searching in your brain for the word, or a rhyming word, that resembles them is apt to be a more difficult way of identifying that word than saying the letters, which goes through the brain's auditory channel.

In our experience, if children are reading at the right level and name the letters of an unfamiliar word out loud, they can sometimes immediately pronounce that word correctly, which may be proof positive that the auditory channel was needed for retrieval! After they name all the letters and successfully pronounce the word, cheer! They have scored a goal. ("See, it was in there. You just had to say it so your brain could find it!") If they still do not know the word after they name all the letters, give them one of the next three cues, depending on the word.

2. *Use the letters and the picture clues.* Pictures often provide clues to words. The child who sees the word *raccoon* and names all the letters, then glances at the picture, may indeed see a picture of a raccoon. The picture, along with naming the letters, often allows children to decode the word. Once the child has named all the letters out loud and studied the picture, we cue them to notice the picture clue:

"I see an animal in the picture that looks to me like a *r-a-c-c-o-o-n.*"

3. *Look for a rhyme you know.* In our word activities, we teach children to decode and spell words based on rhyming patterns. If the unknown word has a familiar rhyming pattern, we cue the child to some of the rhyming words he or she might know:

"We know that *w-i-l-l* is *will* and *s-t-i-l-l* is *still*. Can you make *t-h-r-i-l-l* rhyme with *will* and *still*?"

4. *Keep your finger on the word and finish the sentence; then pretend it's the covered word.* Guess the Covered Word is an activity that helps children use beginning letters, word length, and context to figure out words. It is the "default" cue, the one we use when others do not work. If neither picture clue nor rhyming words help, we cue children to try the covered word activity. Having children read on and then go back is not the preferred method for decoding words because it interrupts their reading. Moreover, we want children to study and process unknown words as they encounter them. However, when children need the clues provided by the rest of the sentence to decode a word, we coach them to use the sentence clues.

Coaching a Missed Word

The procedure just described is what we do when a child stops on a word. If, instead of stopping, the child misreads a word, we let him or her finish the sentence and then have the child return to that misread word. Imagine, for example, that the child reads, "There was not a cold in the sky" instead of reading the sentence, *There was not a cloud in the sky.* At the moment the child misreads "cold" for *cloud, cold* does make sense. But by the end of the sentence, the child should realize that the sentence did not make sense and go back to try to fix the error. We let children finish the sentence to help them develop their own self-monitoring system. If, however, they do not notice any error and just continue to read, we stop them and say something like, "That didn't make sense. Let's look at this word again. Say all the letters in this word." We then give them the appropriate cue to help them figure out the word.

When We Do Coaching Groups

Many teachers do coaching groups while those children not in the coaching group read with partners. Some teachers find time in their weekly schedule to meet with coaching groups outside the guided reading time. In some classrooms, the teacher meets daily with an "after-lunch bunch" and does coaching at that time. We include all children in the after-lunch bunch activities across the week but we include the struggling readers almost every day and the others less frequently. In some classrooms, teachers have a center time each day and do a coaching group which we call a "Fun Reading Club" during that time. Coaching groups last only 10–15 minutes. We do not do before- and after-reading activities to teach comprehension because the children in our coaching group were also in our guided reading comprehension lessons. We do not introduce high-frequency words or teach decoding strategies because these lessons are covered during word activities. We simply choose material at the instructional level of most of the children we intend to include and begin reading it, simulating as we read what children must do during self-selected reading when they tackle text on their own. As the children read and encounter problems, we coach them to apply what they have learned when they actually need to use it.

In some classrooms, special teachers or assistants do coaching groups with children. If you have help coming and have many children that need coaching, you might schedule self-selected reading at that time and have the helping person coach children in their self-selected books. Many teachers like to schedule guided reading when they have help coming. The helping teacher can coach children through the selection, if it is close to their instructional level, or can read that selection to them and then coach them in material at their level.

Finding the time, people, and reading materials to do coaching groups is not easy. But when you add regular coaching in instructional-level material to the good instruction struggling readers receive throughout the day, you will be amazed at the rapid progress these readers can make.

How Coaching Groups Are Multilevel

In coaching groups, we stress that all children are learning to become word coaches. We call them together and model what a word coach does. Then we let children volunteer to be word coaches and coach them on how to coach. We do include struggling readers in coaching groups more often than others, and we choose material at the appropriate level for those children who need coaching. Every group includes some more able readers, however, and the membership in coaching groups changes regularly. Because coaching groups is just one of the formats we use to make our guided reading time multilevel, and because we group children together for all different kinds of reasons, these groups are not viewed by others or the children in them as "low" reading groups.

SUMMARY

Children differ on all possible dimensions. They begin at different points and move forward at different rates. Growth does not happen in equal increments. Spurts and plateaus occur in the development of any ability. The simple fact of individual differences is what makes teaching all children to read and write such a challenging task. In the past, many solutions were tried. Retention, tracking, and within-class groupings according to level were the most common attempts to provide instruction from which all children could benefit. None of these has any research to support its long-term effectiveness in accelerating the literacy development of struggling readers. Multilevel instruction contains multiple things to be learned and allows all students to feel successful. Motivation is directly related to the expectation of success.

This chapter has included a description of how self-selected reading and writing are inherently multilevel and how word activities can be stretched to become more multilevel. Guiding children's reading of text is the most difficult activity to make multilevel because the text is inevitably too hard for some and too easy for others. A variety of formats that teachers use to make guided reading lessons more multilevel were described. When children experience a balanced reading program that includes self-selected reading and writing as well as multilevel word and guided reading lessons, all children can experience success and progress at optimal rates for them.

CHAPTER 6

Assessment

Assessment is part of everything we do in life. Most of us make an assessment of the weather each morning to decide what to wear. We assess the food, service, and atmosphere as we dine at the new restaurant in town. We assess our new neighbors as we watch them interact with each other and move their furniture in. This chapter provides some examples of how you can make assessment an extension of your teaching, rather than just one more chore that has to be done.

WHAT IS ASSESSMENT?

Sometimes, it is easier to define something by beginning with what it is not. Assessment is not grading—although assessment can help you determine and support the grades you give. Assessment is not standardized test scores—although these scores can give you some general idea of what children have achieved so far. Assessment *is* collecting and analyzing data to make decisions about how children are performing and growing. Caldwell (2002) describes four steps for assessment. First, we must identify what we want to assess. Second, we collect evidence. Third, we analyze that evidence. Fourth and finally, we make a decision and act on that decision. Caldwell suggests three main purposes for reading assessment: to determine student reading level, to identify good reading behaviors and to document student progress.

> **RECOMMENDED RESOURCES**
>
> This chapter only begins to discuss the complex topic of classroom assessment. We are indebted to JoAnne Caldwell for her wonderfully written, practical book, *Reading Assessment: A Primer for Teachers and Tutors* (2002). We learned a lot from reading this book and enjoyed all her lively examples and analogies. If assessment is one of the issues you struggle with, we highly recommend this book.

DETERMINING STUDENT READING LEVEL

The previous chapter discussed the inevitability of children reading at different levels and how reading instruction can be multilevel. We also suggested that reading level is not a static entity. Rather, reading level is affected by individual factors within each child, such as prior knowledge and interest, as well as by instructional factors, such as type of prereading instruction, amount of support provided by the reading format, and whether a first reading or a rereading of a selection is being considered.

Despite the fact that reading level is not static, we still need to determine, to the extent we can, an approximate reading level for each child. Knowing the level at which a child is reading early in the school year serves as a benchmark against which to judge how well our instruction is helping each child raise his or her reading level. We need to know how to determine whether the books children are choosing for self-selected reading are too hard or too easy so we can help them make more appropriate choices. We need to have a general idea of each child's reading level so we can decide how much support each child needs to experience success during guided reading lessons with various texts. Finally, we need to determine reading levels because most schools and parents expect and require us to know the reading levels and document progress for each student.

To determine a child's reading level, you need to have the child read passages at different reading levels. Many reading series include graded passages with their reading textbooks. Teachers use these to determine the reading levels of their students. Some school districts and states have created graded passages or selected benchmark books that teachers use to assess reading levels. A number of published Informal Reading Inventories (IRIs) also include graded passages, such as the Basic Reading Inventory (Johns, 2001) and the Qualitative Reading Inventory (Leslie & Caldwell, 2001). These reading passages are graded in various ways. Traditionally, passages were specified as preprimer (early first grade), primer (middle first grade), first grade, early second grade, late second grade, third grade, fourth grade, and so on. Recently, books and passages have been divided into more levels. In the Reading Recovery system, for example, books are divided into many levels; levels 16–18 are considered end of first grade.

Regardless of the source or leveling system of your graded passages, you can use these passages to determine the approximate reading level of each student. Generally, you have children read aloud a passage, beginning with one you think they can handle. As the child reads, you mark the reading in some way that errors can be counted and analyzed. After the child reads the passage, you ask the child to retell the passage or ask questions to determine how much the child comprehends.

Once you have made a record of the child's oral reading and gotten an indication of comprehension from the retelling or the answers to questions, you decide what level of oral reading accuracy and comprehension is adequate. Many arguments and disagreements concern this decision. Most experts recommend that a child have an oral reading accuracy level of about 95 percent and demonstrate comprehension of 75 percent of the important ideas in the passage. The passage

A variety of systems have been developed for marking the oral reading of a child. Most systems work something like this:

In reading this passage, the child read "shooting" for *shooing;* read "quickly" for *quietly,* but then self-corrected (SC); inserted the extra word "his"; omitted the word *finally;* and read "to" for *into.*

Once there was a farmer who lived with his wife and their

ten children in a very small farmhouse. The farmer and his

family were miserable. They were always bumping into

each other and getting in each other's way. When the

children stayed inside on rainy days, they fought all the

time. The farmer's wife was always ~~shooing~~ *shooting* children out of

the kitchen so she could cook. The farmer had no place to

sit ~~quietly~~ *quickly* SC when he came in from *his*∧ work. The farmer (finally)

could stand it no longer. He said to his wife, "Today I am

going ~~into~~ *to* the village to talk with a wise man about our

crowded house. He will know what to do."

---

about the farmer and his wife (above) has approximately 100 words. If you do not count the self-correction (which we would not because self-correcting is a good reading behavior that indicates the child is self-monitoring), the reader made four errors, giving him an accuracy rate of 96 percent. If the child's retelling indicates comprehension of most of the important ideas in this short passage, we will know that this reader can read text at this level quite adequately. We will not, however, know that this is the just right, or instructional, level for the child.

Instructional level is generally considered to be the highest level of text that a reader can read with about 95 percent word accuracy and 75 percent comprehension. To determine instructional level, we must continue to have the child read harder and harder passages until word identification falls below 95 percent or comprehension falls below 75 percent. Instructional level is generally considered

DETERMINING READING LEVELS

1. Use passages or books that have been determined to get increasingly more difficult.
2. Have the child begin reading at the level you think he or she might be.
3. To get a measure of word reading accuracy, record oral reading errors as the child reads.
4. After the child reads, remove the text and ask the child to retell what was read or ask some comprehension questions.
5. If the child's word reading accuracy is approximately 95 percent and comprehension is approximately 75 percent, have that child read the next harder passage. If the child's word reading accuracy is below 95 percent or comprehension is below 75 percent, have that child read the next easier passage.
6. Continue to have the child read until you determine the highest level at which the child can read and still meet the 95 percent word accuracy and 75 percent comprehension criteria. This is the best general indicator of that child's just right, or instructional, reading level.

to be the **highest** level of text for which the child can pass both the word and comprehension criteria.

Once you know the approximate reading levels of all your children, you can use this information to choose materials for guided reading and decide how much support your different readers will need with the various materials. Remember that prior knowledge and interest have a large influence on reading level. Remember that during guided reading lessons, you build both interest and prior knowledge (including meaning vocabulary) before children read. You then choose your format to provide enough support so that they can be successful at meeting the purpose for the lesson. Children can read text that is a little beyond their level if they are given the appropriate support before, during, and after reading. Remember also that the size of the "leaps" children make has limits. If you determine that a child's reading level is late first grade, that child can usually be given enough support to feel successful with some second-grade-level material. However, material written at the fifth-grade level is probably not going to be accessible for that child.

Once you understand how to listen to a child read and retell to determine instructional level, you can use this knowledge during your weekly self-selected reading conferences. We do not do formal oral reading records during these conferences; neither do we want to take an "inquisition" stance as we discuss the text with the child. We do, however, listen to children read a part they have selected, and we do ask them to tell about the most interesting part of the book or what they have learned so far. As they read and tell us about their reading, our informal 95 percent/75 percent meters are running, and if we realize that a child is choosing books that are way too easy or way too hard, we can steer them toward some just right text.

> ### WHY NOT USE STANDARDIZED TESTS TO DETERMINE READING LEVELS?
>
> In many schools, children take a variety of tests that yield a grade equivalent. Teachers get a printout that tells them that Billy reads at 2.5 and Carla reads at 5.5. Being trusting, logical people, they assume that this means Billy's instructional reading level is middle second grade and Carla's instructional reading level is middle fifth grade. Unfortunately, life is not that simple. If Billy and Carla are both in the second grade, most of the passages they read on the test are second-grade passages. Billy's score of 2.5 means that he did as well on the test as average second graders reading second-grade text. Carla read the same passages and she did as well as the average fifth grader reading second-grade passages would have done. We can certainly say that Carla is a good reader—certainly a better reader than Billy. But we cannot say that her instructional reading level is fifth grade because she did not read any fifth-grade passages!
>
> Another reason that we cannot use standardized tests to determine individual reading level is that **all** tests have something called standard error of measurement (SEM). Look in the manual of any test and it will tell you what the SEM is. If the SEM is 5 months, then the score a child achieves is probably within 5 months of the true score. Billy's score of 2.5 has a 68 percent chance (1 standard deviation) of actually being somewhere between 2.0 and 3.0. If we want to be 95 percent sure, we have to go out 2 standard deviations. Then we will know that Billy's score is almost surely somewhere between 1.5 and 3.5.
>
> Across groups of children, these SEMs balance out. One child's score is higher than his actual ability but another child's score is lower. If your class average score is 2.5, you can be pretty sure that your class reads about as well as the average class of second graders on which the test was normed. Standardized scores give us information about groups of children, but give us only limited information about the reading levels of individual children. To determine the reading level of a child, we must listen to that child read and retell and find the highest levels at which they can do both with approximately 95 percent word accuracy and 75 percent comprehension. Unfortunately, no shortcut will get us where we need to go.

IDENTIFYING GOOD LITERACY BEHAVIORS AND DOCUMENTING PROGRESS

Determining reading levels is generally done early in the year, then at specific points during the year, and again at the end of the year. Day in and day out, however, we need to be assessing and monitoring how well students are reading and writing. To do this, we have to know what we are looking for. What are the good reading and writing behaviors? Throughout the chapters of this book, we have described instruction that develops good literacy behaviors. In this section, we suggest ways to assess these behaviors as children engage in literacy activities.

Assessing Emergent Literacy

Chapter 2 described many activities for building the foundation for literacy and concluded that there are seven signs of emergent literacy. These seven signs are the reading behaviors we look for as indicators that each child is moving successfully into reading and writing. These behaviors form the basis for our assessment of beginning readers. We assess these behaviors as children engage in their daily literacy activities.

Many teachers of young children keep a checklist such as the following example. Each day they put the checklists of two or three children on their clipboard and observe and talk with these children as they engage in self-selected reading and writing to determine how well they are developing critical behaviors. Teachers often use a simple system using a minus (–) to indicate the child does not have that behavior, a question mark (?) when the behavior is erratic or it is unclear that the child has it, and a plus (+) to indicate the child does seem to have developed that behavior. Three pluses on three different dates is a reliable indicator that that child has indeed developed that behavior.

Emergent Literacy Behaviors

Name _____   Dates Checked (– ? +)

Pretend reads favorite books, poems, songs, and chants   — — — — — — —

"Writes" and can "read back" what was written   — — — — — — —

Tracks print   — — — — — — —
    Left page first
    Top to bottom
    Left to right
    Return sweep
    Points to each word

Knows reading jargon   — — — — — — —
    Identifies one letter, one word, and one sentence
    Identifies first word, first and last letter in a word

Reads and writes some "concrete" words   — — — — — — —
    Own name and names of friends, pets, family
    Favorite words from books, poems, and chants

Demonstrates phonemic awareness   — — — — — — —
    Counts words
    Claps syllables
    Stretches out words as they attempt to spell
    Blends and segments words
    Identifies rhymes

Demonstrates alphabet awareness   — — — — — — —
    Names some letters
    Knows some words that begin with certain letters
    Knows some common letter sounds

Assessing Word Strategies

As children move from the emergent literacy stages into beginning reading and writing stages, we need to monitor and assess their development of sight words, decoding, and spelling strategies. Chapter 2 contained many activities for developing these strategies. Our assessment, however, must take place while the children are actually reading and writing. The goal of word instruction is to teach children words and strategies they actually use when they are reading and writing. What we want to know is *not* how children spell words during the daily word wall activity but how quickly they recognize these words when reading and how correctly they spell these words when they are writing.

Sight Word, Decoding, and Spelling Behaviors

Name _____   Dates Checked (− ? +)

Identifies word wall words automatically when reading   — — — — — — —

Spells word wall words correctly in first-draft writing   — — — — — — —

Uses letter patterns, picture and sentence cues to decode   — — — — — — —
  Beginning letters of word (*br, sh, f*)
  Rhyming pattern (*at, ight, ain*)
  Endings (*s, ed, ing*)
  Prefixes (*un, inter*), suffixes (*able, tion*) for big words
  Combines letter cues, picture cues, and sentence cues

Uses letter patterns to spell words   — — — — — — —
  Beginning letters of word (*br, sh, f*)
  Rhyming pattern (*at, ight, ain*)
  Endings (*s, ed, ing, er, est*)
  Prefixes (*un, inter*), suffixes (*able, tion*) for big words

Self-monitors   — — — — — — —
  Self-corrects when meaning is distorted
  Self-corrects when nonsense word is produced
  Rereads to correct phrasing
  Rereads for fluency

Reads fluently   — — — — — — —
  With phrasing
  Attending to punctuation
  With expression

Writes fluently   — — — — — — —
  Words are written quickly
  Handwriting is not slow and laborious
  Focused on meaning

There are many opportunities throughout the day to make these observations. During our weekly self-selected reading conferences with children, we ask them to read aloud to us a short part of what they have chosen to share with us. We don't do a formal oral reading record at that time, but we do listen for how fluently they read; how automatically they identify the word wall words; and how they use patterns, context, and other cues to figure out unknown words. When using the partner reading format, we circulate to the different partnerships and ask them to read a page to us. Again, we can note how they use what we are teaching them about words as they actually read text.

Another opportunity to observe their sight word, word identification, and fluency behaviors is when we meet with small coaching groups. We observe their spelling behaviors by periodically looking at samples of their first-draft writing, by analyzing their spelling in writing samples we collect three times each year, and in our revising/editing/publishing conferences with individual children. As with emergent literacy behaviors, the – ? + system allows us to easily record what we observe on each child's word behavior checklist.

Assessing Comprehension Strategies

Chapter 3 described comprehension strategies and a variety of activities to use before and after reading that teach comprehension and foster thoughtful literacy.

Comprehension Strategies—Story	
Name _____	Dates Checked (– ? +)
Names and describes main characters	— — — — — — —
Names and describes settings	— — — — — — —
Describes the goal or problem in the story	— — — — — — —
Describes major events that lead to resolution	— — — — — — —
Describes the resolution to the story	— — — — — — —
Makes inferences and predictions	— — — — — — —
Makes connections To self To world To other texts	— — — — — — —
Expresses a personal reaction/opinion	— — — — — — —
Monitors comprehension and uses fix-up strategies	— — — — — — —

As with emergent literacy behaviors and word strategies, we monitor and assess children's development of these behaviors as we interact with them during comprehension lessons and in our self-selected reading conferences. Because comprehension is so dependent on prior knowledge and interest, we are not so able to feel secure in our judgments that a child can—or cannot—use a particular comprehension strategy. Often, children recall much information and respond to that information in a high-level way when the topic is familiar and of great interest but demonstrate little comprehension of less-familiar, uninteresting topics. We can use some checklists to indicate general use of comprehension strategies, but anecdotal records are also helpful because the teacher can include comments about prior knowledge and interest as well as comprehension strategies. Many teachers find two checklists useful—one for story text and one for informational text.

Comprehension Strategies—Information

Name _____   Dates Checked (- ? +)

Describes major ideas   — — — — — — —

Summarizes important information   — — — — — — —

Accurately recalls important facts/details   — — — — — — —

Organizes ideas appropriately   — — — — — —
    Sequence/chronology
    Topic/subtopic
    Comparisons
    Cause/effect
    Problem/solution

Makes inferences   — — — — — — —

Makes connections   — — — — — — —
    To prior knowledge and experience
    To information from other texts

Expresses a personal reaction/opinion   — — — — — — —
Monitors comprehension and uses fix-up strategies   — — — — — — —

Anecdotal records are the written records that teachers keep on individual children based on their ongoing observation of and interaction with them. We can make anecdotal records instead of or in addition to any of the checklists already discussed. Anecdotal records seem to be most important for noting comprehension behaviors. Comprehension is complex and often checklists just do not seem to capture children's thinking as clearly as you could by making comments, perhaps even including some of your children's "exact words." There are a large number of ways that a teacher can efficiently record and update written observations about individual students. The one we have found to be the most practical uses file folder labels.

Any school supply or office supply store sells file folder labels by the sheet. The user types or writes on the sticky label, peels it off the sheet, and affixes it to the tab of the file folder being labeled. These sheets of file folder labels are also perfect for recording brief comments about children's understanding and engagement, success, or achievement with instructional activities.

The teacher places one or more sheets of file folder labels on a clipboard that he or she carries. When interacting with or observing students, the teacher notices a significant indicator of the child's comprehension (or lack thereof). It is quick, easy, and unobtrusive to record the child's initials, the date, and a brief comment on one of the file folder labels on the sheet in the clipboard. After school, the teacher takes a few minutes and affixes each label used that day to a page for that subject in the child's anecdotal records folder.

Many teachers analyze the anecdotal records for one child each day. At this pace, every student's anecdotal records can be analyzed every 4–6 weeks. The analysis of a child's anecdotal records consists of determining the degree of support in the folder for evaluative statements, which can be written as a narrative description of the child's learning or shared with a parent at a conference. Sometimes, during this analysis, the teacher realizes that not enough observations have been recorded for assessing some important area of the literacy program. When this occurs, the teacher writes the child's initials on one of the file folder labels on the sheet in the clipboard along with a one- or two-word description of the observation needed for that child. While moving through the school day, the teacher then has several labels on the sheet that remind him to obtain particular observations of certain children. No more reliable or valid means of diagnosing or evaluating students' ongoing learning is possible than anecdotal records collected regularly and systematically and consisting of objective and specific descriptions of children's reading behaviors.

Assessing Writing

As described in Chapter 4, writing is perhaps the most complex act people engage in. The best way to determine how well students write is to observe them each day as they are writing, to look at first-draft writing samples, and to interact with them during writing conferences.

You can observe many aspects of writing as you move among the class. Do students struggle to identify a topic for writing? Do students do some planning first when asked to write? Is handwriting easy for them? Are they using resources in the room and spelling patterns they know to spell words? Are they automatically using some of the mechanical and grammatical conventions they have been learning? Do students move confidently through a first draft? Do students revise and edit some as they write, or do they wait until they are publishing a piece? To record these observations, you may want to make a checklist similar to the previous examples but specific to the age and starting point of your students.

In addition to the observations you record, many teachers like to take a focused writing sample during the first week of school. They give the children a prompt to which they all can relate, such as, What Third Grade Is Like or My Most Favorite and Least Favorite Things. They then analyze the sample to determine where individual children are in their writing development and what the class as a whole needs to work on. They put this sample away, and halfway through the year ask children to write on the same prompt again. Once the children have written the second time, teachers return the first sample and let each child analyze the writing growth made. The teacher then analyzes the second sample, comparing them to the first for each child and looking for indicators of things the class needs to work on. The same procedure can be repeated once more at the end of the year.

Writing is a very complex process. No matter how good we get, there is always room for growth. Because writing is complex, it is easy to see only the problems children still exhibit in their writing and not the growth they are making. Having three writing samples on the same topic across the school year provides tangible evidence of growth to both teacher and student.

Assessing Attitudes and Interests

This book began with a chapter that emphasized the importance of children's attitudes toward and interests in reading and writing. If developing avid readers and writers is one of your major goals, you need to collect and analyze some data so that you can identify needs and document progress.

Early in the year, it is important to determine what your students like to read and how they feel about reading. Many teachers start the school year with the following homework assignment: "Next Monday, bring to school the three best books you read all summer." They encourage students to go back to the library to check out a book previously read. If children can no longer find the book, we ask them to tell why they thought it was such a good book. Young children are encouraged to bring favorite books they like to have read to them.

When the children bring their books, we let each child tell why he or she likes the books. Some teachers do this book sharing in small groups. As the children share, we note the titles of the books they bring and their reasons for liking them. This tells us a lot about their current reading interests and also suggests selections for read-aloud books to try to broaden interests.

Some children do not bring three books, or bring books but have nothing to say about them and may not have liked or even read the books. This tells you a lot about the current interests, attitudes, and home environment of these children. It also lets you know that all the efforts you plan to make to encourage and support reading are truly important and needed.

You might want to follow up this "best-books" assignment with another homework assignment to bring in magazines and parts of the newspaper they read. Again, follow up this assignment with group sharing and make notes about what each child brings (or did not bring). Record your results on a Beginning Interests and Attitudes Summary, such as that shown here. In addition to noting what each child shares, summarize the interests of the class by noting which topics and types of books are shared most. You have now assessed your students' entering interests and attitudes and can plan how much and what kinds of motivational activities to do.

Children's Names	Books Shared	Magazines/ Newspapers	Current Interest (none, little, some, much)
Carol	Ramona the Pest Charlotte's Web	none	some
Sheryll	3 Bobbsey Twins mysteries	none	some
Sue Ann	Whales Dinosaurs Runaway Horse	U.S.A Today	much
Travis	none	Sports page	little
Ray	none	Fishing	little
David	3 Star Trek books	Sports Illustrated	some
Jason	Cannonball Death at High Noon Dirty Dozen	Time	some

Topics of interest to many children:
Sports, fantasy

Types of books read:

✓Realistic fiction	✓Science fiction	Historical fiction
✓Mystery	Myths/legends	Folk/fairy tales
Fantasy	Biography	Autobiography
✓Informational	Other _____	

Just as with any kind of assessment, your assessment of reading interests and attitudes should be ongoing. By linking your assessment directly to your instruction, you ensure that your assessment is valid. By assessing interests and attitudes on a regular schedule, you get a more reliable indicator than if you assess only once or twice a year. Also, as in any assessment, you can use a variety of methods to assess interests and attitudes. One of the best methods of assessing is to observe what your students actually do. Many teachers fill out checklists for everyone early in the year and then fill them out again for one-sixth of their class each week.

If you do this all year, you should have six or seven indicators of reading attitude throughout the year and should be able to document which students have better attitudes at the end of the year than they did at the beginning.

Literacy Attitudes

Name _____   Dates Checked (– ? +)

Seemed happy when engaged in reading	— — — — — — —
Seemed happy when engaged in writing	— — — — — — —
Talked about reading at home	— — — — — — —
Talked about writing at home	— — — — — — —
Showed enthusiasm when sharing a book with peers	— — — — — — —
Showed enthusiasm when sharing a piece of writing	— — — — — — —
Showed enthusiasm during self-selected reading conference	— — — — — — —
Showed enthusiasm during writing conference	— — — — — — —
Chose to read rather than engage in another activity	— — — — — — —
Chose to write rather than engage in another activity	— — — — — — —

SUMMARY

Assessment is a part of everything we do. To make any kind of decision, we collect and analyze evidence and then act on that evidence. Literacy assessment includes determining reading levels for children, assessing and monitoring their reading and writing strategies and behaviors, and documenting their progress. The systematic use of checklists and anecdotal records gives you the most valid and reliable results. You can then use these records to document the progress of each child and report that progress to parents and other stakeholders. Assessment in real life is a natural and productive activity. We hope that the practical ideas presented in this chapter help make assessment a natural and productive part of your literacy instruction.

CHAPTER 7

Science and Social Studies Matter to Struggling Readers

When Jimmy was in kindergarten, he wrote about a cow and then drew a picture of it. . . . Large for his age, Jimmy was a shy child and a bit reluctant to speak, although he was well liked by the other children. His social interactions were characterized less by conversation than by actions and gestures. . . . His journal entry on the first day of first grade included an initial consonant for barn, silo, cat, pet, hamster, and grass. By the following May, one of his journal entries was about the number of cows on his family's farm.

"I like cows. We have 80."

In the reader's workshop, Jimmy often spent time studying the farm pages in Richard Scary's *Best Word Book Ever* (1963). In individual conferences, he pointed to a label word such as "corncrib," read it, and then added information from his own experience. In writer's workshop, the first piece he published was entitled "Chores."

"I was sleeping. I had breakfast. I milked cows. I fed calves. I went home."

On a class trip to the library to check out books, he walked over to my side so that our arms touched, nudged me, and still staring straight ahead, asked in his deep raspy voice, "Where's the cow books?" (Duthie, 1996, p. 1)

As the previous excerpt indicates, Jimmy and most other children are primarily interested in their world. Schools must take the responsibility for helping children learn about their world and the broader world. This has always been a responsibility of the schools, but one that elementary schools have not taken very seriously. When you think about what we teach children in schools, you can divide almost everything into knowledge and skills. The abilities to read, spell, write, do math, use the computer, sing a song, play the clarinet, throw a ball, speak a foreign language, and so on are all skills—things you can do. The understanding that there are seven continents, that each state has two senators, that the Civil War was fought in the 1860s, that mammals are warm-blooded animals, and that Martin Luther King

You can learn a lot from reading. Many children like to read about "real" things and "real" people.

led the civil rights movement are all knowledge—things that you know. For many years, our elementary schools have focused on skills and largely ignored knowledge. In many schools with large numbers of struggling readers, teachers are instructed to "teach the basics." The basics usually referred to are the three r's— reading, 'riting, and 'rithmetic. The knowledge part of the curriculum—usually found in the subjects of science and social studies—are too often ignored in the primary grades of many schools that teach a high proportion of at-risk children.

The emphasis on skill subjects and the exclusion of the knowledge subjects often results in a short-term gain and a long-term deficit. In school after school, in which the primary emphasis in grades K–3 is on skills, children perform adequately on standardized tests through the second or third grade and then show steady declines from fourth grade on. Teachers from fourth grade on are supposed to try to teach the knowledge subjects such as science and social studies. They often find, however, that even their average students cannot read the textbooks or can read the words but do not understand what they are reading. Children who can read the words but cannot understand what they are reading are not really reading.

Teachers who are committed to helping struggling readers achieve high levels of literacy must not ignore the prior knowledge/reading comprehension relationship. Children in the primary grades must spend a portion of each day engaging in activities in which increasing their world knowledge is the primary goal. Like most complex problems, there is no simple way to achieve this goal in the limited time available. However, one often-tried simple solution does not work. Having children memorize lists of vocabulary words or isolated facts and then testing them on these generally do not increase their world knowledge. (Perhaps you remember being forced to memorize the elements and abbreviations on the periodic chart in Chemistry or the definitions for some uncommon, unrelated words, such as *abase, abate, abet, ablate, ablaut,* or *abjure* in preparation for the SAT or some other test.)

Learning theorists believe that our brain has two distinct learning systems—the rote system and the associative system (Caine & Caine, 1991). Disconnected facts are stored in the rote system. Storing them here requires much repetition, and once they are stored, they are still quite difficult to retrieve. Most of what we know is stored in the associative system, which is just what its name implies. The facts, terms, and so forth in the associative system are all associated with each other in a vast, complex network. When we find one, we find all the others. When you read or hear the word *brontosaurus*, for example, you not only recognize it as a type of dinosaur, but you think of all the other dinosaur words and facts you know—words like *prehistoric, tyrannosaurus rex,* and *pterodactyl* come to mind immediately. In addition to facts and terms, your associative memory stores places, events, feelings, and emotions. The word *brontosaurus* may "remind" you of a trip to a dinosaur exhibit or of a wonderful dinosaur book you used to have (Whatever happened to that book, anyway?). You may smile as you remember your first crush on a boy or girl who was a "dinosaur nut!"

Our goal in helping children expand their world knowledge must be to help them learn a lot about a number of different topics and to focus on individual

Nell Duke (2000) investigated the question of how much informational text is available to children in first-grade classrooms. She observed 20 first grades, 10 of which were high SES schools and 10 of which were low SES schools, for 4 full days. She recorded what the teachers and children did and what was displayed on the walls. She interviewed the teachers and counted and categorized books in the classroom libraries. In addition to what the teacher read aloud to the children and what children read, she noted what kind of writing the teacher modeled. On average, 3.6 minutes per day were spent in some way dealing with informational text. Only 9.8 percent of the books in classroom libraries and 2.6 percent of the displayed text were classified as informational.

For low SES schools, the percentages were even more dismal. Teachers in schools with large numbers of poor children spent on average 1.9 minutes per day dealing with informational text. Informational books made up 6.9 percent of the classroom libraries and only 1.5 percent of the displayed text was informational. Informational text of any kind is clearly underrepresented in first-grade classrooms, and the lack of this text is even more egregious in the classrooms of poor children.

Lots of wonderful informational books are written just for children.

vocabulary words that are part of this topic knowledge. One of the most difficult decisions faced by teachers is which knowledge to focus on. Children need to know so much, and to teach something well we must invest both time and energy. Most states have established knowledge goals for elementary grades. These goals can usually be found in the science and social studies curriculums. In the remainder of this chapter, we suggest a variety of ways that successful schools and teachers make room in their crowded curriculum for in-depth science and social studies learning.

MAKE INFORMATIONAL RESOURCES THE CENTERPIECE OF YOUR INSTRUCTION

Throughout this book we have emphasized using a wide variety of reading materials. Putting informational books and other materials in the center—rather than on the periphery—of your instruction goes a long way toward achieving dual goals: providing lots of opportunities for children to learn about their world and the world beyond their everyday experiences, and increasing the engagement and motivation of children who love learning about "real things." You can begin to work toward the goal of putting informational resources at the center of your instruction by:

- Reading to children from informational books
- Providing the largest possible range and variety of informational books and magazines as part of the classroom library

- Planning unit and author studies around the writers of informational books for children, such as Gail Gibbons, Dorothy Hinshaw Patent, Jean George, Alexandra Parsons, and numerous others
- Providing print-rich classrooms, including newspaper clippings, magazine articles, brochures, and content-related poetry
- Providing research materials including an updated set of children's encyclopedias, almanacs, and Internet sites if networking is available
- Using informational big books for shared reading—even in the upper grades, for which some wonderful books contain visuals such as graphs, charts, maps, and so on that everyone can see

 WHY INFORMATION BOOKS?

Answer questions

Ask questions

Encourage critical thinking

Stimulate interest and curiousity

Create a sense of wonder

Develop understanding of people, places, and things

Provide additional models and inspiration for writing

Provide rich vocabulary

Stimulate the making of connections

Enlarge store of background knowledge

Contain wonderful and varied visuals:
photographs   drawings   maps   graphs   diagrams

Introduce new authors and illustrators

Provide easy reading without the stigma of "baby" books

Show a variety of text patterns, design, and layout features

Reduce fragmented curriculum and day by creating links to math, science, and social studies

Engage students in multiple ways of knowing/thinking/behaving
—as a historian
—a scientist
—a mathematician

Encourage involvement in learning

USE WHAT YOU KNOW

Many teachers lament that students "know" more than they use. But many teachers do not use what they know either! Often in our classroom observations, we watch a teacher in the language arts block doing wonderful strategy instruction—modeling, demonstrating, posing thought-provoking queries, and using a variety of partner reading, choral reading, and other guided reading formats. Obviously, savvy teachers know and use best-practice teaching strategies. Often, however, these same savvy teachers resort to round robin reading and low-level questions during social studies and science. Why don't teachers, who know how to do good reading and writing instruction, use their knowledge when doing reading and writing activities during science and social studies?

As students, most of us experienced reading in science and social studies as "reading around the room," with each and every student reading one paragraph aloud. Most of us do not remember this fondly. We fidgeted and felt uncomfortable as one of our struggling reader classmates stumbled over all the big words in the assigned paragraph. Some of us counted paragraphs to find the one we would read, and practiced so that we would not make a dumb mistake in front of the whole class. Once our turn was over, we breathed a sigh of relief and daydreamed our way through the rest of the period.

Transfer is difficult and past experience is a powerful force. Because of our own experience with reading and writing in science and social studies, it is hard for us to envision the classes we now teach in dramatically different ways. But we can make this change. Knowledge is power and once we decide we want to use what we know, we are not bound by our past. Some of the activities described in previous chapters belong in science and social studies instruction:

- KWLs, QTAs, and think-alouds
- Drawing and acting, which allow students to use their multiple intelligences to think about content
- Various reading formats, including partner reading, choral reading, echo reading, and ERT, instead of around-the-room reading
- Book club groups, when you can find multiple copies of three or four books related to the topic being studied
- Graphic organizers, including webs, feature matrices, data charts, time lines, double bubbles, and diagrams, to organize the information gained from reading or from field trips, videos, simulations, experiments, and all other various sources of information you provide
- Using these same graphic organizers to organize information before writing summaries and reports
- Shared and group writing formats to write informational text
- Focused writing lessons to model how you write reports, summaries, and other expository forms
- Paragraph frames, to help students learn to write expository text

- Computer programs that help students organize ideas and often provide pictures and other graphics for report writing
- Revising, editing, and publishing phases of writing during language arts time using a piece written during science or social studies time
- Making sure students spell word wall words correctly in all writing—including writing done during science and social studies
- Making Words lesson using science and social studies content words as the "secret word"
- Guess the Covered Word lessons with a social studies or science content-oriented paragraph from a big book or one you have written so that students transfer their cross-checking skills
- Making Big Word Boards from your science or social studies vocabulary
- Modeling how to decode science and social studies big words and pointing out helpful roots, prefixes, and suffixes.

PROVIDE AS MUCH REAL EXPERIENCE AS POSSIBLE

Both research and our own experience tell us that we remember best the real things that we do and see. Books, videos, and Internet explorations help build concepts, but nothing can match the knowledge gained from seeing it, touching it, doing it, hearing it, smelling it. If we are serious about building the knowledge stores of our struggling students, we must constantly ask whether taking our students to see "the real thing" or bringing "the real thing" into the classroom is in any way possible.

Field Trips

Mention field trips to a group of teachers and watch them cringe! Field trips can be expensive, a pain to plan, and exhausting to take! Realizing this, we still must begin our specific suggestions for expanding world knowledge by encouraging teachers to consider the possibility of taking students somewhere outside the four walls of the classroom. Field trips allow students to experience "the real thing." Field trips can be to areas of the playground or places in the neighborhood. Children can walk or take public transportation to the grocery store, the post office, the local mall, a meadow, a pond, or a stream. Trips further afield often require buses, lunches, and so on, but the cost of taking a few trips each year is paid back to you in motivation. Children who go to a museum, factory, park, or theater and who see, firsthand, the things they are studying often form an emotional attachment to the trip and to the things they experienced on the trip. This emotional involvement is transferred to the topic they are studying. Many children have a "Who cares?" attitude toward topics they know nothing about. Taking them on trips to experience real things and real people connected with these unfamiliar topics goes a long way toward establishing critical emotional engagement.

Even a field trip to the sidewalk outside the school can prove truly fascinating. Before you go, read and reread Jean Craighead George's book *Once Upon a Sidewalk*. This book details a day in the life of a worker ant and presents an ant's-eye view of life on, under, and around a sidewalk. The book inevitably creates a real curiosity about the common world under our feet and provides an impetus for taking a careful look at what is going on in our natural environment. The book and field trip provide a wealth of descriptive writing opportunities. A sidewalk field trip can be followed by a playground or park field trip in which children measure and mark a square foot of turf and then observe and record plant and insect activity.

Of course, if you are going to all the trouble of taking them on a field trip, you should get every ounce of learning and motivation possible from the experience. This means you must "hype" the trip and prepare them for what they will see and what they want to find out. Showing them pictures, slides, or a video beforehand of what they will see is a good way to get them thinking about what they will experience. You may do a KWL lesson before going, in which you have them list what they know and what they want to find out. Upon your return, have them fill in the last column listing what they learned. You may also give them each a pocket-sized index card and a stubby pencil and have each student be responsible for finding out and writing down the answer to one or two questions to be shared later with the whole class.

In all schools, field trips are less common today than they were 2 decades ago. Two-parent working families, single-parent families, liability rulings, and the back-to-basics emphasis have put a damper on taking children into the very world that we want them to learn about. In schools with a large number of poor children, field trips are often a real rarity. This is unfortunate because these schools are often located in settings that offer a wealth of nearby opportunities for developing world knowledge. These districts are often poor in terms of funding, but are located in an environment that is rich with opportunities. If we are serious about expanding the world knowledge of at-risk children and about fostering their desire to learn about the world beyond their block and neighborhood, we must reconsider taking them into that world.

Bringing Real Things into the Classroom

When you cannot take a field trip or take *them* to *it*, the next best thing is to bring *it* to *them*. As you plan to have your students learn about a particular topic, look around—beg and borrow objects that are even vaguely related to the topic. Some museums have crates of objects related to commonly studied topics. Some school media centers collect and store "things" that many teachers need. In some schools, teachers take responsibility for gathering objects related to a particular topic and then teach these topics at different times so that everyone can use the same objects.

Whenever possible, use objects that are commonly found in the homes or the environment of your students. When you use these in certain activities or show how they are related to something that you are studying, your students will probably associate the objects with that learning and will think about what they are

Sometimes you can get real people to bring real things into your classroom. This class is doing a unit on safety and rules and is learning more about both from a visiting police officer.

learning when they see those objects in their own environment. When you use common objects, ask students whether they have these at home or have seen them someplace else. Then suggest that the next time they notice these objects, they explain to someone who is with them—parent, brother, cousin, friend, or uncle— how these common objects are related to what they are learning.

For instance, in conjunction with David MacCaulay's book *How Things Work* (1984), bring in an old faucet, a large zipper, or maybe an iron or a camera that does not work. Partially disassemble the object and key the pages of the book that provide diagrams and explanations of how these objects work. Provide an old magnifying glass for closer looks. We can use this same magnifying glass to examine household plants for mites or to examine plant structures or the soil in the pot. We can even observe and describe the children's pets that might accompany them to class for an hour or a day.

Of course, these observations and descriptions can and should be recorded— through writing, drawing, and labeling. (Steve Moline's *I See What You Mean* is an excellent source of varied and creative ways to help students record.) Students can work collaboratively in groups or as a class to create their own book, for example, *How School Things Work* or *How We Care for Our Pets*. If your school is connected to the information highway, you might publish some of the information learned on the Web.

Scavenger Hunts

Have you ever been on a scavenger hunt? Everyone has a list of things to find, a limited amount of time in which to find them, and the team that finds the most things wins. You can adapt the scavenger hunt notion to help your children expand their world and word knowledge (Cunningham, Crawley, & Mountain, 1983). Choose a topic that you are about to study or a piece of literature you are about to read. As you think about what the children will be reading and learning, select words for which you would like to develop meaning and for which children could scavenge for pictures and/or objects.

For the topic weather, for example, a teacher decided that pictures and/or objects could be found to represent

cirrus clouds	blizzard	barometer
cumulus clouds	cyclone	thermometer
stratus clouds	hurricane	meteorologist
fog	monsoon	wind vane
frost	tornado	rain gauge
hail	lightning	rainbow

She made a list of these words and distributed the list to teams of children in her class. She then explained that the class was going to have a scavenger hunt. The teams had 1 week to collect as many objects and/or pictures as they could to represent the words on the list. They could bring one object and one picture for each word. They would get two points for an object and one point for a picture. She then let the teams meet for a few minutes to discuss what the words meant and who thought they could find which objects. When the children protested they could not bring in a hurricane, she responded, "Perhaps you could bring a picture of a hurricane." When children said, "I don't even know what a rain gauge is," she said, "Well, maybe you had better look it up in the dictionary or encyclopedia or ask someone who does know, if you want your team to win the scavenger hunt."

All week, the teacher let the teams meet briefly each day to discuss what they had found and what they still needed. She stressed that they should whisper and keep their finds secret because they did not want the other teams to figure out where they were finding things. When asked whether drawings (of the objects) were allowed, she responded that they were as long as they were well drawn and actually looked like the object being represented. Later, someone asked whether the students could bring "something like the object, but smaller, like a model of it." She responded, "If the model or smaller thing really represents the real thing, it will count as an object."

On the designated day, the children came with the "scavenged" objects and pictures. Each team gathered and laid out their finds. Most teams had pictures—drawn, found, or copied—of almost everything. There were also a surprising number of real objects, including a hand-made rain gauge and one of those small, glass balls with a scene inside that becomes a "blizzard" when you turn it upside down! The students who had thought of this were particularly pleased with their cleverness and the other teams did have to admit that it was "kind of like a model of a blizzard."

The winning team was rewarded for its efforts. They were allowed to create the weather bulletin board! They put all the words up and then made a collage of the pictures brought in by all the teams. They labeled the objects and put them on a nearby table. Then they made a caption in big letters:

WEATHER BULLETIN BOARD CREATED BY WINNERS OF WEATHER SCAVENGER HUNT

and signed all their names.

This first scavenger hunt was a "limited" success. The children learned what a scavenger hunt is and discovered that there are ways to make real things and find models of real things. As the year went on, and after several more scavenger hunts, the children became very clever at hunting and creating. Their world and word knowledge increased, as did their enjoyment in searching for and creating real things and pictures.

DESIGNATE SOME DAYS AS INTEGRATED DAYS

The fragmentation of our curriculum into specific subject areas is frustrating to many teachers and makes learning difficult for many children. For decades, experts have asked why a separate time and curriculum for reading is needed, particularly in the intermediate grades. To become better readers, children have to read something. Why shouldn't that something be related to a science or social studies topic we want them to learn about?

While integrating learning across subject areas makes a great deal of sense, many barriers prevent its implementation. Often, each subject area has its own separate curriculum guide and/or textbook. Each subject also has its own set of distinct goals and objectives. Most schools still require grades to be given in the separate subjects. Finally, in some elementary schools, teachers are, unfortunately, departmentalized, and children move to different teachers for different subjects.

Although these barriers are real and make integration difficult, compelling reasons support integration. The first and most obvious reason is time. When you teach a comprehension lesson using material about Canada or have children research a particular animal and then write and illustrate a class-produced animal encyclopedia, you "kill two birds with one stone." All elementary teachers know that we are constantly adding to the elementary curriculum while never taking anything away. Integrating the skills of reading and writing with the knowledge-oriented subjects, such as science and social studies, is one way to make better use of the time we have (Walp & Walmsley, 1995).

RECOMMENDED RESOURCES

Integration Ideas

Here are just a few of the topics explored on Integrated Days and some of the wonderful informational books related to those topics:

Dolphins (Grades 2–3)

Dolphins Home, Donna Bailey and Chris Butterworth (Steck-Vaughn)

Different Kinds of Dolphins, Donna Bailey and Chris Butterworth (Steck-Vaughn)

The Sea World Book of Dolphins, S. Leatherwood and R. Reeves (Harcourt, Brace, Jovanovich)

Dolphins! June Behrens (Children's Press)

Dolphins, Norman Barrett (Franklin Watts)

Whale and Dolphin (Raintree-Steck-Vaughn)

Dolphins, Margaret Davidson (Scholastic) Harder book

Early America (Grades 2–4)

Sarah Martin's Day: A Day in the Life of a Pilgrim Girl, Kate Waters (Scholastic)

Colonial Crafts: The School, J. H. Corwin (Franklin Watts)

If You Lived in Colonial Times, Ann McGovern and B. Turkle (Scholastic)

The Boston Coffee Party, Doreen Rappaport (Scholastic)

Sam the Minuteman, N. Benchley (HarperCollins)

George Washington: First President, Carol Greene (Children's Press)

The Connecticut Colony, D. B. Fradin (Children's Press) Harder book

The Civil War Era (Grades 4–5)

Turn Homeward Hannalee, Patricia Beatty (Morrow) Harder book

Caddie Woodlawn, C. R. Brink (Scholastic)

Across Five Aprils, Irene Hunt (Follett)

Freedom Train: The Story of Harriet Tubman, D. Sterlin (Scholastic)

The Perilous Road, W. O. Steele (Scholastic)

Rifles for Waitie, H. Keith (HarperCollins)

The Civil War Soldier at Atlanta, W. Sanford & C. Green (Children's Press)

Slave Dancer, Paula Fox (Dell) Harder book.

The Boys' War, Jim Murphy (Clarion Books).

Dinosaurs (Grades 1–3)

Digging Up Dinosaurs, Aliki (HarperCollins)

Dinosaur Story, Janna Cole (Scholastic)

Dinosaur Time, Peggy Parrish (HarperCollins)

The Littlest Dinosaurs, B. Most (Harcourt, Brace, Jovanovich)

Baby Dinosaurs, P. Dodson and P. Levangis (Scholastic)

Eyewitness Books: Dinosaurs (Albert Knopf)

Over 65 Million Years Ago: Before the Dinosaurs Died, R. Moody (Macmillan)

Life and Death of Dinosaurs, P. Chenel (Children's Press)

The Dinosaur Is the Biggest Animal That Ever Lived and Other Wrong Ideas You Thought Were True, S. Simon (HarperCollins)

Prehistoric Marine Reptiles, J. A. Massare (Franklin Watts)

The Last Dinosaurs, Douglas Dixon (Gareth Stevens)

Life Cycles—Frogs (Grades 1–5)

Life Cycles: The Frog (Raintree-Steck-Vaughn)

Frogs, B. Watts (Franklin Watts)

Tadpole Diary (Rigby)

The Tadpole (Raintree-Steck-Vaughn)

The Frog in the Pond (Gareth Stevens Books)

Frogs and Toads, J. Dallinger (Bancroft-Sage)

Eyewitness Juniors: Amazing Frogs and Toads (Albert Knopf)

A variety of sources exist for integrated-curriculum books. A few of the best are currently available:

A to Zoo Subject Access to Children's Picture Books (3rd ed.), Carolyn W. and John A. Lima (R. R. Bowker, 1989)

Eye Openers! How to Choose and Use Children's Books about Real People, Places and Things, Beverly Kobrin (Penguin, 1988). This book lists activities and children's books that can be used to study Hawaii, Australia, Japan, Italy, Kenya, and Brazil.

Multicultural Explorations: Joyous Journeys with Books, Mary Ann Heltshe and Audrey Burie Kirchner (Teacher Ideas Press, 1991)

Children Exploring Their World: Theme Teaching in Elementary School, Sean Walmsley (Heinemann, 1993)

Social Studies through Children's Literature, Anthony D. Fredricks (Teacher Ideas Press, 1991)

Adventures with Social Studies (through Literature), Sharron L. McElmeel (Teacher Ideas Press, 1991)

Books You Can Count On, Rachel Griffiths and Margaret Clyne (Heinemann, 1991)

Have You Read a Good Math Lately?: Children's Books for Mathematical Learning, David Whiten and Sandra Wilde (Heinemann, 1992)

Science through Children's Literature, Carol M. and John W. Butzow (Teacher Ideas Press, 1989)

True Stories: Nonfiction Literacy in the Primary Classroom, Christine Duthie (Stenhouse, 1996)

Relevance and application are equally compelling arguments for integration. Many children do not see any reason for learning to read, write, and compute. When reading, writing, and math are taught as separate skills, children often do not apply them at other times or to other subjects. The difficulty children experience reading their content-area textbooks can be partially traced to the fact that they have spent most of their time learning how to read stories. Assessment data in math shows that children can solve almost any problem if it is all set up for them. When presented with a story problem that requires them to decide which operations to perform on which numbers, however, their mathematics abilities are abysmal. Rarely in life are we confronted with straightforward numbers to multiply or percentages to figure. Children who cannot apply their reading, writing, and math skills to real-world situations are not being educated to succeed beyond the walls of their classrooms.

Realizing that integration across subject areas saves time, makes the skills more relevant, and provides constant opportunities to apply the skills being learned, teachers in some schools have begun setting aside one day each week as an "Integrated Day." On Integrated Day, the usual schedule of separate subjects and the use of separate textbooks is abandoned. The *topic* is the focus for that day and all activities—reading, writing, math, art, music, and so on—are chosen because they help children learn about that topic.

Teachers who teach an Integrated Day report that both they and the children are much more excited about learning when they have a whole day to pursue a topic and find out a lot about it. Children look forward to this day as a break from the routine of subject-structured days. Teachers enjoy planning for this day; they *find* time for the children to work together on projects and *to do* some creative activities that often get ignored in the busy elementary school day. When we first started doing one Integrated Day each week, Friday was the day that most teachers chose. After several years of experimenting with the Integrated Day notion, most teachers now like to have their Integrated Day on Monday. They use the whole day on Monday to get the topic really going and to get the children involved with research and creative projects. For the rest of the week, children can continue working on these projects at other times during the school day or at home. Teachers who use Monday as Integrated Day, initiating their special topic, often spend an hour or more on Friday afternoon to let children share what they have done or learned and also to use it for closure of the topic. In classrooms where Monday is the Integrated Day, the normally "blue" Monday often becomes everyone's favorite day of the week!

INTEGRATE SCIENCE AND LANGUAGE ARTS

The combination of science and language arts may sound like a strange one. If subjects are combined, language arts is more apt to be put with social studies, and science is often linked with math. Compelling reasons, however, support linking language arts curriculum with your science curriculum.

The federally funded NRRC—National Reading Research Center—carried out research on ways to improve literacy instruction. One of the main thrusts of the NRRC was student engagement.

> At the NRRC, our over-arching goal is to study how to cultivate self-determining readers who are the architects of their own learning. Our research is unified by an engagement perspective which suggests that productive learners are motivated, strategic, knowledgeable and collaborative. Engaged students participate in literacy activities to gain knowledge, perform tasks and enjoy literary experiences. (Guthrie, McCann, Hynd, & Stahl, 1998, p. 1)

The engagement perspective of the NRRC was partly motivated by data that show that a huge number of students are aliterate—choosing not to read despite good reading ability. Recent NAEP (National Assessment of Educational Progress) data indicate that 25 percent of fourth graders and 50 percent of eighth graders report reading *once a month or less* for their own interest! Clearly, the literacy problem in this country goes beyond decoding and comprehension. Readers are not just people who *can* read; they are people who *do* read. They select books that appeal to them and set aside time to read for their own pleasure and information.

NRRC carried out many classroom-based research projects during its 5 years. Two of them linked language arts and science, and this linkage came about because the researchers asked themselves questions such as,

What turns elementary kids on?
What are they interested in?
What do they want to learn about?

The answers to many of these questions lie in the domain we call science. Kids observe things—animals, plants, weather, physical phenomena, stars, and so on. They have a natural curiosity about what is happening and why. The unusual linking of science and language arts makes sense when you consider that the content and process of science are natural motivators for children's learning.

One language arts–science linkage research project took place in six third-grade classrooms (Morrow, Pressley, Smith, & Smith, 1997). Two of these classrooms were designated as control classes and carried out their language arts and science instruction as they had in past years. Instruction was carried out using basal readers and science textbooks. Language arts was allotted 90 minutes daily for a total of 7½ hours each week. Science was given three 45-minute periods each week for a total of 2 hours and 15 minutes. Two other classrooms, designated as literature classrooms, continued teaching science in the traditional way for the same 2 hours and 15 minutes weekly, but divided the language arts tie between the basal reader and literature. Teachers read to the children daily; engaged the children in a variety of writing, dramatizing, and retelling activities related to books read; and provided time and a variety of books for independent reading.

The other two classes, designated science/literature classrooms, also divided their language arts time between basal reader instruction and literature, but their science time was also divided between textbook reading and literature. Five science books were read and responded to for each science unit throughout the year. Students were given time to read science informational books and encouraged to write about what they were reading.

At the end of the year, a large amount of data was collected including standardized test results, writing samples, book title recognition measures, and attitude measures gathered through teacher and student interviews. Students in the science/literature classrooms scored significantly higher on all literacy measures and on two of the three science measures. Perhaps, more importantly, students in both the literature and science/literature classes read more than students in the basal/textbook–only classrooms, and students in the science/literature classrooms read science on their own more often than children in the literature classrooms.

A final encouraging outcome relates to student attitudes toward science. The majority of students in the two science/literature classrooms reported that they liked science wheareas the majority of students in the other four classrooms reported that they did not like science because it was "boring!"

The other classroom-based research study that integrated language arts and science was CORI (concept-oriented reading instruction). The CORI framework was first tried out in one fifth-grade classroom and in subsequent years was extended to a variety of upper-elementary and middle grades in many different sites.

In CORI classrooms, teachers spend 2 hours daily in an integrated science and language arts block. During this time science is real hands-on science; textbooks are used rarely and only as resources. The language arts focuses primarily on reading "real" books—both fictional and informational (no basal readers allowed!)—and on writing in personal logs. Students record what they are thinking and learning and the products—posters, books, letters to parents, and so forth—they are using to communicate what they are learning.

In addition, teachers provide some other blocks of time during the week to accomplish language arts goals that do not fit well with science content. Most teachers schedule 2 hours for Writer's Workshop writing in which children explore their own topics and ideas, unconstrained by the science topic. Most teachers also have a separate spelling time in which they use some topic-related words and some pattern words. Many teachers read aloud books related to the topic, but they also read grade-level favorites that are unrelated. This description focuses on the 2-hour science–language arts block, but keep in mind that these teachers actually spend more than 2 hours a day when you add in the hours given to Writer's Workshop, teacher read-aloud, and spelling.

Each CORI classroom studies three science topics: one life science, one physical science, and one earth science. In third grade, for example, they studied the adaptation of animals to their environment and focused specifically on birds. They also did units on the solar system and weather. For each unit, students go through four stages. In each stage, important literacy strategies are taught.

The first stage is called Observe and Personalize. During this stage, students observe phenomena such as clouds or crickets. They collect things such as the crickets or water samples. They carry out experiments. They activate prior knowledge and generate questions such as, Where do crickets go in the winter? The second stage is called Search and Retrieve. Students use a variety of books, computer databases, and other sources. They learn to locate information using the table of contents and index. They take notes and outline information. In the third stage, Comprehend and Integrate, they use information from a variety of sources to synthesize information. They analyze, summarize, make inferences, and draw conclusions. The final stage, called Communicate to Others, involves the students in writing, making videos, drawing maps, and producing a variety of things that allow them to share what they have learned. Much of the learning done in CORI classrooms is done in teams composed of three to five students. Teachers do whole-class strategy instruction as needed and then support teams as they work though the various stages.

Research with the CORI model has been carried out in a variety of different settings across several years. The results, though complex, support the idea that achievement and motivation are increased when science and language arts are linked. For detailed results and more about the instructional model, we highly recommend that you read "Growth of Literacy Engagement: Changes in Motivations and Strategies during Concept-Oriented Reading Instruction" (Guthrie, Van Meter, McCann, et al. 1996).

Motivation matters when it comes to literacy achievement. As children go through school, their motivation for school and reading decreases. The less they like to do it, the less they do it. How much children read is the best predictor of how well they read. If we want all our children to read and write as well as they possibly can, we must find ways to combat the problem of decreasing motivation. We can capitalize on children's natural affinity for science by integrating some of our reading and writing instruction with science topics. Their science knowledge will increase as will their motivation to read. Having more science knowledge and spending more time reading results in better readers.

ORGANIZE YOUR SPECIAL TEACHERS TO SUPPORT SCIENCE AND SOCIAL STUDIES

All over the country, schools are rethinking how special teachers are being used to support children with learning problems or who find learning to read difficult. One possibility that is being tried in some schools involves special teachers supporting classroom teachers in the areas of science and social studies. This support takes a number of different forms. In some schools, the remedial reading or resource teacher is scheduled into the classroom during science or social studies, and the classroom teacher and special teacher team up to work with all the students. The special teacher might use the knowledge of books and other materials to find more interesting and readable books. If nothing but the textbook is available, the special teacher might rewrite important portions of the text, making them simpler and clearer. Special teachers might teach reading-strategy lessons focused on building prior knowledge and vocabulary. They might help children learn to deal with expository text structure. They might model how to read graphs, maps, and other visuals. They might help students learn to write reports and summaries.

Another possibility that is being tried involves the special teacher working with only those students designated as having learning or reading problems, but still focusing on science or social studies content. Whether the special teacher works in the classroom or in a room down the hall, the remedial time is scheduled during science or social studies and the special teacher provides instruction in reading and writing covering the same content being covered in the classroom. Again, special teachers will find or rewrite simpler, clearer text, develop prior knowledge and content vocabulary, and help students learn how to read and write informational text.

Learning to read is a complex process. Children who are struggling with reading need help with all aspects of reading and they need more time and practice to learn effective reading strategies. When the special instruction they need is provided during science and social studies time instead of during language arts time, they get an extra "dose" of literacy instruction. When the content of that instruction is part of the classroom science or social studies curriculum, they increase, rather than fall further behind in, their knowledge stores.

TRANSFORM EVERY STUDENT INTO AN "EXPERT"

All the activities described in the chapter so far have been based on having the teacher select the topics around which to develop knowledge. The last activity is centered on the various interests of each child. Many children have a hobby or a passion for some topic about which they willingly dig and devour information. As they learn about this topic, they increase not only their knowledge of this topic, but of their general knowledge as well. Children who collect baseball cards, and can give you the stats for all their favorite players, learn a lot about baseball, but they also expand their general knowledge. Any baseball enthusiast knows the meaning of the general words *average, rare, trade, manager, major,* and *minor.* In addition, baseball card collectors learn about geography and economics. Professional baseball teams are located throughout North America. Students can locate these cities and mark them with a replica of a team banner. Students can develop some basic economic knowledge while learning about the prices offered for baseball cards. Listing price trends, basis for pricing, and tallying prices of cards owned by members of the class are all activities that foster basic economic knowledge.

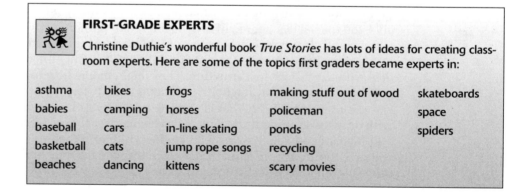

FIRST-GRADE EXPERTS

Christine Duthie's wonderful book *True Stories* has lots of ideas for creating classroom experts. Here are some of the topics first graders became experts in:

asthma	bikes	frogs	making stuff out of wood	skateboards
babies	camping	horses	policeman	space
baseball	cars	in-line skating	ponds	spiders
basketball	cats	jump rope songs	recycling	
beaches	dancing	kittens	scary movies	

Children who become fascinated with a topic learn, of course, about that topic. In addition, they learn the meaning of some words used in that specific topic that could have a wider, more general use. They also learn how to find and evaluate information about that topic—a skill we call *research* or *inquiry*. Perhaps the most important thing they learn, however, is that learning and gaining knowledge (when you care about the topic) is an intrinsically motivating and satisfying pursuit. Children who become interested in and pursue one topic derive so many academic and attitudinal benefits that we believe all elementary children should be encouraged to become experts at something! The strategy we use to help children become experts is called You Be the Expert.

To get children interested in becoming experts, it is important to help children see that people can become experts in all kinds of topics. Invite some experts into your class to share their expertise. Make sure children understand that a person's area of expertise is not necessarily the same thing as that person's livelihood. Perhaps you, the teacher, have something you know a lot about and keep up with. Begin with this. Do you collect antiques? Watch birds? Grow roses? Track hurricanes? Bring to class some things—books, magazines, and so on—that relate to your expert knowledge; share this knowledge and enthusiasm with your children. Then invite friends, neighbors, relatives, other teachers, or staff members to come and share their expertise. Talk with the children about their hobbies and interests and have a time each week when they can bring in some thing that they know a lot about to share with the class. You may be amazed at what your children know and are interested in.

Once children understand that people become experts by devoting time and energy to learning about a specific topic, and once they learn that the number of topics for which a person can develop expertise is practically infinite, let each child choose a topic about which he or she can be the expert. Allot some time each week for your experts to share the new things they have learned. Encourage the children to bring sources of information and to show where they found certain

TWO-LANGUAGE CHILDREN AS EXPERTS

A classroom that includes a Jamaican child, a Hmong child from Cambodia, a Mexican child, or a Jewish Russian child is not difficult to find. Each of these immigrant children could easily still be acquiring English as their second language, yet each is an expert on cultural and world knowledge of which many other children are wholly unaware. Too often, these children are viewed as having substantial deficits in world knowledge because their expertise does not match the curriculum in our schools. We like to think of these children as experts—experts whose specialized knowledge can be tapped to broaden the world knowledge of others in the classroom. We might have them provide us with knowledge of the geography or the climate of their native land or with training in speaking their native language. We might have them develop our knowledge of the history of their cultural group. We might work to make sure that our classroom has books that reflect their culture and that we incorporate their knowledge into our discussions.

facts. Help them find a variety of ways (scrapbooks, notebooks, file folders, etc.) to keep up with what they are learning. As children share, encourage other children to ask questions. If the experts cannot answer the questions, point out that an expert is always adding more facts and knowledge and suggest that your experts try to find out the answers before the next "expert share."

SUMMARY

Helping children expand their knowledge stores should be a major goal of every teacher. This goal is particularly important when teaching children whose families may not be able to provide them with enrichment experiences. Because knowledge expansion is an enormous and never-ending goal, it is never completely finished or "mastered" and is not easily measured. When considering how to promote literacy for struggling readers, it is easy to focus on the small, visible components of reading and writing and lose track of the knowledge/reading/writing/thinking connection. To read and write about a variety of topics, you must have a lot of specific and general world and word knowledge. Successful schools for at-risk children achieve a balance between the need to teach skills and the need to expand world knowledge. These schools understand that children can learn to read and read to learn simultaneously, and that the most powerful classroom lessons reflect both goals. This chapter has offered a variety of ways teachers get organized and use their precious time to do it all!

CHAPTER 8

Extra Support for Students Who Need It Most

Throughout this book we have described ways in which classroom teachers provide support for children who find learning to read a challenge. Taking into account the new criteria for what children must do to reach the basic proficiency standard, we have emphasized instruction in which children develop thoughtful literacy. Many children who are currently just a little below level can achieve basic and even proficient levels of reading achievement if their elementary literacy instruction includes the following:

- Lots of reading and writing (as described in Chapter 1)
- Activities designed to produce fluent decoders and spellers, even of big words (as described in Chapter 2)
- Comprehension lessons in which children learn to think about, compare, and evaluate what they read (as described in Chapter 3)
- Writing lessons in which children learn to write thoughtful responses to what they are learning and reading about (as described in Chapter 4)
- Multilevel instruction that has a variety of things to be learned and allows everyone to experience success (as described in Chapter 6)
- An emphasis on applying reading and writing strategies to learn science and social studies content (as described in Chapter 7)

FORM AN AFTER-LUNCH BUNCH

An after-lunch bunch is a small group that gets together for 10–15 minutes after lunch (or at another time—just choose another name for it!) and reads easy books "just for fun." For example, in one first-grade classroom in January, the teacher was doing guided reading in primer- and late preprimer–level materials. When the children were partner reading, they could all read the primer with a partner's help. The teacher knew, from observing the partners during partner reading, however, that four of the first graders were missing many words and were not really at instructional level in these books.

The teacher decided that these children needed some additional reading with easy early preprimer–level materials. Thus, the after-lunch bunch was formed. Membership in the after-lunch bunch changed daily, but the teacher made sure that the four children whose needs had instigated the formation of this group were in the group often but not every day. Every child was included in the after-lunch bunch every week, but the best readers were only included once each week. Thus the membership changed daily, but the group always included a majority of children who needed some easier reading and other children who were good reading models. No child ever suspected that this was "a low group" (and in fact it wasn't!).

Each day when the children returned from lunch, they would check the list posted at the back table to see whether they were in the after-lunch bunch that day. The six children who found their names gathered eagerly at the back table "to read some fun books with the teacher." The children read for 10–15 minutes, often reading through several easy stories. Sometimes these stories were found in old preprimers; sometimes they were "skinny books" made from old preprimer stories. Sometimes the teacher was able to find several copies of "real" books to share that were easy enough to read. During this after-lunch bunch, no comprehension strategies were taught as they are during guided reading. The teacher did however coach them on how to figure out words, and meaning was always emphasized.

The after-lunch bunch idea can be used at different grade levels and with a variety of materials. Teachers find it most useful for guided reading when they have just a few children who are not at instructional level with the materials the class is using. If children share books, you can do an after-lunch bunch with only three or four copies of the easy material you have selected. It is critical for the children to view the after-lunch bunch as a chance to "just read and enjoy" some fun material and to see that the membership varies. No child is in the same group every day, and some good reading models are always present.

SCHEDULING EASY READING TIME

After-lunch reading can also be after-school reading (or even before-school reading if school opens later). We have seen programs similar to the one described above that involved teachers, parents, and children after school. In some cases the reading and special education resource teachers work on "flex-time" and begin their school day a bit later than other teachers to be available to organize the after-school reading for this extended day program, at no additional cost. In one of these schools each teacher schedules a single child to stay after school each day (except Friday) to work with individually for 15–20 minutes. The child then joins the after-school children for some fun easy reading with a small group.

SCHEDULE 30 MINUTES OF OPEN-CENTER TIME INTO YOUR DAY

We know what you are thinking. You are thinking that you cannot get it all done now, much less with 30 minutes less time! We are going to try to convince you that you can get back your 30 minutes in increased productivity during the rest of the day, that students need time to pursue their own interests, and that freeing you up to work with individuals and small groups on the most pressing needs is a valuable use of your time.

First, let us consider what "open centers" are—and what they are not. Open centers contain "things" kids like to work with and opportunities to pursue their own interests. Open centers usually do not change very much, although a new center is often added that connects to a current theme or unit. Open centers often contain the following items:

Legos or other building materials
Puzzles
Board games
Computer with games, drawing, and publishing software
Computer linked to the Internet
Math manipulatives
Math games
Science manipulatives
Play-doh or other sculpting material
Chalk, paint, or other drawing material
Markers, paper, stamps, and other writing/drawing materials
Children's magazines
Children's encyclopedia and other reference books
VCR and monitor showing a Reading Rainbow book or other video

From this list, you should get the idea that open centers contain "open-ended" materials, things children can enjoy and learn from on their own not unlike the way they might play at home, if they lived in this kind of enriching environment. Open centers do not contain worksheets or assignments. Although students do "produce" things in some centers, these are things they choose to make. Students are not required to complete things and turn them in, and nothing is graded or checked on.

To get open centers to work, you must have rules and routines and spend whatever time is required making sure everyone understands and follows them. Decide on a way of determining who goes to which center. Because children follow their interests, it is not necessary or even desirable that every child go to every center. In many classrooms, children are designated as days of the week and do a variety of things on their day. On Mondays, the Monday children share in the Authors Chair, conference with the teacher during self-selected reading time, and so on. Use this or some other system to let children choose centers. On Monday, the Monday children choose first and then the Tuesday, Wednesday, Thursday, Friday children choose. But on Tuesday, the Monday children are the last to choose because the order is Tuesday, Wednesday, Thursday, Friday, Monday. The number of children allowed at each center is determined, and once children choose a center, they stay in that center for the remainder of the 30 minutes. Appoint one child in charge of each center for a week. Choose a child who often chooses that center, and let center leaders go to their centers and get materials ready a minute before others go to the center. At the end of center time, the center leader sees that all of the center materials are stored and ready for the next day.

Before beginning center time, use 30 minutes to have some class members role play what should happen in each center, how center materials are treated, and the quiet voices required if everyone is to work in centers. Stop the role plays regularly and ask the children who are watching what is being done right and what needs to be done differently. Do not begin centers until all children understand, even if they do not perfectly carry out, what must happen in the centers. When you begin open-center time, spend whatever part of the 30 minutes is required getting kids to the centers, making sure they know what they are allowed to do there, reminding them not to migrate to other centers, and making sure centers are tidy and ready for the next day. If children are not used to caring for materials and working independently, it may take several weeks of your persistent reminders to teach all your children what is expected. Do not hesitate to close a center—sending the members back to their desks—if the whole group at the center was not following procedures. If an individual child is not cooperating, sharing, using a quiet voice, and so on, send that child back to his or her seat. Some teachers require that the children sent back to their seats use this seat time to write an explanation of what they were doing and what they should have been doing. They are not allowed to choose a center the next day until a satisfactorily written explanation is produced.

Eventually, if you are determined and persistent, your centers will work almost without you. Leaders will care for materials, and children will know which days they get to choose first. The occasional child who must be removed will, after sulking for a few minutes, write the required explanation so that he or she can go to centers the next day. Once this happens, you can begin to reap the benefits of this time. Explain to the children that, on some days, you need to use some of their center time to work with them individually or in small groups. Explain further that because you are taking some of their time today, they get first choice of the centers tomorrow, regardless of which day of the week they are. Now you have some uninterrupted time to do any number of things: to tutor individuals, to work with small after-lunch bunch groups, to do individual running records, to catch a child up who has been absent for a week, or to chat with a child who needs some attitude adjustment as well as some of your undivided attention.

The notion of balance in classrooms is a critical issue. We must balance the instructional approaches we use because children learn in different ways. We must allocate time to different subject areas because many important things need to be learned. One way in which many classrooms are out of balance is addressed by the concept of open centers. Children who are exploring through manipulating, drawing, playing games, and so on are learning, but they are pursuing their own interests and learning in a way for which they are best suited. If you consider Gardner's (1993) important concept of multiple intelligences and you look at what happens across an entire school day, you often do not see many learning opportunities for children whose intelligence is more visual/spatial, musical, or rhythmic. Because centers contain a variety of activities and because children choose their center, the learning possibilities are greatly expanded.

Open centers also create a more balanced classroom day by freeing up the teacher to do whatever is most needed on that day for particular groups or individuals. When every minute of every day is allocated to a particular subject and the teacher has just that time to teach that subject to everyone, individual needs go unmet. One of the great frustrations of teaching is seeing something that desperately needs to be done and in many cases even knowing what to do about it but not being able to find the few minutes it would take to do it. Classrooms with smooth-running open-center time provide teachers opportunities to do the little things that add up to big differences in a particular child's learning.

Now, if you are convinced that you need some open-center time, where will it come from? In most classrooms, a lot of time is wasted in transitions. Teachers who are looking for 30 minutes should clock how long it takes to settle down after lunch and how much time they spend waiting for everyone to get ready. In some classrooms, 15 minutes is spent taking attendance each day, and children spend 15 minutes getting ready to go home! To find that 30 minutes, try carving 3–5 minutes off transitions, attendance taking, getting ready to go home, and so forth and see whether it cannot be done. If your school day ends at 3:15, imagine it was ending at 2:45. You do not want to leave any subject out, but could you "tighten it up a bit" and find 30 minutes? Most school days contain 30 minutes of slack, and this 30 minutes could provide you and your students with a more balanced, less frustrating day.

FIND AND TRAIN A TUTOR FOR YOUR MOST NEEDY CHILD

In many classrooms, teachers are overwhelmed by the scope of the literacy problems our children have and by how much needs to be done. If we have lots of struggling readers, we may realize that we cannot do everything, so we end up doing nothing. Think now about the one child you have who is most behind in reading and writing and is not receiving any individual help. Perhaps this child is just learning to speak English or has not attended school regularly. For whatever reason, this child's reading and writing level is well below that of the other children.

Most children who are far behind in reading and writing can make considerable progress if they have a strong classroom program and some one-on-one tutoring. Before thinking about where you might find this tutor, you must decide what you would train the tutor to do. The most important component of any successful tutoring program is through the repeated readings of materials at the child's instructional level. So your first task is to find some materials that are just right. As described previously, disagreement exists about what exactly constitutes instructional level, but materials in which the child misses no more than five words per hundred and that are interesting to the student are ideal. Fortunately, you have a wealth of easy materials to choose from. The best list of easy-to-read books can be found in Marianne Lanino Pilla's *The Best High/Low Books for Reluctant Readers* (1990). In this book, she describes 374 books that she has found to be accessible and appealing to reluctant readers. Of course, new books are being published at a phenomenal rate, so you should be constantly on the lookout for easy books that appeal to your students.

In addition to high/low series of books, many other books have a particular appeal to struggling readers. Many teachers find that their students like to read books that relate to movies and TV shows, such as the *Star Wars* books and *Voyager* books. Many struggling readers enjoy books about real things, such as David Macaulay's books *Pyramids* and *Cathedral* or the Time-Life *How Things Work*, *Ripley's Believe It or Not*, and *The Baseball Encyclopedia*. Cartoon characters such as Garfield and Heathcliff are enormously popular with some intermediate-aged children. Comic books have long been a mainstay of preteen reading and actually require sophisticated reading skills to follow what is happening.

So your first task is to find some books that will interest your student and that the student will be able to read with some help from the tutor. If your student is a "nonreader" or such a beginning reader that you cannot find anything, you will have to create the materials. This is not as hard as it sounds. Simply sit down with your struggling reader and write an introductory paragraph of five or six sentences about him.

Carlton is nine years old. He goes to Washington School. He is in the fourth grade. Mrs. Cunningham is his teacher. He likes Washington School. He likes Mrs. Cunningham too.

This paragraph will become the reading material he reads with the tutor for the next several days until he can read it fluently and knows most of the words in it. When he demonstrates to you that he can do this, ask him what else he would like the book to tell about him and have him watch while you write the second page:

Carlton has six brothers and sisters. Their names are Robert, David, Manuel, Thomas, Patrice, and Jackie. They live on Willow Road. His father works at the Ford place. His mother works at Ken's Quik-Mart. His cousin, Travis, lives with them too.

RECOMMENDED RESOURCES _____

Easy but Interesting Books

Any list of high/low books is out of date before it is published, but the following list is a sampling to give you some idea of the variety available and to entice you to find some books that will appeal to your kids:

Eek: Stories to Make You Shriek! (Grosset and Dunlap). Easy-reader chapter books in which children experience scary, spooky—but not violent—adventures.

Eye Witness Books (Dorling Kindersly). Science and social studies topics—rocks, birds, machines, and so forth in an attractive, highly visual format.

Bridgestone Early Reader Science (Capstone). Reading levels 1–3. Our favorite is the transportation set, featuring bulldozers, fire trucks, freight trains, and tractors.

Capstone High–Low Nonfiction (Capstone). Dozens of theme sets on reading levels 3–4. Our favorites are the set on lizards and the one on racing, which includes hot rods and stock cars.

The Reading Scene (Continental Press). Each book contains four (7-page) stories. Mysteries, biographies (including those of Bruce Springsteen and Bill Cosby), and young adolescent problems are the major topics covered.

Galaxy 5 (Fearon, David S. Lake Publishers). This science fiction series of 6 books (60 pages each) follows the adventures of the crew of the spaceship *Voyager* as it establishes a colony of humans on a far-off planet.

Laura Brewster Books (Fearon, David S. Lake Publishers). This mystery series

of 6 books (60 pages each) finds a jeans-clad Laura Brewster roaming the world and solving mysteries for her insurance company employer.

Sportellers (Fearon, David S. Lake Publishers). This series of 8 (60-page) books gives a fictionalized account of how stars in various sports train and grow.

Tom and Ricky Mystery Series (High Noon Books). This series of 10 (45-page) books, and several other series also published by High Noon, have reading levels of first and second grade and are particularly helpful in providing easy reading material to very poor readers for whom English is a second language.

Great Lives (Scholastic). This is one of several themed collections available. The series focuses on biographies of famous Americans and offers links to social studies topics.

Concept Science (Modern Curriculum Press). This series includes 44 titles, such as *Earthworms Are Animals* and *Our Changing Earth*. The books are available in Spanish.

World of Dinosaurs (Steck-Vaughn-Raintree). This series includes 10 books and offers short, easy-reading opportunities about a most popular topic.

The procedure continues with the teacher creating the pages of Carlton's book and the tutor reading and rereading them with Carlton until he can fluently read each page and most of the words. Future pages tell about any pets Carlton has, places he has gone, friends and what they do together, foods he likes to eat, jobs he does at home, things he does not like, and so forth. Once Carlton can fluently read this beginning book, he will have a good bank of known high-frequency words and should begin being tutored in one of the easiest high/low books.

Once the material has been chosen or created for the child to read, tutoring procedures follow a predictable pattern.

1. The child rereads pages for several days. After reading each page, the child puts checkmarks on index cards next to previously missed words that he or she was able to read correctly today. Words with three checks are "retired."
2. The tutor and child preview a new book or several new pages of a book, naming things, talking about what is happening in the pictures, and reading any headings or labels.
3. The child reads one page without help from the tutor, figuring out words in whatever way he or she can.
4. The tutor points out good strategies the reader used: sounding out an unfamiliar word, using picture clues, going back and correcting at the end of a sentence, and so on.
5. The tutor then points out any words that the child did not read correctly and helps the child figure them out by showing the child how the picture, the letters in the word, and the sense of the sentence help with that word.
6. The tutor writes the missed words on index cards along with the page number on which they were missed.
7. The same procedure is repeated with each page. Pictures, headings, and labels are discussed. The page is read by the child unaided. The tutor points out good strategies the reader used and then gives help with missed words. The missed words are written on index cards with the page number.
8. When several pages have been read and three to six missed words are written on cards, the tutor and child return to the first page read that day. The missed words are displayed in front of the child, but they are not pronounced by the tutor or the child. When the child has finished the page, he puts a check next to any word correctly read in the text this time. The tutor and the child talk about words that were not correctly read and how they can be figured out. The child continues to reread pages with the index-card words for that page visible as he reads, checking those correctly read when the page is finished and getting help with those incorrectly read.
9. The word cards are put in an envelope and clipped to the book and are ready for the next day's reading.
10. Together, the tutor and the child write in a notebook a sentence or two summarizing what was read today. The child and the tutor first agree on what to write. Then the child writes, getting help from the tutor with spelling as needed. The tutor and child decide on one word each day to add to the child's portable word wall folder. This folder has the alphabet letters and spaces for words needed. By having the folder open while writing, the child can quickly find a word he or she remembers deciding that he or she needs to learn to spell.

A	B	C	D	E	F
are	before	can't	don't	enough	first
also		could			favorite
about					

G	H	I	J	K	L
getting	have	I'm		know	let's
		into		knew	

M	N	O	P	Q	R
myself	new	one	people		really
		our			

S	T	U	V	W	X	YZ
said	then	until	very	want		your
school	there			was		you're
	threw			wear		
	to			whether		

For Carlton's book, this procedure should be varied somewhat. Because Carlton knows almost no words, each sentence should be written on a sentence strip, read, and then cut into words. Carlton should reassemble the words to match each sentence in the paragraph. Eventually, he should make the whole paragraph by matching and assembling the cut-apart words. Carlton should write a sentence at the end of each day, perhaps choosing his favorite sentence from the paragraph and then trying to write it without looking with spelling help from the tutor. He and the tutor decide on a word each day to add to his word wall folder, and Carlton learns to find and use these words to help him write his sentence each day.

As you can tell, the trickiest part of this tutoring is finding the right book. If you find a book in which the child is missing a word every 20 words or so, the reading is fluent enough so that the child can figure out words and self-correct. The number of missed words you write on index cards is small enough so that the child is able to learn these words and accumulate the three checks necessary to retire them. Once you have the tutoring set up, you need to monitor the progress of the child. When children are accumulating few index-card words, it is time to move them to slightly harder books. Now how can you find this tutor? Consider these possibilities:

1. Do you know a parent who drops off or picks up at school every day and could stay 30 minutes or come 30 minutes early? Many parents are on a tight schedule, but most schools have some parents with the flexibility to spend 30 minutes tutoring a child if they know they are needed and have a specific, workable tutoring system such as that just described.

2. Does a capable lunchroom worker or bus driver have 30 minutes a day to spare? Some part-time workers would love to have the opportunity to make a difference in the life of a child. Some schools even have money to pay this person a little extra each week for the extra hours worked.

3. Does a high school nearby begin or end earlier or later than your school? Many high schools encourage (or even require!) volunteer service by their students. Perhaps a future teacher would love to have the experience tutoring your child could offer.

4. Does your school have older students, one of whom might be your tutor? Ask a teacher friend who teaches older children if some student could afford the half-hour it would take each day to tutor your child. The schedule could be staggered so that the tutor did not miss the same thing each day, or the tutor could come when other students are going to band, chorus, and so forth.

5. Do you have a student who could be the tutor? If you are an intermediate teacher and you have a sophisticated, nurturing, budding teacher in your classroom, you may already have the help you need. Most intermediate-aged children are not sophisticated or dedicated enough to do this, but there is often one in every class.

6. If you cannot get one person to come for 30 minutes every day, could you get four people to come for 2 hours 1 day each week? One school found four retired people willing to give up one afternoon each week to tutor children. Two teachers worked together to find and train these tutors. On their day each week, each tutor worked individually with four children, two from each class. Each tutor knew the procedures and each wrote a note in the child's notebook for the next day's tutor, telling how far they had gotten and pointing out any "good things" the child had done that day. On Friday, the classroom teachers took turns meeting with each child being tutored while the other teacher read to both classes. During this Friday time, they monitored the progress of each child and decided when to move each child to higher-level books. They also wrote a note in the child's notebook letting the tutors know how much progress each child was making and how appreciative they were of the help.

> **A MODEL FOR VOLUNTEER TUTORS**
>
> The University of Virginia sponsors a volunteer tutoring program. The program is organized by reading specialists and graduate students. Their job is to determine reading levels for children and take running records on books read. They put critical words on cards in pockets in the back of books. When a child has read that book and learned the words, these word cards are added to the child's shoebox word bank. The tutor makes a duplicate set of word cards to replace those in the pocket. Each child's shoebox word bank has an alphabet strip and sound boxes taped on the outside. For more details, see Invernezzi, Juel, and Rosemay (1997).

PARTNER OLDER STRUGGLING READERS TO TUTOR YOUNGER STRUGGLING READERS

This idea is based on a tutoring program set up at Webster Magnet School in Minnesota (Taylor, Hansen, Swanson, & Watts, 1998). Fourth graders who were reading at beginning third-grade level tutored second graders, most of whom were reading at primer level. The second graders were all participating in an early-intervention program in their classroom in which they read books on their level. The fourth graders spent 45 minutes on Monday and Tuesday with the reading coordinator or with their classroom teacher preparing for their 25-minute tutoring session on Wednesday and Thursday. On Monday, the fourth graders selected a picture book to read to their second grader and practiced reading the book. They also practiced word recognition prompts that they would use when their second grader read to them. On Tuesday, they practiced again and developed extension activities to develop comprehension strategies, including story maps and character sketches. They came up with several good discussion questions based on the picture book they were planning to read.

On Wednesday and Thursday, the fourth graders met with their tutees. During this session, they listened to their second grader read the book currently being read in their classroom's early-intervention program. While listening, they helped their second graders identify words by giving them hints: "Look at the picture"; "It starts with *pr*"; "Sound in and out in chunks—what would this part be (covering all but the first syllable)?" Next they read from the picture book they had chosen, built meaning vocabulary from the book, led a discussion based on their discussion questions, and did the comprehension extension activity.

On Friday, the fourth graders had debriefing sessions with their teacher in which they discussed how their tutees reacted to the book, how well their word recognition prompts were working, the success of their discussion and comprehension activities, as well as problems encountered and progress noticed. They also wrote a letter to project coordinators detailing the successes and problems of that week. They received a response to their letter on Monday.

Data reported on this project show that both the second- and fourth-grade struggling readers made measurable progress. This is not surprising because this program combines all the elements essential for reading growth. Second graders were getting daily guided reading instruction in materials at their level in their classrooms. In addition, during the tutoring session, they were reading material at their level to someone who knew how to help them with word recognition. They were also increasing their knowledge stores and comprehension strategies as they listened to their fourth-grade tutor read the picture book to them and as they engaged in the discussion and comprehension activities. Fourth graders got lots of practice using the material at their instructional level, reading the picture book, and learning word recognition and comprehension strategies, as they prepared and carried out the tutoring with their second grader.

Getting this to work would take some organization and if you have a reading coordinator/specialist at your school, it would be good to get him or her involved. Given the results reported and the "just plain sensible" nature of the cross-age tutoring program, you are almost guaranteed to "get your money's worth" out of the time required to set up such a program.

COORDINATE WITH REMEDIAL READING AND RESOURCE ROOM TEACHERS

Many struggling readers participate in remedial or resource room instruction in addition to classroom reading instruction. Such programs can provide much-needed support for the children, but they can also result in a confusing and unhelpful conglomeration of reading lessons and activities. Special programs are most effective when they provide supportive instruction that is designed to ease the difficulties that participating children are having in their classrooms.

To accomplish this, however, means that remedial and special education teachers must be familiar with the classroom reading program. New federal regulations for remedial and special education programs promote cooperative planning of instruction between classroom teachers and specialist teachers. In addition, the support instruction must be designed to improve classroom performance. The goal of these regulations is to accelerate children's reading development to move them back into the classroom with no further need for assistance.

Struggling readers who participate in remedial or resource room instructional support programs are the very children who need the kind of reading instruction that is coherently planned and richly integrated. We have seen a variety of ways in which classroom teachers work with support teachers to develop such programs.

RECOMMENDED RESOURCES

Early Success is a small-group intervention program for grades 1 and 2 based on Barbara Taylor's Early Intervention in Reading model, which many classroom teachers have found very useful and usable. For older students, *Soar to Success* provides programs for grades 3–8. *Soar to Success* uses real books and a reciprocal teaching framework for instruction. Both programs have a solid research base. (*Early Success* and *Soar to Success* are both published by Houghton Mifflin.) Information about these programs can be found on their website, http://www.hmco.com.

In one school, the support teachers come into the classrooms to work with participating children. They support the children's progress through both the basal and trade books that are used in the core-reading/language arts program. The special teachers may have the children reread a story and work on fluency and self-monitoring behaviors. At times, they reteach a strategy lesson from the basal or model summary writing for a *Weekly Reader* article. These teachers work with both small groups and individuals depending on the classroom and the students. With support teachers in the room working at supporting progress through the core curriculum, less time is needed to meet and plan instructional roles.

In another school, the support teachers work in the classroom occasionally but more often work on extending classroom reading lessons in another room. In this case, the coordination is achieved through the use of a traveling notebook that the teachers have children carry back and forth each day. Both teachers jot down comments about what they are working on and the problems or successes the children had that day. The notebook allows the support program teacher to monitor core-curriculum lessons and to develop lessons that extend or support this learning.

In another school, the support teachers work only with the trade books that children are reading in the classrooms. The support teachers focus on extending comprehension of the stories being read in the classroom by working with children to develop scripts from books and stories, and to develop performances of these. Another example of classroom/special teacher coordination is found in one school where the sixth graders who attend the remedial program read trade books linked to their social studies curriculum. With the support of the specialist, these struggling readers read historical fiction and biographies; this adds greatly to their background knowledge and allows them to be active participants in social studies class discussions. A similar link could also be made between reading and science.

What is common among the very best remedial and special education programs is that children spend most of their time actually reading and writing in a way that supports classroom success. The support children receive from the specialist teacher provides immediate returns in improved reading and writing during classroom instruction.

INCREASE THE SUPPORT YOU ARE PROVIDING YOUR TWO-LANGUAGE CHILDREN

A decade ago, in many parts of the country, teachers did not have children in their classrooms whose first language was not English. This is no longer the case. All over the country, in urban and rural areas, children come to school speaking little or no English. These children usually take longer to become literate. This is not surprising because they must learn another language at the same time that they are expected to learn to read, write, and increase their content knowledge. No agreement exists about the best way to help these children achieve literacy. Bilingual programs provide some instruction (including reading and writing) in the first language of the child as he or she is learning English. Bilingual programs, as their name suggests, have as their goal that the child becomes literate in both languages. In ESL programs, more emphasis is placed on the child's acquiring English and providing support for the child as English is acquired. Many teachers have strong opinions about the ESL versus bilingual issue, but often they have no choice but to provide the best literacy instruction they can for their two-language children.

Many of the strategies described in this and other chapters of the book that help struggling readers in general also help two-language children. The following list contains instructional practices generally agreed to support the literacy of all children having difficulty, including two-language children. You are probably already doing most of these and may indeed be doing more than you realize.

   1. *Cooperative groupings.* Christian Faltis, in his excellent book *Joinfostering: Adapting Teaching Strategies for the Multilingual Classroom,* has many practical tips for making small-group work more productive for two-language children. These include the following eight tips:

- Keep group size at three or four so that two-language children feel a need to participate.
- Encourage everyone to participate using devices such as talking chips in which each person puts down a chip after speaking and no one is allowed to add a second chip until everyone has put one down.
- Play Paraphrasing Passport in which each person must paraphrase the previously given idea before giving a new idea.
- Conduct three-step interviewing in which pairs of children interview each other about a question and then share the results of the interviews with the group of four.
- Make sure that group members all face each other so that they can hear each other clearly.
- Make sure that group tasks promote positive interdependence in which students cannot successfully complete the task without the active participation of all members of the group.
- Teach individual accountability with activities such as Paraphrasing Passport, three-step interviews, and Numbered Heads.
- Play Numbered Heads, an activity in which each member of the group is designated by the numbers 1, 2, 3, or 4. As each task or question is posed to the group, the whole group discusses and agrees on a response that is then given by whatever numbered head the teacher calls out.

   2. *Partner activities.* Two heads are better than one! Whether it is partner reading or writing or a think-pair-share activity children learn from each other. This is particularly true for two-language children, who are often hesitant to talk in a group. Your child, who is learning English, will benefit more from the partnership if you consider carefully with whom to partner him or her. Look for a child who is nurturing, clever in explaining things, and alert to nonverbal signals. If you have another child who speaks the same language as the child you are supporting, but who is more proficient in English, you may want to partner these children together if your concern is with content learning because that child's bilingualism may allow things to be explained. But if your concern is primarily language development, you may want to rely on a nurturing partner who does not speak the first language of the child being supported.

3. *Graphic organizers for reading and writing.* Webs, time lines, double bubbles (Venn diagrams), and story maps show relationships without using all the connecting words that are often confusing for children learning English. Using these devices before reading helps two-language children focus on important words and makes the purpose for reading clearer. When used as organizing frameworks before writing, they help fledgling English writers create more coherent texts.

4. *Picture walks and other attention to visuals.* A picture is worth a thousand words for children learning a new language. Use picture walks before reading, and let your students name what they see in the picture and then try to find a written word on the page to match the spoken word. Help all your students, but especially your children learning English, to become excellent interpreters of diagrams, maps, graphs, and other visual displays that require minimal word reading. Finally, instead of always requiring a written or spoken response, have your children respond to their reading using visuals—pictures, diagrams, graphs, and so on. An excellent source for lots of ways to use visuals and lots of ways to have children learn to create visuals is Steve Moline's *I See What You Mean: Children at Work with Visual Information.*

5. *Real things.* Real things are always motivating to children, and for children learning a new language, they are crucial. Point to things in your room as you give directions. Bring in things that connect with what your students are going to read during guided reading. Make sure that your science, social studies, and math activities are as centered in manipulatives as possible.

6. *Predictable text.* Predictable text, in which sentence patterns repeat and pictures support the words, help two-language children get a jump-start in reading and expand the oral sentence patterns they can use in speaking.

7. *Reading to children.* It would be hard to overstate the benefits of reading to children from a variety of different books. If you have two-language children in your classroom, be alert for idioms, multimeaning words, homophones, and other language peculiarities that make sense to you but are always difficult when learning a new language. Read the book for enjoyment and/or information and then return to those difficult language structures and use the full context of the book, pictures, and so on to clarify the meaning of the word or phrase.

8. *Providing time for self-selected reading and conferencing.* Self-selected reading time is critical for children learning a new language. They need to be encouraged to read and reread books, and they need help in choosing books with pictures and predictable text. When you conference with them, let them show and tell you what they liked and then ask them to find some parts that were confusing to them so that you can help them understand. You may want to give your two-language child a pack of little sticky notes to stick on confusing places so that they can quickly find the things they did not understand. You may also want to let them choose a friend to read with them during self-selected reading time so that they can get lots of language about the book they have chosen.

9. *Prereading activities that build prior knowledge and set purposes and postreading activities that follow up purposes and help students monitor comprehension.* These help all readers but are critical for children trying to read and comprehend in a language that they are learning at the same time.

10. *A print-rich classroom.* Rooms with a word wall, a theme board containing both words and pictures, environmental print, labels, and signs all promote reading, writing, and language development.

11. *Every-pupil response activities.* Activities such as Making Words and others in which all children, rather than just one child, respond promote student engagement and are less threatening than activities in which one child is called on and singled out. Teachers with two-language children can also make use of a variety of every pupil's response techniques, including using yes/no cards, numbers of fingers held up, and a variety of gestures to help students stay involved and to show what they know as they develop their oral language facility.

S U M M A R Y

Most classrooms contain two levels of struggling readers. Some children have a literacy level that is close to grade level but need to become more thoughtful readers and writers. Often they need more experience with text found in science and social studies and with the big words that comprise these informational texts. Most of these struggling readers can achieve basic and even proficient levels of reading and writing if their elementary years are rich in the type of instruction described in the previous chapters of this book.

This chapter has described a variety of ways teachers can organize and "mobilize" to meet the needs of children whose literacy levels are way below the levels of others in the class. Teachers who have several children for whom the material read in guided reading is not at instructional level can hold short after-lunch bunch easy-reading sessions. Everyone is included on some days, but the children who really need this extra reading are asked to join the group more often. Teachers might find the time to meet with this easy-reading group and to meet other individual needs by scheduling 30 minutes of open centers sometime in the day. In addition to freeing up the teacher to meet whatever needs are most pressing that day, the open-center time allows children to pursue their own interests in a variety of ways.

Children who find learning to read particularly difficult often benefit from a period of regular tutoring in addition to all the classroom instruction. If carefully structured, tutoring can be provided by a variety of people, including older struggling readers. The most effective teachers are informed about what is happening to their children when they are with special teachers and work with those teachers to provide a "nonfragmented," "noncontradictory" instructional program. Finally, many two-language children need additional support in learning to read and write. Eleven tried-and-true classroom practices that enhance the learning of all children, including two-language children, were described.

CHAPTER 9

A Day in a Building Blocks Kindergarten Classroom

In previous chapters, you learned that many children have had 1,000 or more hours of "informal" literacy encounters before coming to school. From these encounters, they develop critical understanding about the nature of reading and writing and the "I can" attitudes toward their inevitable inclusion into the literate community.

1. They know that when you read or write, you are trying to understand or communicate some information or story.
2. They know reading and writing are two important things that everyone who is bigger than them can do and that they too must learn to do because they want to be big.
3. They know from the overwhelming adult approval and pleasure at their fledgling attempts at pretend reading, at reading some signs and labels, and at writing that they are succeeding at mastering this mysterious code.

Our major literacy goal in kindergarten should be to simulate the reading and writing encounters many children have had that led them to develop these critical understandings and attitudes. It is important to think of at-risk kindergartners primarily as children who have had few experiences with print, stories, and books. Thinking of these children as "inexperienced" creates a different view of their instructional needs than thinking of them as "developmentally delayed," "language impaired," "slow," "unready," or any of the other labels commonly given to children who enter school inexperienced in literacy activities. The critical nature of providing these children with a print-rich, story-rich, book-rich classroom becomes clear when we take this view. The rest of this chapter is devoted to how one day might look in a Building Blocks kindergarten.

8:00–8:45 Choice Centers

The children arrive at different times, depending on buses, rides, and so forth. They come to the classroom immediately and, once in the classroom, come to one of the many centers in the room. During this time, they can choose to go to any center as long as there is space at that center. Each center has a limited number of tickets that are laminated and strung with yarn. The children choose a ticket, put the ticket on, and then go to that center. They can stay at each center as long as they like but must return that center's ticket and get another one before moving to another center.

The teacher spent a lot of time and effort at the beginning of the year helping the children learn what they could and could not do at each center, how to clean up the center before they left, and so on. This initial effort paid off; now there are seldom problems with behavior and routines during center time.

During center time, the teacher circulates throughout the room, greeting children and helping them get the day off to a good start. As always, she has her file folder labels on a clipboard, and when she notices accomplishments, problems, or other things that she wants to remember, she records them by putting the child's initials, date, and the comment she wants to make on one of the labels. At the end of the day, she peels off these labels and attaches them to each child's anecdotal record folder. Today she jots down notes about the child "reading" a little book in the library corner to a stuffed animal, noting that his voice sounds like a reading voice and that he is doing a good job of telling a story that matches the pictures. She also notes that another child is drawing at the writing table and "reads" her drawing when asked by the teacher. Also at the table is a child who has created strings of letters in rows and "reads" her "writing." The notes describe the different levels of conceptual development that each child exhibits about writing.

The teacher tries to talk to each child during the morning center time and spends a few extra minutes with the children she has identified as being most needy. For her children whose English is limited, either because English is not their first language or because they have had few real conversations with adults, she makes sure to engage them in some conversation about what they are doing at the center. She points to things in the pictures they have painted or to their block construction and fosters their talk with her by asking what they are doing. She asks them about the little books that they are "reading" and about the writing they produce. Because these conversations are one-on-one and are related to something they actually are doing, the children are more willing to talk than they are in a small-group or whole-class setting. She also notices that the children talk with each other more during center time. In fact, knowing that listening and speaking are major goals of kindergarten, she encourages this child-to-child talk as she visits the various centers and engages the children in conversations in which she gets them to talk to one another about what they are doing.

8:45–9:15 Opening, Calendar, Morning Message

When the teacher goes to the rocking chair and sits down, the children realize that center time is over. They quickly clean up what they have been working on and come sit on the floor in front of her. The teacher begins the big-group activities with the usual questions: What day is it today? What was yesterday? What day will tomorrow be? What is the date? What is the weather? How many days have we been in school? The children answer each question, then find the word cards (Thursday, Wednesday, Friday, March 24, windy) to finish the sentences on the sentence strips in the pocket chart. They count the twelve bundles of "tens" and the eight "ones" and talk about what they will do today in kindergarten.

Now the teacher picks up a black marker and gets ready to write on a large piece of lined chart paper. She writes the morning message on the chart paper as all her children watch. She does not talk (as she did at the beginning of the year) but instead writes quietly as the students read quietly her daily greeting—"Dear Class." She begins her message by asking what day it is. The children respond, "Today is Thursday." She asks the children how to spell *today*, and they quickly answer, "*t-o-d-a-y*." They also know how to spell *is* and *Thursday*. Those children who are not sure look on the sentence strips in the pocket chart nearby to help spell Thursday. The teacher writes three more sentences: March is a windy month. Today is a windy day! Can we fly a kite outside?"

After she finishes the morning message by writing *Love* and her name at the end, she lowers the chart paper and asks, "Who can count the words in these sentences?" The teacher calls on a student who could not count when school began and praises him for correctly counting the words in each sentence. Next, she asks, "What do you notice?" The children notice many things—the words they know, the capital letter at the beginning of each sentence, the periods, exclamation point, and question mark at the end of the sentences, and so forth. To end this big-group session the teacher leads the children in some of their favorite marching and moving songs and closes with some fingerplays using familiar rhymes; she knows that a few children still need this practice to strengthen their phonemic awareness.

9:15–9:45 Shared Reading

The teacher takes out the big book *Brown Bear, Brown Bear, What Do You See?* by Bill Martin. It is clear from the children's response that they have read this book before. First, the teacher points to the name of the book on the cover. She reads, "Brown Bear" with the children. Next, she points to the author's name, Bill Martin, as she reads that with the children.

Before reading the teacher begins the lesson by reviewing the colors and animals in this book. First, she holds up a brown circle and asks, "What color is this?" Then she asks, "What animal in the book is brown?" She encourages the students to remember what animal is coming next and what color it is. At first this is easy, but after several animals the children become confused. She continues putting the red, yellow, blue, gray, purple, green, pink, white, black, and orange circles in a row in the pocket chart and talks about which animal is that color. "Now, let's read this story together and see whether we put the colors in the right order and remembered all the animals in this book."

The children join in and share the reading of this big book with the teacher. She points to the words as the children read in chorus with her:

"Brown bear, brown bear, what do you see?"

Before turning the page she asks the children whether they remember what animal is next. The children know the red bird is next. She turns the page, and the children are delighted to see that they are correct. Led by the teacher, who continues to point to words, they all read:

"I see a red bird looking at me.

Red bird, red bird, What do you see?"

The teacher and the children continue in this manner until they have completed the book. After the book has been read and enjoyed one more time, the teacher reviews the sequence of this book by talking about the colors in the pocket chart and the animals they read about. Did they put them in the right order? Yes!

The teacher gets the wiggles out by having the children move like the animals in the book. She then passes out color circles to the children, although fewer colors are passed out than are in the book. The teacher then puts on a tape recording of their favorite color song by Hap Palmer. The children stand up, sit down, and march around the room as they sing along with the tape and follow the directions for whatever color circle they are holding.

9:45–10:15 Writing

After this brief but essential break, the children settle back down while the teacher picks up a marker and gets ready to write. She thinks aloud about what she might write. She models different levels of writing on different days. Sometimes she drites, both drawing and writing on a blank page. Other times she writes a few sentences. Still other days she adds to some sentences written previously and writes a complete paragraph. As she writes, she models invent-spelling some words for the children. She says the word aloud very slowly and writes down some letters to represent the sounds she hears. In this way she demonstrates for the children many different levels of writing and shows them that all these ways of writing are acceptable.

On this day she writes two sentences:

Mr. Hinkle will vizit us after lunch.

He will bring his pet turtl.

She does not read the words aloud as she writes them, except when she models invented spelling for the children by saying a word very slowly. The children watch closely and try to read what she is writing. Many of them recognize the words *Mr., lunch,* and *pet.* She then draws a simple picture to illustrate the sentence and labels the drawings of Mr. Hinkle and the turtle. Even though (or perhaps because) she is not artistic, the children love to watch her draw. Once her drawing is complete, she reads what she has written, pointing to each word as she does. The children are amazed to hear that Mr. Hinkle, who teaches fourth grade, has a pet turtle. They also point to her stick figure drawing of him and remark that they cannot wait for Mr. Hinkle to see his picture! The teacher promises to hide it before he arrives!

The teacher asks the children what they are going to write about today. As each child tells the teacher what he or she is going to write about, they stand up and go back to their tables where their writing journals are waiting for them. As the children write, the teacher circulates around the room, encouraging or coaching children as needed.

10:15–10:45 Recess/Snack

As the children line up to go outside, the teacher picks a child and asks the child what letter she or he wants the children to be as they go outside. The child thinks and decides that they should all be M's today. The teacher lets that child lead the line, and all the children march to the playground because *march* is the action they have learned for the letter *m.* (Earlier in the year, they learned an action for each consonant letter. Now, they review this every day by performing the correct action on the way to the playground. On days when they have to stay inside during recess, they play games in which they review all their letter actions.)

When they return to the classroom, they find some peanuts on each of their desks. They look up at the food board and notice that the teacher has attached a picture from the peanut jar to the space under the letter *p.* As they munch on their peanuts, and whatever else they might have brought for snack time, they review the other foods on their food board. So far, only five letters have food pictures attached to them:

b–bananas, *d*–donuts, *m*–milk, *j*–juice, *p*–peanuts

The children are curious about what foods might go with the other letters. They make the sounds of the letters and try to predict what they might find for a snack one day. One child says he hopes there are hamburgers for *h,* but another child protests, "She won't bring us hamburgers for snacks!" The teacher picks up on their conversation and helps them think about possibilities for the various letters. She suggests that, as they eat lunch today and when they eat meals and snacks at home, they should look at the packages and think about what letters begin the names of these foods.

10:45–11:45 Assigned Centers

During this time, the children go to centers once more, but, unlike the morning hour when they choose centers and activities, now they are assigned to centers and the children all rotate through all the activities. Today, the teacher has set up four centers, and children are to spend 15 minutes in each. Before they go to the centers, she directs their attention to each center and makes sure they know what they are going to do.

In the math center today, she has put a pile of the laminated words used in yesterday's Being the Words activity for *Brown Bear* and has designated eight baskets with a number from 1 to 8. The children's job in the math center today is to take the words from *Brown Bear*, count the letters in each word, and put them in the appropriate basket. She points out the baskets designated 1–8 and helps the children see that some words only have one letter and that the longest words have eight letters. She reminds the children that, at the math center, they work with their partner and take turns counting and then checking each other. She has a math partnership come up to demonstrate how one child picks up a word, counts the letters, and points to the basket that the word goes in. The partner's job is to play teacher and respond with encouragement, "Right!" or to give help, "Let's count those letters again." After each word is counted, the partners switch roles. The one who counted first becomes teacher for the second word, and so on.

The children have been working with partners in the math center, alternating the teacher/student roles for several weeks now. They understand the procedures, and even though they have not counted letters in words before, they have counted all kinds of concrete objects. She reminds the children that they will spend 15 minutes in the math center and will not have time to count the letters in all the words: "Just count and sort until your math center time is up," she encourages them.

The activity at the next center takes little explanation. The children are making their own take-home books patterned on the *Brown Bear* book. Their book is about the animals you might see in a zoo. Each day they make a page by tracing the printed sentence at the bottom and drawing a picture to illustrate that page. On one side of today's page, they trace:

I see a yellow lion looking at me.

Printed on the back is the sentence:

Yellow lion, yellow lion, what do you see?

The teacher picks up one of these dittoed sheets and reads it to the children. She also points to several books that are opened to display various lions and reminds the children that their lion should be yellow, but that it can be as big or as scary or as cuddly as they like. "People who draw the illustrations in books use their imaginations to make their illustrations different from anyone else's," she says.

The third center that the children visit today is the listening center. Here they listen to a tape of two books about real animals. The teacher picks up the books and quickly shows them some pictures, reminding them that they have been studying animals and reading books about how real animals live and what they do, and have also been reading silly books about imaginary animals. Today, they listen to two books about real animals and perhaps learn some facts to add to the animal chart this afternoon. As she says this, their eyes turn to a data chart made by stringing yarn along a bulletin board. Going down the chart are the names and pictures of some animals that are being studied. The columns across are labeled with words such as *eat, move, live, body covering,* and so forth. The teacher reminds them that the chart is not yet finished; where there are spaces they need to add information for the animals that are listed as well as add five more animals. The teacher reminds them that because there is only one book, the group leader of the day gets to turn the pages and must try to hold the book so that everyone can see.

Finally, the teacher points to the writing center. The writing center has a variety of things to write and draw on and with. Besides paper, index cards, labels, postcards, and old stationery are available. The teacher reminds the children that she wants them to write something in addition to drawing something, and that scribble writing and one-letter writing is fine as long as they know what they are writing.

For the next hour, the children rotate in 15-minute blocks through each of the four centers. The children are assigned to groups, each of which contains the whole range of children—from those most experienced with print to those least experienced, and from the most agreeable to the most difficult. Each group has a leader for the day. This child is "in charge" at the center and sees to it that materials are put away and are ready for the next group as they leave each center. As the children work, the teacher circulates with a clipboard and file folder labels in hand. She stops for a few minutes at each center and makes observations and/or gives help as needed.

While observing in the math center, she notices one child counting the letters in a word, from right to left. She stops and explains to this child that we always have to start the other way when we read words and that it is important to always go a certain way when we look at the letters in a word. She then helps the child count some letters correctly and notes this directional confusion on a label that she will attach to his folder. Having seen one child do this, she is alerted to this problem, which other children might have. As the group rotates into the math center, she notices that several children are counting the letters from right to left. She notes this on labels and makes a note to herself to pull these children together soon and work on left-to-right directionality with them.

As she observes the children in the listening center, she notices that two children are very inattentive to the tape. One child has a very limited use of English.

The other is a very "antsy" child. She worries about their inattentiveness and decides to think about ways to alleviate it; she makes these notes on the labels.

The children doing the yellow lion page of their take-home book are busy tracing and drawing. Again, she notices some children tracing the letters from right to left. She explains that they must go the other way when they read and that they should trace this way to get in the habit. She helps them get reoriented and again jots a note to herself to pull together the children who lack this print orientation. She begins compiling a list of these children. She asks several children to read their page to her and to touch the words as they read; she notes their success on labels, which she will attach to their folders later.

As she stops in the writing center, she is once more reminded that all children can write, if whatever writing they do is accepted. She picks up a paper that is clearly a list in scribble writing and says, "Read what you wrote to me." The child proceeds to point to each scribble and tells her that these are foods he likes to eat and he then reads his scribbles about the foods. The teacher notes on the child's label that he can read his own scribbles, seems to have top–bottom and left–right orientation, but has not written specific letters yet. Another child has made a drawing of himself and his pet and has labeled the drawing with his name and his pet's name. One child is writing sentences that have many correctly spelled words in them and other words that are clearly readable from his invented spelling. Another child is listing animals, copying the words from the newspaper animal board, from the list of animals on the side of the data chart, and from a book on animals he has picked up from the bookshelf next to the writing center.

The teacher reminds herself that children have various levels of experience. Some children arrived at school understanding that writing is talk written down, but many did not. Some had been writing at home for a long while. Others did not hold their first pencil until starting school. Knowing this and knowing the importance of providing many experiences with written language, she has all the children write every day. She encourages children to write words in any way they can, but some children will not write them unless they know they are writing them correctly! She realizes that by providing acceptance for a variety of writing levels and by providing words available in the room support for children who have to do it right, she allows children to write in whatever ways they can.

11:45–12:15 Lunch

Just before the children line up, the teacher reads the lunch menu. Usually, she just reads it to them, but, capitalizing on their interest in the letters that begin the names of favorite foods, she generates some little riddles to give them clues about the foods on the menu and the beginning letters of the food words.

> "Today, you are having another food that begins with a *p*. The one you are going to have just has cheese on it. I like it with cheese and with another *p* word—*pepperoni!*"

The children make happy sounds as they realize their favorite food—*pizza*—is on the menu.

> "With your pizza, you will have something that is very nutritious and contains lots of vitamins. It has lettuce and other vegetables and begins with an *s*."

Most children guess salad.

> "For dessert, you will have something that comes in different flavors and colors. Sometimes it is yellow, sometimes brown, sometimes white. Today it is white with chocolate frosting and begins with the letter *c*."

The children guess cake and have no trouble guessing that their beverage is the *m* food from their food board—milk.

12:15–12:45 Reading to Children and Self-Selected Reading

When the children arrive back from lunch, some children go to their tables; others go to a corner of the room that contains all the predictable big books that they have read this year; others go to the reading corner that has puppets and stuffed animals in addition to books. An observer would have trouble figuring out which children were supposed to go where, but the children know exactly where to go. Each child has 1 day to read in the reading corner, another day to read big books, and three other days to read at their seats. This procedure has been in place for 2 weeks now and is working quite well. Having all the children spread out in the room created problems because not enough good "spreading-out places" were available. This new arrangement seems to have just the right balance of freedom and structure so that the children spend most of their time actually reading (or pretend reading, if that is what they are doing!).

Reading at their tables, the children find trays of books there. The trays contain a variety of books and are rotated so each table gets a different tray each day. One tray is filled with animal books—the topic they are studying in a combined science/social studies unit. Included in the tray are the two books children listened to at the listening center this morning. Many of these books are too hard for most of the children to read, but they love talking about the pictures and do find some animal names they recognize.

A second tray contains books gathered up for the last topic studied—weather. The children enjoy looking at these books, most of which have been read to them. Many children can read the predictable books, such as *What Makes the Weather?* and *Our Friend, the Sun*. Another tray of books contains "oldies but goodies," which the children request to have read again and again. All children can make some attempt at reading favorites such as *Go Dog Go, Clifford the Big Red Dog,* and *The Three Little Pigs*.

A fourth tray contains class books. The books written during shared writing and illustrated by the children are perennial favorites of the children. The first class book contains a photo and a few sentences about each child in the class. This is still one of the most popular books and is reread almost every day by someone. Currently, they are writing and illustrating a class book about animals that will be added to this tray when it is finished.

Two trays of library books also are available. One tray contains books checked out from the public library and the other contains books checked out from the school library. The teacher has arranged with both libraries to check out 20–30 books to keep in the classroom for a month. She chooses two or three children to go with her on a special trip to the public library every month to return the old books and pick out new ones for the public library tray. By the end of the year, all children will have made this special after-school trip. For many children, it is their first trip to the public library, and some of them (and their parents!) are amazed that you can get books to take home "for free." At the end of the year, the whole class makes a trip to this library again, and most of the children get library cards. The monthly trips with two or three children to the public library and the library card field trip takes extra time and effort, but the teacher feels that introducing these children to a free, unlimited source of reading material early on makes the time and effort worthwhile.

Each day, when the children return from lunch, they read books. They can read by themselves or, if they use quiet voices, with a friend who sits near them. The children who go to the book corner often read to the puppets and stuffed animals that reside there.

When the children have read their own books for about 10–15 minutes, the teacher chooses several books or parts of books to read to the class. She chooses from a variety of books, often reading a few pages from an informational book, an old favorite (that the children never tire of having reread to them), and a new book. As she reads aloud, the teacher talks about print and artwork, allowing children to "see" how a good reader thinks while reading. She turns the book to face the children and shows them features of the book.

Today they have a guest reader, Mr. Hinkle. He sits in the rocking chair and shows his turtle to the children gathered at his feet. He talks to the children about the turtle and then reads them a book about turtles. When Mr. Hinkle finishes the book, the teacher reminds the children of the three ways children in kindergarten can read books: (1) They can read the words; (2) they can retell the story; or (3) they can read the pictures. The teacher tells the children that most kindergarteners cannot read all the words in the book about turtles. She asks the children how they could read this book if they picked it up from one of the trays. The children quickly tell her they could "read" the pictures.

12:45–1:15 Math

This half-hour is devoted to math. Today children graph their favorite colors and then their favorite animals from *Brown Bear*. Each child is given a bag with buttons inside to graph by color on a laminated mat the teacher passes out. When they finish, they may quietly help the other children at their table.

1:15–1:45 Shared Writing—Predictable Chart

The teacher talks about what a windy month March has been. They talk about the kites they made in the Art Center last week and about the time the wind caught a kite they took out at recess and how the kite soared high into the sky. Then the teacher shows the predictable chart she wrote with their help on Monday and finished on Tuesday. Looking at a piece of lined chart paper, the teacher and the class read the title and the first line together:

> "If I Were a Kite!"
> "I would fly to"

She reminds the children that the first response is from Justin who would fly to New York. She reminds them how she repeated his sentence saying the words and writing them. Each child repeated the predictable phrase, "I would fly to" and finished it the way they wanted. On Wednesday they all "touch read" the sentence they dictated to the teacher.

Today they will build these sentences. The teacher has chosen Raheem's sentence. After writing it on a sentence strip, she cuts the words apart. She gives one word each to five children and hands Raheem his name. Sentence Builders is a favorite activity; children love "being the words" and building sentences in front of their classmates. *I* knows his place at the beginning of the sentence. A little girl has the word *would* and matches it to "would" on the chart and gets in the second spot. The next word is *fly,* and the child with that word counts to three and becomes the third word in the sentence. "*To*" excitedly says, "I know this word. I can read *to!*" She gets in the fourth spot in the sentence. The last word in this sentence is *Kentucky.* One rather large kindergarten boy says, "I am the longest word. I go next. I am *Kentucky.*" Raheem quickly gets in his spot at the end. He knows that the names always go at the end! Once the words are in place, the children who are not being the words for this sentence read the sentence as the teacher moves behind each child holding a word card. The teacher praises the students for doing such a good job. The teacher writes and cuts apart two more sentences and different children get their turns being the words and building the sentences.

Next, the teacher shows the children how she takes her cut-up sentence and pastes the words in the right order at the bottom of a piece of paper. She explains how she is going to illustrate her sentence at the top of this paper. The teacher gives each child in the class their cut-up sentence and a large piece of paper on which they will paste the words in the correct order, then illustrate. Each child makes a page for the class book, *If I Were a Kite.*

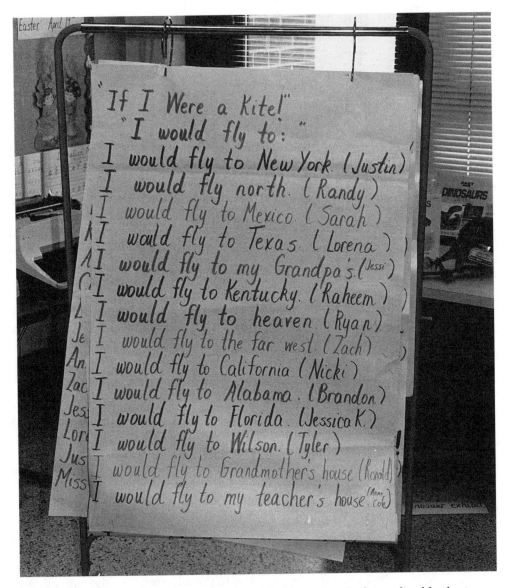

In March, this class studied about, made, and flew kites. Here is the predictable chart on which the teacher recorded where the children would choose to fly if they were a kite.

1:45–2:15 P.E.

As the children march to P.E. class, the teacher leads them in a whisper version of a favorite song, ditty, or rhyme. Today they are marching along to one of the raps recorded by African American poet Lindamichellebaron (*The Sun Is On*, book and tape available from Harlin Jacques Publishers, 507 Panache Suite, 200 Fulton Ave., Hempstead, NY 11550). This use of rhythm and rhyme serves the children because it is fun and helps them develop their phonemic awareness.

2:15–2:45

On three afternoons, the children have this half-hour once again to choose activities in the various centers. One day each week, they go to the computer lab. On another day, today, their "big buddies" from the fifth grade arrive to read and write with the children. Each fifth grader is assigned one kindergarten buddy. They bring a book that they have practiced reading and read it "lap style" to their kindergartener. They then let the kindergartner choose a book to read to them. (It took some explaining, but the fifth graders have learned that pretend reading is a critical beginning reading step, and they now accept whatever kind of reading their kindergartner does.) Next, they write whatever their kindergartner would like them to write in that child's "All About Me" book. They have learned to talk with the child about "the interesting things that have happened since I came last week" and to record some of these things in simple sentences. These weekly journals are records of lost teeth, new jackets, birthdays, family moves, births, and deaths. The children love to have someone record what has happened in their lives, and once today's record is made, they pester their big buddies to "read all about me from the beginning of the year."

2:45 Daily Summary/School–Home Connection

The children prepare to go home. They talk about what they have done today and what they will do tomorrow. They look forward to finishing their pages for the class book on kites. They also are ready to do another page in the take-home zoo animals book they are making.

The teacher lets each of them choose a little book, an index card, and a pencil to put in a reclosable bag. Each night, their "homework" is to read the book to someone or have someone read it to them, and to write or have someone write something for them on the card. Today, given their interest in how foods are spelled, they are to try to copy some names of foods they like from the boxes and cans that they find at home.

Once the children are gone, the teacher peels the file folder labels off the backing and attaches them to the appropriate children's folders. She thinks about how each child is developing in his or her literacy and looks again at the list of literacy goals she has for them:

1. They pretend read favorite books and poems/songs/chants.
2. They write in whatever way they can and can read what they write even if no one else can.
3. They "track print," that is, show you what to read and point to the words using left–right/top–bottom conventions.

4. They know critical jargon, can point to just one word, the first word in the sentence, just one letter, the first letter in the word, the longest word, and so on.

5. They recognize and can write some concrete words—their names, names of other children, and favorite words from books, poems, and chants.

6. They are developing phonemic awareness—including the ability to clap syllables, recognize when words rhyme, make up rhymes, and stretch out words.

7. They can name many letters and tell you words that begin with the common initial sounds.

8. They are learning more about the world they live in and are more able to talk about what they know.

9. They can listen to stories and informational books and can retell the most important information.

10. They see themselves as readers and writers and as new members of the "literacy club."

She feels that, even though they are at very different places, all her kindergartners are making progress toward achieving these critical understandings. Even though some children arrived without print, story, and book experience, her classroom is organized to immerse these children in literacy experiences. These experiences with print, stories, and books form the base for her instructional planning. She thinks about whole-class, small-group, and individual activities she can do tomorrow to further their development.

CHAPTER 10

A Day in a Four Blocks Primary Classroom

The activities described in the kindergarten chapter (Chapter 9) are equally appropriate in first grade, particularly at the beginning of the year. Some children spend the summer in print-rich home environments, but others have few such experiences from the day they leave kindergarten. Re-immersing all children in print-rich classrooms goes a long way in fostering easy and early reactivation of the concepts and strategies they developed last year. Print-rich classrooms, shared reading and writing, opportunities for every child to read and write daily, rhymes and chants to develop phonemic awareness, and opportunities to expand knowledge through science and social studies units are the cornerstones of successful literacy programs for at-risk first graders. The 10 goals listed at the end of the previous chapter are the goals that first-grade teachers must evaluate and work toward as they begin the year.

As children demonstrate that they have the emergent literacy knowings under varying degrees of control, first-grade teachers must provide activities that further the development of reading and writing. We organize important primary-grade activities within a framework we call Four Blocks. These blocks—Guided Reading, Self-Selected Reading, Writing, and Working with Words—provide numerous and varied opportunities for all children to learn to read and write. For more information about Four Blocks, see *The Teacher's Guide to the Four Blocks* (Cunningham, Hall, & Sigmon, 1999) or go to http://www.wfu.edu/~cunningh/fourblocks. The rest of this chapter is devoted to what 1 day in a Four Blocks primary classroom might look like.

8:30–8:50 Opening

The children enter and prepare for the day. When they have their gear stowed, they gather around the teacher. They share things that have happened to them over the weekend, do some calendar activities, and talk about the events planned for the day. Next, the teacher reads a new informational book with lots of pictures of seeds and the plants that grow from them. She tells the children that they will learn much more about seeds and plants as they begin their new science unit. As she finishes reading the book, she places it in the tray labeled Seeds and Plants, which has many other books in it. As she picks up three or four of the other books and shows a few pages of each, she reminds the children that each time they start a new science or social studies unit, she gathers up books from both the school and the public library and puts them in a special tray. The children are all anxious to look at the books, but it is time to get on with other things. They know, however, that this tray of books will be waiting for them during self-selected reading time. Finally, the teacher shows them a seed catalog that she has brought from home, quickly flipping through it and pausing briefly to show a page or two of the illustrations. She then puts the catalog on the tray also.

8:50–9:20 The Working with Words Block

The 2 hours and 15 minutes designated for reading/language arts in this class are divided into four blocks of 30–40 minutes each. The first block this teacher does is the words block. Activities in this block are designed to help children achieve two critical goals. To read and write independently, children must learn to automatically recognize and spell high-frequency words, which occur in almost everything we read and write. They must also learn to look for patterns in words so that they can decode and spell the less frequent words they have not been taught. To accomplish these two goals, the teacher depends on a daily word wall activity and a second activity designed to help the children become better decoders and spellers.

The children are seated at their desks, and because today is Monday, they are eager to see what five new words will be added to the wall today. The teacher looks at Roberto, who just arrived in her classroom last Wednesday, and realizes that he does not really know what the word wall is for. She decides to use this opportunity to remind the children about the importance of the words selected for the word wall.

The teacher begins by directing the children's attention to the bulletin board word wall. She asks the children how many words they think are currently on the word wall and gets some wild guesses. She decides that this is a good math opportunity and leads the children to count the words. There are 95 words. She then asks someone to explain to Roberto how many words are added each Monday and how she decides what words to add.

The children explain that five words are added each week and these are the most important words. When asked what "most important" means, the children explain:

> "You use them all the time," "You can't read and write without them," and "A lot of these words aren't spelled the way they should be, so when you want to write one of the word wall words, you look up there to remember how to spell it instead of trying to figure it out."

"Why are the words arranged according to their first letter?" the teacher asks.

"To make it easier to find them. When you need the word, you just think how it begins and then you can find it faster."

"Why are the words different colors?" she asks.

"To make the word wall pretty," one child explains.

"Well, it does make the word wall pretty to have the different colors, but does it help us in any other way?"

"It helps you remember the words that look almost alike, which word is which—*then* is pink and *them* is green and I can find *them* quicker if I look for the green one under the *t*."

Satisfied that the children understand why learning to read and write these words is so important and how to find them when they need them in writing, she goes on to show the children the five new words that she will add today. She reminds the children of the selections they had read last week during the guided reading time and that she had introduced them to many new words as they read these selections.

"It was hard to choose only five words, but I chose the ones that you see most often in books and that I think you all need when you write. I also chose one word that occurs fairly often but that also begins with a letter for which we don't have any words yet. Some of you have been complaining about not having any words that begin with *q* or *z*, and I have told you that not many words begin with those two letters. But I have been on the lookout for a *q* or *z* word in one of our selections, which you might see in books and need in your writing. Last week, as you were reading, I spotted one."

As she says this, she puts the word *question,* written with a black permanent marker on yellow construction paper, on the word wall next to the *q.* "Remember that everyone kept telling the boy not to ask so many *questions* in the story you read. *Question* will be our word wall *q* word." She then writes *question* on the overhead as the children write it on their handwriting paper. She reminds the children of the proper letter formation as she writes each letter. They seem pleased to have a *q* word on the word wall and are amazed that it is such a big word. The teacher leads them to count the letters in *question* and points out that many of the words we read and write most often are pretty short words.

Taking less time, she adds the other high-frequency words to the wall that were introduced last week during guided reading—*about, where, many, this*—and demonstrates correct letter formation. She has the children write the words on their half-sheet of handwriting paper. Once they have written them on the front, with the teacher's direction for handwriting, the children turn their paper over to the back, and the teacher gives clues to the five words that were just added to the word wall. "The first word I want you to practice is our new *th* word. Who can remember what it is?" The children respond, *"this."* The teacher then points to *this* and has them clap rhythmically and chant the letters three times—*"t-h-i-s, t-h-i-s, t-h-i-s—this!"*

After clapping and chanting the word, they write it on the back of their handwriting paper. The teacher does not demonstrate how to write *this* this time, but she does remind them to make the letters just as they did on the front. She continues to ask them to identify, clap, and chant in this manner, and to write the other four new words that were just added to the word wall. After they have written all five, she demonstrates how to write them once again, and the children check their own papers.

She finishes the word wall activity by reminding the children that on Monday when five new words were added, they practiced only those five new words. "From now on this week, I will pick different words from the wall to practice." (On days when old words are being practiced, the procedure is for the teacher to call out any five words, the children clap and then write them. Next, they check the words for correct letters and handwriting by tracing around the word as the teacher traces around the same word on the board or overhead.)

One child points out that if they had 95 before they added today's words, they must have 100 now. Several children look skeptical about this, so the teacher lets them count the words once more; sure enough, they have reached the magic number—100! The children seem very pleased to have 100 "important" words on their wall and to finally have a word for *q*. The teacher promises to be on the lookout for a *z* word in one of the selections they read so that every letter will have at least one word!

Next, the children go to the second activity in the Words block; today they are making words. (On other days, the activity might be Guess the Covered Word, Using Words You Know, or an activity with lots of rhyming words.) The Monday children at each table (who, of course, are the people in charge on Monday!) pick up the letter tray that is on their table and distribute the needed letters to each child. For this particular lesson, each child has five consonants, *c, r, r, s, t,* and two vowels, *a* and *o.* In the pocket chart at the front of the room, the teacher has large cards with the same seven letters. Her cards, like the small letter cards used by the children, have the uppercase letter on one side and lowercase letter on the other side. The consonant letters are written in black and the two vowels in red.

The teacher begins by making sure that each child has all the letters that are needed. "What two vowels will we use to make words today?" she asks. The children hold up their red *a* and *o* and respond appropriately. The children then name the consonants they have and are surprised to notice that they have two *r*'s. The teacher tells them that sometimes you need two of the same letter to make certain words and that they will need both *r*'s to spell the secret word that ends the lesson.

The teacher then writes the numeral 2 on the board and says, "The two-letter word I want you to make today is a word that you already know—*at.* She watches as the children quickly put together the letters *a-t* and she checks to see that Roberto is able to follow along. She sends someone who has correctly spelled *at* to the pocket chart to make *at* with the big letters and to put an index card that has the word *at* written on it along the chalkledge.

Next, she erases the 2 and writes a 3 on the board. "Add just one letter to *at* to make the three-letter word *sat*," she instructs. She chooses a child who has arranged his letters correctly at his desk to make *sat* with the big pocket chart letters. The lesson continues with children making words with their individual letter cards, a child going to the pocket chart to make the word, and the teacher putting a card with that word along the chalkledge. (The teacher does not wait for everyone to make the word before sending someone to the pocket chart, and some children are still making their word as the word is being made with the pocket chart letters. Before starting to make another word, the teacher reminds the children to fix their word to match the one made with the big letters.) Directed by the teacher, the children change *sat* to *rat*, *rat* to *rot*, *rot* to *cot*, and *cot* to *cat*. "Now, we are going to work some magic on the word *cat*," the teacher explains, "Don't take any letters out and don't add any either. Just change the places of the letters and you can turn your *cat* into *act*. After we read stories, we like to *act* them out." The teacher has the children say the word *act* slowly, stretching out the sounds to figure out where to move the letters to transform *cat* into *act*.

The teacher erases the 3, writes a 4 on the board, and asks the children to make *Rosa*. "We read a story earlier this year about a girl named Rosa who was unhappy about always being too little. Make the name *Rosa*." She observes them saying "Rosa" very slowly, emphasizing each sound, and then finding their letters. She is pleased to notice that almost everyone turns the *R* card to display the capital *R*. She had been including at least one name in almost every Making Words lesson, and the children were getting very good at remembering that names need capital letters. Next, they make *coat* and then *oats*.

The teacher erases the 4 and writes a 5 and tells them that if they add just one letter to *oats*, they can turn *oats* into *coats*. She then has them, without adding any letters or taking any out, transform their *coats* into *coast* by changing the order of the letters. She helps them say the words *coats* and *coast* slowly and to listen for how these words sound. Most children are able to move the *s* and the *t* around to make this change; she notes their growing phonemic awareness. "Now make one more five-letter word by changing just one letter and turn your *coast* into a *roast*."

As a child is making *roast* at the pocket chart, many of the other children are manipulating all their letters, trying to come up with a word. They know that each lesson ends with a word that uses all their letters, and they always like to figure it out. The teacher walks around looking for someone with the secret word, and just as she is about to declare that no one can figure out the secret word, so she will, she notices a child who has made the word and sends that child to the pocket chart where he makes the word *carrots*.

After making the words, it is time to sort for patterns and to use those patterns to read and spell a few new words. The teacher has the children read all the words they have made, now displayed in the pocket chart:

at	sat	rat	rot	cot	cat	act
Rosa	coat	oats	coats	coast	roast	carrots

She picks up *at* and says, "Who can come and hand me three words that rhyme with *at*?" A child hands her the words *sat, rat,* and *cat.* She then has someone find the word that rhymes with *rot—cot,* the word that rhymes with *oats—coats,* and the word that rhymes with *coast—roast.* The children spell the rhyming words and decide that these words all have the same letters from the vowel on. The teacher reminds the children that words that have the same spelling pattern usually rhyme and that knowing this is one way many good readers and writers read and spell words.

She shows them an index card on which the word *lot* is written. "What if you were reading and came to this word and didn't know it? Don't say this word even if you know it, but who can go and put this word with the rhyming words that help you figure it out?" A child places *lot* under *rot* and *cot* and all the children pronounce all three words and notice that they have the same spelling pattern and rhyme. The same procedure is followed with another rhyming word, *flat.*

"Thinking of words that rhyme helps you when you are trying to spell a word too. If I were writing and wanted to write *boats,* which of the rhyming words that we made today would help me?" The children decide that *boats* rhymes with *oats* and *coats* and will probably be spelled *b-o-a-t-s.* "If I were writing about foods I liked

a	o	c	r	r	s	t

The letters you need to "make words" tonight are at the top of the page. Write capitals on the back. Then, cut the letters apart and see how many words you can make. Write the words in the blanks.

Take-Home Sheet for Making Words

and I wanted to spell *toast,* what rhyming words would help me?" The children decide that *toast* rhymes with *roast* and *coast* and will probably be spelled *t-o-a-s-t.*

Finally, she shows them their take-home Making Words homework sheet. The letters *a, o, c, r, r, s, t* are in boxes along the top and beneath are larger boxes for children to write words. "When you show this to someone at your house, do you think they will figure out the secret word or will you have to tell them?" she asks. Most children think that this will be a "toughie." They always enjoy their Making Words homework sheet. They cut the letters apart, write the capitals on the back, and fill the boxes with the words they can make—including some made in class and others they think of. Parents and older siblings often get involved and because the letters formed the secret word made in class that day, the children are always smarter than anyone else and enjoy stumping their often "competitive" families!

9:20–10:00 Guided Reading

In this classroom, the Words block is followed by the Guided Reading block. On some days, they do a shared reading in a big book. The teacher reads the book first and the children join in on subsequent rereadings. On other days, the teacher guides the children's reading in selections from basal readers, literature collections, or trade books, of which they have multiple copies. For today's lesson, the teacher has chosen *The Carrot Seed* (Krauss, 1945). As often as possible, the teacher tries to find reading material that ties in with the children's science or social studies unit. *The Carrot Seed* is perfect for their current seeds and plants unit.

The teacher picks up *The Carrot Seed* and points to the title. She asks, "What word do we see here that we made with an *s* added in our Making Words lesson?" The children quickly identify the word *carrot.* The teacher then points to the word *seed* and asks the children to look at the picture on the cover of the book. She asks them to think about what the boy is doing and what word the letters *s-e-e-d* might spell. The children realize that the boy is planting something; using the picture clue and what they know about letters and sounds, they are able to figure out the word *seed* and read the title of the book, *The Carrot Seed.*

Next, the teacher directs the children to look at all the pictures in the story and to think about what is happening. "You know that we can read lots of words we haven't seen before if we look at the pictures, think about what is happening, and then think about what words we might read to tell what is happening." She leads the children on a picture walk in which they use the pictures to make predictions and develop some vocabulary. First, they look at the pictures and identify the characters—a little boy, his mother, his father, and his big brother. The children all know the word *mother;* she writes it on the board and underneath it writes *brother.* She underlines the *other* in both *mother* and *brother* and asks the children what they know about words that have the same spelling pattern. The children respond that the words usually rhyme, and the teacher leads them to figure out the new word *brother* from their known word *mother.* The teacher follows the same procedure to help them decode the new word *weed* based on the rhyming word *seed.*

Next, the teacher leads them to decide what the boy is doing on certain pages. On the first page, they decide that the boy looks like he is planting the seed. The teacher asks them to say the word *planted* slowly and decide which letters they would use if they were making the word *planted.* The children decide that they hear a *p-l* at the beginning and that it ends in *e-d.* "Look on this page and find a word that might be *planted.* Put your finger on it when you find it." The children quickly find and say the word *planted.*

The children look at other pages and decide that the boy is pulling up weeds and sprinkling the plant with a watering can. The teacher has them say the words and think about which letters they would use to make the words *pull* and *sprinkle.* Now they search the text for these words. Throughout this phase of the lesson, the teacher develops useful strategies for children to use as they read. This lesson, using pictures to predict specific text content and attending to sounds in spoken words, represents an attempt to support children's development of the integrated strategy, using both the meaning and sounds of words in combination with one another.

Having guided them to look at the pictures, to talk about what was happening, and to use that knowledge to figure out some unfamiliar words, the teacher then asks them to make some predictions about what they will find out as they read the story with a partner. Finally, she tells them what they will do when they gather back together after reading the story. She shows them six index cards on which she has written the words:

carrot seed	mother	little boy
carrot	father	big brother

She also shows them that she has written the word *everyone* on 17 other index cards. The children read the words with her, and she tells them that after reading she will shuffle and distribute the cards, and they will get to play a part in acting out the story. Everyone will get a part, even if their part is to be part of the *everyone.* Because they do not know which card they will get, they should read the story and think about what they would do for each part, no matter which card they get.

The children go to read the story with their partners. The teacher has partnered up struggling readers with better readers. The children have learned to take turns reading pages and to help each other when help is needed. The teacher reminds the children to examine the pictures before beginning to read and to help figure out, but not tell each other, an unknown word. She then reminds them of the steps they have learned for figuring out words that they do not recognize immediately:

1. Put your finger on the unknown word and say all the letters.
2. Use the letters and the picture clues.

3. Try to pronounce the word by seeing whether it has a spelling pattern or rhyme you know.

4. Keep your finger on the word and read the other words in the sentence to see whether it makes sense.

5. If it does not make sense, go back to the word and think what would have these letters and would make sense.

She also reminds the children that when their partner is reading a page, they are to play teacher, and if their partner is having trouble with a word, they should go through the steps, instead of just telling what the word is.

The partners go to designated places and read the story. The teacher circulates, with clipboard and labels in hand, and makes notes on how fluently the children are reading. She praises the partners who are helping other children use the steps to figure out unfamiliar words by telling them that they could "soon have her job" and that "they are great little teachers!"

It takes only about 7 minutes for the partners to finish reading. When she notices they have finished, she hands each of them an index card indicating what part they will play in the story reenactment. She then gathers the children around her again and has them retell the story, with emphasis on what the main characters do. The child who got the seed card will be put on the floor and lie there, motionless. The carrot will be pulled from the ground and wheeled away by the little boy. The mother, the father, the big brother, and everyone will shake their heads and say, "It won't come up!" The little boy will plant, sprinkle, pull weeds, and finally wheel the carrot away proudly.

Space is cleared in the center to make room for a stage, and *The Carrot Seed* is acted out. This low-budget, off-off Broadway production lacks props, costumes, and rehearsal, but no one seems to care. The children take their places, and the story is retold with the events happening in the correct sequence. The only complaint comes from the children who are part of the "everyone" and who want starring roles instead! The teacher assures them that tomorrow they will reread the story and act it out again, and more people will get the "big parts"!

10:00–10:15 Break/Snack

The children and the teacher go outside and take one brisk walk around the school, singing a favorite marching rhyme on their way. Once inside, they all have juice and crackers. Many children in this school do not eat nutritious meals, and the ones who need it most either brought no snack at all or brought junk food. The teacher has prevailed on those parents who can send something to send large cans of juice and boxes of crackers or to donate money so that she could buy juice and crackers at the local warehouse. Many parents donated willingly because they did not have to send something each day, and when everyone had juice and crackers for a snack, their children could not pester them to bring junk! Arranging for the juice and cracker morning snack took some time and preparation, but the teacher knew that some children needed this healthy snack; she also could not stand to watch some of them eat while others sat there hungry. During this break, the teacher talks with the children about the kinds of seeds and plants that produce much of the food they are eating. She even thought to bring in some raw carrot slices for everyone to munch on and a whole raw carrot for all to examine.

10:15–11:15 Math and Science or Social Studies Unit

During this hour each morning, the class does math and activities related to their science or social studies unit. On some days, it is impossible to integrate the two so they do one or the other or divide the hour between the two. Today, she integrates a math lesson with the new science unit on seeds and plants. She passes out containers filled with various kinds of seeds. She then leads the children in a variety of counting, sorting, predicting, classifying, and weighing activities with the seeds. The children work in groups at their tables, sorting the seeds by putting the ones that are alike together, estimating, counting to see how many of each type of seed they have, and graphing to show which seeds they have more and less of. The teacher gives out simple balance scales and has the children predict which seeds weigh the most and the least. They then weigh the different seeds and determine that it would take "more than they have" of the tiniest seeds to weigh as much as one of the largest seeds. The children are particularly amazed by how tiny carrot seeds are.

When the hour allotted for this hands-on math/science activity is almost over, the teacher shows the children some pages from the seeds and plants book that she read to start the day. She helps the children identify the seeds and the plants that grew from them. The children are amazed to realize that hickory nuts, acorns, and white beans were once all seeds. They remember seeing seeds like the little ones they had when eating cucumbers and apples. The children then regretfully dump all their seeds back into the containers, and the teacher promises that they will do more exploring and computing using the seeds tomorrow.

11:15–11:50 Writer's Workshop

Each day after math/science, the children have their Writing block. This block always begins with the teacher writing something on the overhead as the children watch. As she writes, she thinks aloud, modeling the way she thinks about writing. This think-aloud writing supports children as they develop into readers and writers. She writes about a variety of topics and in a variety of formats. Today, she decides to capitalize on the children's interest in the new seed and plant unit by writing about some of the things they found while exploring with the seeds.

She sits down at her overhead, pen in hand. The children settle down on the floor in front of her, eager to see what she will write about today. They watch and listen as she thinks aloud about what to write.

"I always have so many things I want to write about on Mondays. I could write about going shopping this weekend and finding my car with a flat tire when I came out of the store! I could write about the funny movie I watched on TV. I could write a list of the different seeds I ordered from the seed catalog this weekend. But I think I will write about what we did with the seeds this morning because you all seemed to have so much fun with them."

The teacher writes a description of some of the activities the children have just done. As she writes, she models for them how she might invent-spell a few words. (Early in the year, she told the children that she used to love to write when she was their age and that she would write all kinds of things. She wrote stories and kept a diary and was always making lists. She pretended that she was a great writer and wrote wonderful books for children to read. She explained that, of course, when she was their age, she could not spell all the words she needed, so she just put in all the letters she could hear so she could read it back. She told them that she used to invent-spell the big words and would show them how she used to do this at the beginning of each writer's workshop.) As she writes, she stops and says a word aloud slowly and writes down the letters she can hear. She also looks up at the word wall a few times and says, "I can spell *many* because we just put it on our word wall" and, "I will look at *some* on our word wall because *some* is not spelled the way you think it should be." When she is ready to write the last sentence, she picks up the book and says, "I can use this book to help me spell the names of some of the seeds we had." She also omits one ending punctuation mark and fails to capitalize one word.

When she is finished writing, she says, "Now, I will read it to make sure that it makes sense and that it says what I wanted it to say." She reads aloud as the children watch. As soon as she finishes, the children's hands are raised, volunteering to be editors. She gives one boy a different color marker to go to the overhead and lead the class in helping her edit her writing. Each editing convention the children have learned so far is covered, and the class checks her draft for these. When they find something that needs fixing, the editor fixes it. Possible misspelled words are circled, capitals and punctuation marks are added. The boy who is editing makes changes and insertions like a pro! So far, they have learned five things to look for. They read the short paragraph and put a check on the bottom as they check each of the five things:

1. A title is in the middle.
2. Every sentence makes sense.
3. Every sentence begins with a capital and ends with a punctuation mark.
4. People and place names have capital letters.
5. Words that might be misspelled are circled.

The writing minilesson takes approximately 10 minutes, including the editing. The children are then dismissed from the big group to do their own writing. The children are at various stages of the writing process. Five children are at the art table, happily illustrating their books. When asked why they get to make books, they proudly explain that you have to write three pieces first. Then you pick the best of the three and get a friend to be your editor—"just like we do for the teacher at the overhead." Then you get to go to the editing table, and the teacher helps you edit. Then you copy it in one of these books (holding up a premade half-sheet construction paper book that is covered and stapled). One child who is illustrating a book about her best friend proudly turns to a blank last page in her book and says, "That's where she's going to write about me." When asked what the teacher might write, the author responds, "She's gonna say, Nikita is 7 years old. She has three brothers and four sisters, and this is her fourth book!—something like that!"

Four children are at the editing table with the teacher. She is helping them do a final edit of their pieces in preparation for copying them into books. A pair of children are helping each other edit before proceeding to the editing table. The other children are working away at their desks, in various stages of producing their three pieces so that they too can get to the art table. Children write about whatever they chose to. Some days, they continue writing on something they started the day before. Other days, they start a new piece. This morning, some children write about seeds and about what they did with the seeds. Another child pages through the seed catalog and writes a list of all the seeds that they want to order. Other children write about things they did over the weekend. The teacher's minilesson and her pondering about what to write each morning always gets the children thinking about what to write. The children often write about what the teacher writes about, although the teacher neither encourages nor discourages them from choosing the same topic. Many children can be seen glancing up at the word wall when they realize that the word they are trying to spell is up there. Some children have a book open to use as a reference for ideas and spelling.

The classroom is a busy working place for about 15 minutes. Then, with a signal from the teacher, the children once again gather on the floor and the Monday children line up behind the Author's Chair! (All the children are designated by a day of the week; on their day they get to share!) The first child reads just two sentences of a piece that was started today. He calls on various children who tell him that they like the topic (dinosaurs) and give him ideas he might like to include. One child suggests a good dinosaur book for him to read. The second child reads a completed piece. She calls on children who tell her they like the way she stays on the topic (her new baby sister) and ask questions ("What's her name?" "Does she cry all night?" "Is this the only sister you've got?") The third and fourth children read some unfinished pieces and receive praise and suggestions. Nikita is the final Monday child. She reads her book and shows her illustrations and then hands it to the teacher, reminding her to "write about me on this page!" The sharing takes approximately 9 minutes, for a total of 34 minutes of Writer's Workshop.

11:50–12:30 Lunch/Recess

Each day, as the children are lining up, the teacher reads the lunch menu to them. Today, she tells them that one of the foods they are going to have for lunch is made mostly from seeds. She then reads the menu. No one can figure out that peanut butter is the food made mostly from seeds. Many children seem quite astonished! The teacher decides that a peanut butter cooking activity would be a great tie-in to the unit.

12:30–1:45 P.E./Library/Art/Music/ Open Centers/Coaching Groups

During this time each day, the class is scheduled for their time with the specialists. They do not have specialists for the whole time each day; they also use this time to go outside or to the gym or library or to do music or art. On some days, they have open-center time for part of this time. The teacher also uses this time to meet with small coaching groups and teach them how to be word coaches.

1:45–2:15 Self-Selected Reading

Each day, the teacher begins this block by reading aloud to the children for 10–15 minutes. After reading to them, she dismisses them to their tables for their own reading time. The teacher has arranged books into several plastic crates and has put one crate on each of the five tables. The crates contain a variety of books, including some related to the science unit—seeds and plants; some old favorites, such as *Are You My Mother? One Fish, Two Fish,* and *Robert the Rose Horse;* some class books; and some books the children had written. The trays are rotated each day so that all the children have lots of books to choose from without leaving their seats but do not see the same old books every day.

The children eagerly read the books. As they read, the teacher conferences with the Monday children. Each child brings the teacher a book that he or she has selected and reads a few pages from that book. The teacher makes anecdotal notes about what the Monday children are reading and about how well they are reading. She notes their use of picture clues, their attempts to figure out unknown words, fluency, self-correction, and other reading behaviors. She also asks them what they like about the book they are reading and sometimes suggests another book they might like to read.

2:15–2:30 Daily Summary/School–Home Connection

During this time, the children prepare to go home and the teacher helps them talk about what they have learned today and what they could talk about at home. Because so many of these children come from homes in which English is not the spoken language, she feels that promoting as much home/school talk as possible is important. She help them recall the seeds they learned about in the book and what they did with the seeds. She reminds them that they ate peanut butter— made mostly from seeds—at lunch. She makes sure they have their song sheets from music class and asks them whether they think someone at home would enjoy learning the song. She reminds them of *The Carrot Seed* and has them think about their part in the reenactment. She distributes the Making Words homework sheets and reminds them to bring them back tomorrow so she can see what other words can be made from these letters that she had not been smart enough to think of!

Next, she gives them their take-home word wall and has them find and highlight the five new words with their yellow crayon. "Be sure to show your family that we finally have a *q* word—*question*—on our word wall and that we are looking for a useful, important word that begins with the letter *z*." She also reminds them to tell about what they wrote about during Writer's Workshop and what they were reading during self-selected reading. She reminds the Tuesday children that tomorrow is their day to do everything special and that they should decide which book they want to share with her during their conference tomorrow. Finally, she gives them a science homework assignment:

> "Look around your house and street and try to find three different kinds of seeds. You might find these seeds in your kitchen. Sometimes, the seeds might be part of a food. Some seeds can be found outdoors. Bring these seeds in if you can. If not, write down their names so you can remember them when we share what you have found first thing tomorrow morning."

After the children leave, the teacher attaches the labels on which she has written anecdotal comments to each of their folders. She then puts a clean sheet of labels on her clipboard. She writes the initials of each Tuesday child on several labels so that she will remember to take note of their progress and problems tomorrow. She also writes the initials of several other children and a few questions on several other labels to remind her to observe the problem areas she was concerned about for particular children tomorrow: Solves math problems? Using self-correction strategies? Using strategies taught for figuring out unknown words? Really reading during self-selected reading? Then she begins to organize the materials for tomorrow's science lesson—planting beans in cups and watching them sprout. Of course, the children will observe, sketch, and write descriptions of the growth of the bean plants over the next 2 weeks.

CHAPTER 11

A Week in a Big Blocks Intermediate Classroom

Throughout the chapters of this book, we have tried to convey to you that, when working with children who find learning to read difficult, the earlier we start teaching them to read, the better. Children who receive the kind of instruction provided in Building Blocks kindergartens and Four Block primary classes are usually reading and writing when they reach the intermediate grades. They do still need good instruction but have achieved some basic literacy skills and, perhaps more importantly, view themselves as readers and writers. They have—in the current lingo—the right attitude!

Unfortunately, children who have experienced many years of frustration and failure have developed, justifiably perhaps, the wrong attitude! They say with their eyes, their bodies, and, sometimes, boldly with their mouths:

"I won't do it!"
"You can't make me!"
"Reading and writing are dumb and stupid and sissy!"
"I don't care!"
"Who needs it?"

What most of them really mean is

"I can't do it!"

Throughout this book, when describing activities for intermediate-aged, still-struggling children, we have tried to describe activities that involve real reading and writing and that provide for success on a variety of levels. Six principles are behind the activities we have described:

1. All children can learn to read and write—and all of them really want to.
2. Success precedes motivation, and once children see that they can be successful, they will participate; thus, teachers must engineer success!
3. Real reading and writing are intrinsically motivating.

4. Traditional seatwork is a waste of time.
5. Children learn from each other.
6. The mastery model is wrong; teachers must teach for and look for improvement, growth, and approximation—not perfection.

The intermediate classroom where struggling readers become readers and writers is not the traditional classroom. You cannot just make "a few little changes" and transform the children. Things must change—and these changes are fairly radical.

One thing that must change is the way grades are determined. Grades must be based on effort and not on some notion of grade level and the tests in the teacher manuals. This is difficult for everyone to accept because we all want to have high expectations and maintain standards for students. But no one will work if they know they are going to fail no matter what! If children come to you reading and writing 2 or 3 years below grade level, they cannot pass grade-level tests and standards. If they know they are going to fail regardless of effort, they will not try! If they do not try, they cannot learn!

Once you decide to grade on effort primarily and you clearly communicate this to the students, your students will be motivated to "hang in there" and to "give it another try." It is not your fault that they come to you functioning far below grade level. It is not your job to get them all to grade level or to fail them if they cannot get there. It is your job to teach them and to help them move toward a literate future. You cannot do this if you must fail them for their illiterate past.

Another thing that must change is the schedule. In many intermediate classrooms, time is allocated to more than a dozen different subjects during the day. In some cases, even the language arts are broken down into separate areas: reading, writing, spelling, language, and handwriting. Add to this list math, health, science, social studies, P. E., music, art, foreign language, guidance, and computers. The instruction cannot help being in small, isolated segments when all these separate subjects are presented every day. In addition to being choppy and fragmented, this type of scheduling is antithetical to our current understanding of how people learn. The associative theory of learning described in Chapter 6 demonstrates that we learn when we associate the material with other things and events. We do not learn by memorizing facts and practicing small skills. Rather, we learn as we work with information, applying what we are learning to solve problems and to achieve goals. In classrooms in which intermediate-aged children are transformed into readers and writers, teachers do whatever is within their power to help children make connections. They take whatever time is allocated to them and create a schedule that allows for as much integrated learning as possible.

The final big change that must be made relates to how the teacher and the children work with one another. An intermediate classroom that succeeds cannot be one in which the teacher teaches the whole class all the time, nor can it be one in which children are assigned to static reading groups, based on achievement levels, that rotate to meet with the teacher while the other children complete seatwork assignments. Intermediate-grade children span the whole range of reading and writing abilities. Instruction that treats them all the same or that arbitrarily divides them into three groups will not meet their diverse needs. The intermediate classroom, in which many struggling readers are learning and growing, is one in which various kinds of cooperative learning arrangements are used. Children read, write, edit, and research with partners and in small groups. Teachers who succeed with older struggling readers spend a great deal of time early in the year role playing and modeling these cooperative ventures and make the "working together" atmosphere a top priority in their classrooms. They have a "we're all in this together" and a "united, we stand, divided we fall!" attitude. They work with children to help them learn how to work with one another.

Those of you who actually teach intermediate-aged, struggling readers are probably thinking, "Easier said than done!" You are right. It is not easy to change your grading system, to develop a less choppy schedule, or to get your students working together, but it is essential and it can be done. Teachers in schools all over this country make up their minds, close their doors, and restructure their classrooms so that children can become more literate. If children have failed in the past, it will take them a while to get on board and to realize that in your classroom things are different. But most do realize eventually. They are still children, despite their sometimes grown-up facade, and they have the same primary needs that all children, and indeed all humans, have. They want to succeed, to be liked, and to know that they "are somebody."

Given all they must accomplish, intermediate teachers cannot usually do everything every day in the same way that primary teachers can. In addition, intermediate-aged children need larger blocks of time to pursue reading, writing, and research. We call our intermediate-grades literacy framework Big Blocks because we schedule larger blocks of time and integrate at least one subject area with our reading and writing instruction.

In the remainder of this chapter, we describe a week of instruction in an intermediate Big Blocks classroom. We assume a 5½-hour instructional day (330 minutes, not including recess and lunch). We assume that 40 minutes of each day is given over to specials—music, art, computers, P.E., foreign language, and so on—and that another 50 minutes is allocated to math. We further assume that, as in most states, 120 minutes should be allocated to the language arts daily, 50 minutes to science, 50 minutes to social studies, and 20 minutes to health. In our classroom, however, the teacher alternates between teaching a social studies unit and a science unit each week. Health is combined with science, when possible, and, thus, a combined science/health unit might merit 2 weeks. If the curriculum demands it, a week-long health unit is taught. Most 9-week grading periods contain four week-long social studies units, four week-long science units, and one week-long health unit.

Thus each day, we have 240 minutes available to teach language arts and one topic from science, health, or social studies. This allows us to meet the guidelines for content subject teaching in most states whereas reducing the fragmentation found in classrooms that schedule each subject every day. We make every effort to foster reading and writing development, even during content topic time. Students develop strategies for comprehending informational text and for writing factual reports as they learn the content of their science, social studies, and health subjects. Of course, schedules differ from school to school and from teacher to teacher within a school. For our example, we assume the following daily schedule:

8:15–8:30 Arriving and Settling in (children arrive at different times, depending on buses, breakfast, and so on; attendance taken, routines, and so on). (noninstructional time)

8:30–9:10 Language Arts—Self-Selected Reading (40 minutes)

9:10–9:40 Language Arts—Working with Words (30 minutes)

9:40–10:30 Math (50 minutes)

10:30–10:50 Break/Recess (noninstructional time)

10:50–11:50 Language Arts/Unit Time (60 minutes)

11:50–12:20 Lunch (noninstructional time)

12:20–1:40 Language Arts/Unit (80 minutes)

1:40–2:20 Special Subject (40 minutes)

2:20–2:50 Language Arts/Unit (30 minutes)

Once we know the time frame we are working with, we can decide what happens. Not all components can be included every day, but all the important ones should be implemented on a regular basis. A successful teacher of struggling readers might follow these time allocation guidelines:

Every Day (No Matter What!)
- Teacher reads to the class from a book.
- Teacher reads something to the class from a newspaper, magazine, riddle book, joke book, book of poetry, or other "real-world" source.
- Children read something they choose from a large and varied selection.
- Children learn more about the topic they are studying.
- Children do a word wall activity with high-frequency, commonly misspelled words and/or with topic-related big words.

Two or Three Times a Week
- Children participate in guided reading activity.
- Children participate in a focused writing lesson.
- Teacher models topic selection and writing a short piece.
- Children write on a topic of their own choice.
- Children work with words—looking for patterns, learning how to chunk and decode big words, and so forth.

Once a Week

- All children share something they have written.
- All children share something they have read.
- One-third of class revises, edits, and publishes a piece of writing.
- Children read to their little buddies.
- Children do research related to topic.

This is what 1 week of instruction might look like using the allocated 250 minutes and making sure that all the activities in which we want children to engage happen as often as we have decided.

8:30–9:10   Self-Selected Reading

Many important things must be done each day in an intermediate classroom. Every activity wants more time than it can be allotted. Interruptions and schedule changes sometimes force activities to be "scrapped" or postponed until tomorrow. The teacher in this class has decided that the most crucial goal for her students is that they all become readers—people who choose to read even when they are not forced. All her students can read some although many do not read at grade level (and a few read above grade level). She knows that the major determinant of how well they will read by the end of the year is how much they read. She also knows that many of her students do not read on their own at home and view reading as "something you have to do in school." The teacher knows that she can provide two activities that have the greatest potential of getting her kids "hooked on reading"—reading to them and giving them consistent and ample time to read materials of their own choosing. To make sure that reading to the class and giving them time to read does not get crowded out as the day goes on, she schedules it first thing every morning.

Each morning she reads two pieces to the class. The first piece she reads is a "quickread," and she tries to make it as current and "in sync" with the interests of her students as she can. On Monday mornings, the teacher usually brings in a newspaper and shares some of the more interesting tidbits with the children. Children are encouraged to bring in interesting things from the weekend paper too. Pieces shared are added to the collage-style newspaper board. Other mornings, the teacher reads from informational books, magazines, joke and riddle books, pamphlets, and so on. The message that the children begin with each day is that reading is an essential part of their real world.

The second piece she reads each day is a book—or a chapter of a book. She chooses books of high interest to readers at this age but of varying genres so the children are exposed to a variety of literature. She tries to include equal numbers of fiction and nonfiction titles and is always on the lookout for good multicultural books. This week, she is reading *Get On Out of Here, Philip Hall* (B. Greene, 1981). When she finishes each book, many children always want to read it for themselves. Those who want the book write their names on little slips of paper. She pulls one slip (without looking) and hands the book to that lucky winner. The other slips are also pulled and used to make a waiting list in the order they were pulled, just like they do at the library.

This procedure is perceived as fair by the children, and the chapter books that the teacher reads aloud always have waiting lists. Even children who could not read the book by themselves the first time can often read and enjoy it once they have listened to it read aloud. Whenever possible, the teacher tries to read a book aloud by an author who has written similar books or by one who has several books in a series. Children who are on the waiting list for the book are often delighted to get a similar book to read in the meantime. The class does not know that the teacher has hidden away a copy of Greene's *Philip Hall Likes Me, I Reckon Maybe* (1974).

Next comes the students' time to read. Many children have a book at their desk that they are in the middle of reading. Other children choose a book from the trays of books that rotate to different tables each week. Each tray is filled with a wide variety of books, including some high-interest, easy vocabulary books and some informational books with lots of pictures. Children are grouped by days of the week, a fifth of the class for each day. On day 1, the day 1 people can read anywhere and anything in the room, including newspapers, magazines, joke books, the newspaper board, and so on. On the other days, they stay at their seats and read books. In this way, everyone gets a chance to "spread out" and read anything 1 day each week, but most of the class is seated quietly at their desks reading books.

While her students read, the teacher holds quick conferences with one-fifth of her students each day. The students have been taught how to prepare for the conference; they come to the conference with the pages they want to read and talk about marked with a bookmark. When making the schedule for the daily conferences, the teacher spreads out her most struggling students across the 5 days—beginning each day with a conference with one of her struggling readers and giving that reader a few additional minutes. The teacher views these weekly conferences as "conversations" rather than "interrogations," and all her students look forward to their weekly one-on-one time with her.

9:10–9:40   Working with Words

This half-hour each day is devoted to words. The goals are that children (1) learn to spell the high-frequency words that they need in their writing, (2) learn to read, spell, and develop meanings for big words that are part of the science, health, or social studies topic they are studying, and (3) learn to decode and spell unfamiliar words—particularly polysyllabic words.

Monday is usually the day on which a new unit of study begins, so the teacher adds 10–12 unit-related big words to a Big Word Board. These words are related to the unit topic for the week. As the teacher puts the words on the board, she helps the children associate meanings for the words. This week's unit is on pollution. Twelve words are added to the Big Word Board:

pollution	environment	recycle
pollutants	environmental	conservation
resources	chemicals	fertilizers
pesticides	combustion	renewable

Each week, the teacher tries to include some words that have the same root—pollution/pollutants, environment/environmental. As she introduces the words to the children, she helps them distinguish the different forms of the words from one another. She helps them understand that *pollution* is the word we use to describe the whole problem and that *pollutants,* including *fertilizers, chemicals,* and *pesticides, are some of the things* that cause pollution. Although the word *pollute* is not included on the board (the number of words must be limited if children are really going to focus on them and make them part of their listening/speaking/reading/writing vocabularies), she writes it on the chalkboard. She reminds the children that an *e* at the end is often dropped when endings such as *tion* and *ant* are added, and helps them see that "*pollute* is what you do that causes the problem of *pollution.*" In a similar way, she helps them understand that the *environment* is the surroundings in which we live, and *environmental* is the word we use as a describing word. "We can say that pollution is a problem for our environment or that pollution is an environmental problem." She has the children contribute several sentences describing how pollution is a problem and using the words *environment* and *environmental* to help them develop a sense in their listening vocabulary of when each word is used.

The other words get introduced and the teacher alerts the children to similar morphemes and meanings. *Recycle, renewable,* and *resources* all begin with the prefix *re* and have related meanings. "When you *recycle* something, you use it again. *Renewable* resources, such as trees, will grow again." The teacher also writes the word *nonrenewable* on the board and helps the children think about what the addition of *non* does to *renewable* and to think of some *nonrenewable* resources.

The words *pollution, combustion,* and *conservation* are discussed. Then the teacher writes the words *pollute, combust,* and *conserve* on the board, drawing their attention to how the word changes as it is used differently in both speaking and writing. Throughout this introduction phase, the teacher talks about the words, defines them, uses them in sentences, and focuses on word structure and other cues.

Once all the words have been introduced and attention has been devoted to their meaning and to similar chunks, the teacher leads them in a clapping/chanting activity similar to the cheering you would hear at a basketball game. The children say each word, clap and chant its spelling, and then say the word again. The teacher leads

them to spell the word in a rhythmic way, pausing briefly between the syllables—
"pollution—p-o-l___l-u___t-i-o-n—pollution, pollutant—p-o-l___l-u___t-a-n-t—pollutant."
The lesson ends with each student writing the 12 words in a vocabulary notebook.
One of their regular Monday night homework assignments is to write a sentence
and/or draw a picture giving a personal example for each word.

In addition to helping intermediate children develop a store of big words,
many struggling readers still misspell (or do not know how to spell) common
words that are needed in their writing. This classroom has a word wall of frequently misspelled words. The teacher began the word wall at the beginning of
the year with words she knew many of the children would misspell. Five words
were first added to the wall:

they   were   friend   from   said

The next week, she added five more frequently written but often misspelled
words:

are   what   because   could   once

As the year went on, she became alerted to words many children were mis-
spelling in their first-draft writing and added words the children evidently
needed. She also added homophones, putting a picture or word clue next to all
but one of the words:

to   two   too   there   their   they're   buy   by   write   right

Now the word wall contained the contractions that the students used a great deal:

can't   didn't   won't   wasn't   we're   let's

Five high-frequency words were added to the word wall each Tuesday. After
adding the five new words, the teacher calls out the five new words for the week
and five review words. The children clap, chant, and write these 10 words. The
teacher is adding five new words this week:

new   knew   doesn't   terrible   until

Each Wednesday, Thursday, and Friday, the children write big words and
word wall words in a variety of ways. On some days, the teacher simply calls out
five words from the Big Word Board and five from the word wall of frequently misspelled words and has the children clap, chant, and write them. On other days,
she gives clues to the words or does the Be a Mind Reader activity, and the children have to guess the word. She also dictates short sentences that can be made
by combining words from the Big Word Board and the word wall. Regardless of

what activity she uses to review these words, she always involves the children in some chanting and writing because these activities focus their attention on all the letters in the words. In addition, when children are writing, she encourages them to use invented spellings or whatever resources they have for spelling words. The teacher insists, however, that the words from the Big Word Board and the word wall be spelled correctly because they are so readily accessible. Students' eyes can be seen going to the board or the wall when they are writing.

On Monday and Tuesday, most of the 30 minutes devoted to working with words is consumed with introducing, adding, and reviewing words on the board and the wall. On the other 3 days, however, a quick review activity takes only 5–10 minutes; the remaining time is devoted to activities designed to help them see patterns in words. Generally, the teacher does a Making Big Words activity on Wednesday, an activity designed to teach particular prefixes or suffixes on Thursday, and everyone's favorite—"The Wheel"—on Friday.

9:40–10:30   Math

10:30–10:50   Break/recess

10:50–11:50   Unit Time

This time is usually devoted to learning about the topic, expanding both world and word knowledge. Whenever possible, the teacher uses real experiences—experiments and demonstrations during science, simulations, and imagined journeys during social studies. At least one day each week includes a guided reading activity, and another day includes a focused writing lesson. The students are taught strategies for reading and writing informational text and study strategies, including note-taking and summarizing. Sometimes, the focused writing lesson is a follow-up to the guided reading activity, and sometimes the two are topic related but not related to each other. On Fridays, the student usually brainstorm questions they would still like to know the answers to and go to the library to find answers to the questions. Students work in pairs to find answers.

This week, the topic being studied is pollution. On Monday, they watch a video that shows some of the most serious sources of pollution and begin to fill in some information on the data chart graphic organizer on the following page. The video described some general pollution problems but was not specific to the geographic area in which the school is located. The teacher finishes the lesson by asking students to write down the three pollutants that they think are most problematic where they live. For homework they are to interview two adults about pollution in the local area and determine what these adults think the most significant problems are.

Tuesday's lesson begins with the students sharing what they found out in their interviews with the two adults. Most had talked with someone about the problem and were surprised to learn how high the level of concern was. The teacher shares some newspaper articles from local sources that she has been saving until this unit. More information, particularly in the last column, Our Area, is added to the data chart.

Environmental Pollution			
Where	**Causes**	**Possible Solutions**	**Our Area**
Air			
Water			
Soil			
Land			

On Wednesday, the teacher leads the students in a guided reading activity in which they read about what can be accomplished with recycling. She uses a KWL to help them organize and connect what they knew before and after reading. Their homework assignment for Wednesday night is to find out what they can recycle from their homes and where to take the recyclables.

Thursday begins with a discussion of their home recycling efforts. The teacher then describes some recycling efforts that are being made by various businesses. She explains that on her recent plane flight, the flight attendants were collecting cans and other recyclables separately. The school secretary comes in and explains how copying and computer paper are being recycled. Next, the teacher gives out a list of local businesses. Included on the list are stores and fast-food restaurants that the children visit on a regular basis. She does a focused writing lesson in which she demonstrates for the children how to write a list of questions they can ask to find out what, if anything, a business is doing about recycling. As the children watch, she writes a list of questions to ask her brother, who works at a car dealership.

After watching her write her questions, she lets each child decide who or what business they will interview and has each child make a list of questions to ask. She helps the children see that some of their questions might be just like hers:

> Do you have a place to collect recyclable aluminum cans?
> Do you have bins in all the offices for recyclable paper?

Other questions were particular to a car dealership:

> What happens to the old oil when you do an oil change?
> What happens to old tires and worn-out car parts?

She gives the children the option of doing the interview by themselves or with a classmate, assuming that the pair can get together over the weekend to do the interview. The children who are going to interview together pair up to make the list of questions. The others do theirs by themselves. The teacher circulates and helps each child make a readable list.

Normally, on Fridays, the class goes to the library to do research designed to answer the unanswered questions they have about a topic. This Friday, however, the teacher decides to have them do some "field research." She gets the class together and asks them to predict what kind of litter and how many pieces of it they might find in the area surrounding the school and where that litter might have come from. Once they have made their predictions, she divides them into teams, arms each team with a trash bag, and gives them 20 minutes to see how much litter they can pick up in the designated area.

Dividing the children into teams is a problem in some classes. The children fuss about who they are with and who gets to do what. In this classroom, however, the teacher has a system for forming teams and distributing responsibilities. She uses this system quite often, and it is perceived as fair by all the students. She uses a deck of playing cards, taking out as many numbers as she has children present today. She has 27 children present and decides to form six groups of four and one group of three. Thus, she takes out all four suits of the cards numbered 1–6 and three of the 7s. The cards are dealt and children form teams based on the number they get! Sometimes, she uses the suits to designate who will do what. Today, she writes these responsibilities on the board:

- *Spade*—Carrier—Carry trash bag.
- *Club*—Leader—Lead the team in whatever direction this person chooses; team must "follow the leader."
- *Diamond*—Tallier—Tally the trash collected into different categories as team counts it.
- *Heart*—Reporter—Report team's results to the rest of the class.

As she writes these responsibilities, the different class members cheer and grumble as they get responsibilities they like and others they eschew. As in real life, everyone wants to lead and no wants to "carry the load," but the children accept what they get because they have seen the cards shuffled and dealt. They know that it was "the luck of the draw" and not teacher favoritism that determined their "fate." (The team that has only three members is lacking a tallier, and the teacher tells them that the reporter will have to double up and also be the tallier for their group.)

The class goes out and collects the litter. As they collect each item, they count and tally their "treasure" and then add up the results for the reporter to report to the class. As each group reports, the children tally the results reported by the groups. Finally, they compare what they actually found to what they had predicted. They decide that much too much litter is around, that most of it came from students, and that some of it can be recycled. They sort out the recyclables, decide who can take it where, and take the rest out to the big dumpster.

This unit, like some others, extends into the following Monday. The class has done a good job of interviewing local business owners and employees, and many children are encouraged by what they have found. Others discover that there was still much to be done that was not being done. After discussing their results on Monday, the teacher leads them in another focused writing activity. This time, they watch as she writes a letter to her interviewee (her brother), thanking him for taking time to be interviewed, praising him for the good things the car dealership is doing, and suggesting that someone needs to find out what is being done with all those old tires that are just being hauled away.

The students use her model to write their own letters. The teacher uses some of the time to help them revise and edit their letters as needed. Then they copy the letters to make them as "readable" as possible and deliver them to their interviewees (including one to the school principal with suggestions for increasing recycling at the school).

11:50–12:20   Lunch

12:20–1:40   Guided Reading or Writer's Workshop

Each day this time is used for guided reading lessons and for children to write, revise, and edit on topics of their own choosing. It varies according to what they need to do. Most weeks, the teacher does guided reading lessons on Mondays and Tuesdays and Writer's Workshop on Wednesdays and Thursdays. On Friday, the children often have a choice of whether they want to read or write or do some combination of both during this hour.

The teacher uses a variety of materials and a variety of formats for guiding their reading. The children in this class read on many different levels, and the teacher tries to make sure that over the week, children read something at their instructional level or easier during this time. Sometimes, she finds two or three pieces, similar in genre, topic, or theme that different students can read. Whenever possible, she finds something related to the topic being studied, but often the reading done at this time is unrelated to the topic.

This week, they are going to read two stories. The stories are not about pollution (one is about a current-day family that survives a fire and the other is set in the old West), but the teacher sees possibilities for tying in what they have been learning about pollution to both stories. The story about the family that survives the fire is from a grade-level basal and is too hard for many of the students to read by themselves. The other story is from another series that features stories of interest to intermediate-aged children, have more vocabulary control, and are much easier to read.

She decides to have them read the fire story on Monday. Because this story will be difficult for many of her students, she reads the first three pages of the story to them. Before reading, she begins a character web on the board. The class has done character webs many times before and knows that they need to decide on a couple of adjectives that best describe the main character in the story. They know that they will fill in details next to the adjectives the teacher has chosen and then try to come up with other adjectives that they think "sum up" the main character.

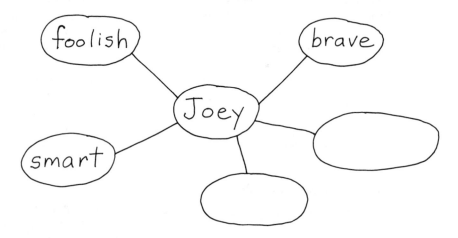

The teacher reads the first three pages of the story and the children listen so that they can tell her what to fill in as evidence that Joey was brave, smart, or foolish. They are also thinking of adjectives they would use to describe Joey.

When the teacher finishes the three pages, the children are eager to offer support for all three adjectives and to suggest others. The teacher writes some of their supporting statements out next to the adjectives and adds the other adjectives that they suggest. She then tells them to finish the story with their partners and to come back ready to add more adjectives and more support for the other adjectives. She reminds them as they read that they should "think" just as they did when she was reading to them: "Think about Joey and his role in the fire and decide what word you think best sums him up and why you think so."

The children then go to read with their partners. Each struggling reader in the class is paired up with a better reader. The teacher had to change the partnerships several times but finally paired up most of the children with someone they liked and who would help them without making it too obvious. Most of the partnerships alternate between periods of oral and silent reading, with partners first reading a page to themselves and then alternating the lead role in discussing, summarizing, or asking the other partner questions. They may reread sections aloud to clarify a point or to emphasize a major point. At times, they take turns reading pages to each other. The teacher encourages them to "help with words they don't know" by focusing on the use of appropriate strategies. Generally, better readers do not intérrupt to correct or supply a word to their partner. Instead, they respond as their teacher does, by saying, "That didn't sound right," or "I didn't get that."

As the partners read, the teacher circulates with her clipboard in hand. She has attached file folder labels to the clipboard and written the initials of six children whose reading she wants to monitor today. (These six children are six of her average readers. Tomorrow, when they read the selection from the easier basal, she will monitor six of her struggling readers.) She stops and asks each child to read aloud very softly and then asks the child which adjective they think is best and why. She makes notes on their labels about their reading fluency and their ability to think about characters. She spends about 2 minutes with each child she is monitoring and notes that each child is able to read the story fluently and could think about and justify character traits.

After about 12 minutes, the teacher notices that many of the partners have finished reading the story. She tells them to start a list of adjectives and justifications while the others finish. After another 4 minutes, she signals the class to join her and help complete the web. (One pair has still not finished reading the story; she tells them to continue and join the group as soon as they finish.)

The class joins her and suggests many more adjectives and justifications for each. She adds the adjectives and writes in a few words of justification next to each. She ends the lesson by letting each child vote on the one adjective that they think best describes Joey. She tallies the votes next to each and reminds the class that the story did not tell us directly what kind of person Joey was. We had to figure out what kind of person he was the same way that we figure out people we meet in real life. Just as we do not always agree about people we meet in real life, we also do not always agree on characters we read about in books. What matters when you read is that you think about the characters and decide what *you* think!

Finally, she tells them, "The story wasn't about pollution, but did it have anything to do with pollution?" The class talks about it and decides that if the newspapers had been recycled and if the old paint had been disposed of, the fire probably would not have happened. They also talk about the air pollution caused by the smoke from the fire.

On Tuesday, they read a story about a family homesteading in Iowa. Before reading, the teacher begins a Then and Now Chart and has the children brainstorm some of the differences they thought would exist in their lives if they were transported back to the prairieland of the 1800s. Once again, the partners read the story together. Today, the teacher has put the names of some of the struggling readers on the labels. She makes notes about their reading fluency and their comprehension of this material, which is closer to their instructional level. When the partners finish reading, they reconvene and complete the chart. The teacher then has them vote on whether they would have rather lived then or now. (*Now* won hands down!)

Finally, she asks them whether the homesteaders had to worry about pollution. A lively discussion ensues as the children realize for the first time that pollution is a relatively new problem for society to contend with.

On Wednesdays and Thursdays, this time is used for Writer's Workshop. Each day, the teacher models how to think of topics and writes a short piece on the overhead. She tries to write a variety of pieces so the children see that writing can take many forms. She has told the children that she used to write a lot when she was their age—most of her writing was for herself and she did not let anyone else see it. They know that she used to keep a diary and write in it every night. Sometimes, she writes in her diary still, the way she did when she was their age. They think it is hilarious when she writes as an intermediate-aged child. She does not read aloud what she is writing, except when she is inventing the spelling of a word. During invented spelling, she says the word slowly, exaggerating the sounds. The children are always eager to see "what she will write today."

On Monday, she decides to write an imaginary diary entry. The children always recognize when she is doing this because she writes the date and "Dear Diary":

> **February 14, 1967**
>
> **Dear Diary,**
>
> **Today was valintin's day. I was so exsited! I sent my best valintin to YOU KNOW WHO! He sent me one too but it wasn't a speshul one he sent a speshul one to ANITA! YUK! I got 23 valentins in all. My Dad bought me some a big box of candy and it was very exspensiv. It cost $1.59!**

The children were all reading along as she wrote. They laughed when she sounded out how to spell *valentine, excited, special,* and *expensive.* They could not imagine that you could ever buy a big box of valentine's candy for just $1.59. When she finishes writing, she says, "Now, I will read it all to make sure it makes sense and that it says what I wanted it to say." She reads it aloud as the children watch. As soon as she finishes, the children's hands are raised, volunteering to be editors.

She reminds the children that a diary entry probably would never be edited because it is personal writing and is certainly not meant to be public. But to provide practice (and becuase it was not a true entry!), she lets them edit it. She then hands a girl a different color marker, and the girl goes to the overhead and leads the class in helping the teacher edit her writing. They use a class-created editing checklist that has seven things to check for:

1. A title is in the middle.
2. Every sentence makes sense.
3. Every sentence begins with a capital and ends with a punctuation mark.
4. People and place names have capital letters.
5. Words that might be misspelled are circled.
6. The writing stays on the topic.
7. Things people say have commas and quotes (She shouted, "Help!").

Each editing convention the children have learned so far is read; the class then checks for these features and volunteers what they think needs fixing. Possible misspelled words are circled; capitals and punctuation marks are added. They decide that a diary entry does not need a title but that it does need a date and a "Dear Diary," both of which this entry has. Some children think that only the first letter of *Anita* should be capitalized, but others argue that it was all in caps for emphasis and that, if it were your diary, you could write it that way!

After this writing minilesson, the teacher takes the children who are publishing a piece this week to the back table with her while the other two-thirds of the class pursue their own writing. Some children begin new pieces. Others continue writing an already begun piece. Some children look in books to help them get ideas and for words they want to spell. Children also looked at the word wall and Big Word Board when they need spelling help. They can be heard saying words very slowly and listening for the sounds they want to represent as they invent-spell some words, just as their teacher did.

The third of the class that the teacher takes with her is composed of a whole range of students. She divides the nine children into three trios and has them read their stories to each other. The children have learned how to help each other revise and edit and know that on the first day they focus only on revising for meaning. When one person reads his or her piece to the other two, the listeners cannot see the writing. They are listening for something they like about it and for something they can suggest to make the piece more clear or more interesting. It takes about 5 minutes for each member of a trio to read the piece and listen to the praise and suggestions. While they are doing this, the teacher circulates and adds her own praise and suggestions.

Once the children have all read and listened, they return to their seats and make whatever additions or changes they choose to. They do the adding and changing right on the page because they have learned to write all first drafts on every other line in their writing notebooks, leaving space for revisions. The teacher circulates, giving encouragement and suggestions to the revisers and those working on first drafts.

On Thursday, they have their second Writer's Workshop of the week. Once again, the teacher writes, but today she claims to be in a poetry mood, so she writes the following cinquain about pollution:

Pollution
Pollution
Scary, Disgusting
Trash, Chemicals, Pesticides.
They threaten our environment.
Recycle!

As she writes today, she makes it obvious that she is getting the spelling of many of the big words from the Big Word Board. After writing, she reads it aloud and then chooses a boy to be the editor. Once again, the editor and the class read through the checklist and help her edit the piece.

The children who are publishing this week bring the piece they revised for meaning yesterday to the back table. The teacher then pairs eight of the children up with partners of similar writing ability. These partners help each other edit using the editing checklist and the procedures used each day when a student edits the teacher's writing. The teacher takes for her partner the child who is having the most difficulty communicating through writing. (When dividing the class into thirds for revising and editing, the teacher makes sure to put the three children having the most difficulty writing in three different groups.) This child needs more help from the teacher, but the teacher is able to use the blank lines to write in words and to help the child produce a piece that he can copy over or type on the computer and can illustrate and be proud of.

As the partners finish helping each other, they bring their pieces to the teacher who reads them and helps fill in needed words, punctuation marks, and so on. Misspelled words are corrected and other obvious problems are fixed. Once the piece has been through a "teacher edit," the children publish it in some form, depending on the piece and how it will be displayed or shared. Some children type their piece into the computer and then print it out. Other children copy their piece on some special paper and illustrate it. Still other children make a book from their piece.

On Friday, during this hour, children are engaged in a variety of activities. This Friday, like most Fridays, the children whose week it is to publish are copying, typing, or illustrating their finished pieces. This is also a time during the week when children can do more reading and research on their expert topic. Each child has been designated class expert on a topic of that child's choice. Every 3 weeks they take a portion of this Friday time to share new information they have learned about their topic. Today is not an Expert Share Friday, but children who are not publishing can choose to spend this time in the room or in the library finding out more about their expert topic. Several children spend this time "just reading"—a Friday afternoon activity encouraged by the teacher. Several children who know that next week is their week to revise, edit, and publish a piece are busy finishing up the piece they have decided to work with. The rules for this afternoon time are simple. It is a time for reading and/or writing, and children can do whatever they choose to as long as what they are doing involves reading or writing.

1:40–2:20   Special Subject

2:20–2:50

The last minutes of any school day are difficult to structure and, in many classrooms, are just "waiting-to-leave" time. When teaching struggling readers, however, we have no time to waste. In this classroom, the teacher has a different activity each day. Children look forward to it, and it also helps her accomplish some of her weekly goals.

Monday   On Mondays, the children get ready for Tuesday's reading to the kindergarten children. Every Monday after lunch, some kindergartners bring favorite books from the kindergarten. On a sticky note attached to each book is the name of the kindergarten child who would like to have that book read to him or her tomorrow. (The teacher and the kindergarten children have chosen a book for each child.) The books are quickly distributed to the big buddies, who then practice reading that book in preparation for tomorrow's reading. Some children tape record their reading to check how they sound. The teacher reminds her big kids of the steps in reading the book to their little buddies:

1. Read the book title and author's name and ask your little buddy what she or he thinks the book will be about.
2. Look through the book, talking about the things you see in the pictures before reading.
3. Read the book and help your little buddy talk about it. Ask questions that get your little buddy involved with the book:

   What do you think will happen next?
   Would you like to do that?

4. When you finish reading, ask your little buddy to find his or her favorite page and tell why it was the favorite.
5. Go through the book again and let your little buddy tell you what is happening or help read it to you if some parts are very easy.

The children eagerly read the books, which include such classics as *Robert the Rose Horse, The Little Red Hen,* and *Caps for Sale.* The teacher sits with one boy who is a very hesitant reader and who needs her help to read this book successfully tomorrow. She leads him to look through the pictures and to predict what will happen, in the same way that she wants him to do so with his little buddy tomorrow. As they look at the pictures, she supplies words and phrases needed so he can successfully read the book. She then reads and enjoys it with him. She praises him for his reading and asks him to read it with her once more as soon as he arrives at school tomorrow so that he will be able to read it with expression and enthusiasm.

Tuesday   The kindergartners arrive and the big buddies read to their little buddies. The intermediate-grade teacher and the kindergarten teacher circulate, stopping to listen to children read and helping them engage their young listeners with good "reader involvement" questions. The kindergartners come with all their gear, prepared to go home from here. Many of the big kids walk out with their little buddies in tow.

Wednesday   On Wednesdays, the children are divided into groups of four (using the deck of playing cards again), and each child has 5 minutes to read about or tell about something they have read this week. The cards are passed out and the children get together wherever the teacher has put that number. (The teacher places big number cards around the room—1 at the back table, 2 at her desk, 3 in the corner, and so on.) They share in alphabetical order of the suit they get—clubs, diamonds, hearts, spades. The teacher sets her timer for 5 minutes; the children have become good at preparing for this 5 minutes. Most know right where to find the scary, funny, silly, or fascinating part of the book that they want to read. Some children have riddle and joke books with the best riddles and jokes ready to share. The teacher circulates, making notes on her clipboard labels about books children choose and whether the accuracy and fluency exhibited while reading suggest that the book was an appropriate choice. When the timer sounds, she says, "Diamonds," and the second person in each group gets her or his 5 minutes. If a few minutes remain after all four people have had their turns, the teacher asks different children to share something particularly interesting with the whole class.

Thursday   On Thursdays, the same procedure is used to have children share writing that was used on Wednesday to share books. Cards are dealt. Children go wherever the teacher has put their number and have 5 minutes to share something they have written or that they are in the process of writing. Usually, but not always, the children who are revising that week share their piece. Other children read a piece they have decided to revise next week. Still other children read a piece they have just begun and tell what else they intend to write. If the child finishes reading before the 5 minutes are up, the reader can call on the listeners to tell "things they liked." The teacher makes notes on her clipboard labels indicating what different children have written about and have chosen to share.

Friday   Once again, Friday varies. Usually, the teacher takes a few minutes to have the children who have just published something show it to the class. On some Fridays, the whole class has an Expert Share. On this Friday, the teacher is nearly finished with a chapter book, and the children are eager to see how it ends, so the teacher devotes the entire last 35 minutes to finishing reading the book aloud to the class, letting them respond to it, and drawing slips to see who gets the book and to form the order of the waiting list.

Each day, when the children leave, the teacher removes the labels from the clipboard and puts them on the outside of each child's folder. (Inside this folder are samples of writing, reading responses, and other work.) As she puts on new labels with new comments, she looks at the previous labels and considers how each child is growing. Sometimes, as she reflects on the different children whose reading and writing she has focused on that day, she thinks of other questions she has about that child's literacy development. She then puts this child's initials, tomorrow's date, and a few words to remind her of what to look for on the label and spends some time focusing on the same child again tomorrow. Although some children are focused on more often than others, she tries to focus on each child at least once a week. The combination of weekly anecdotal records and samples of writing and reading responses kept in the folder gives the teacher a basis for deciding how well children are progressing toward becoming more literate, as well as information that guides her whole-class, small-group, and individual instruction.

CHAPTER 12

Beyond the Classroom: Things Worth Fighting For

We wrote this book to help classroom teachers provide the highest-quality literacy instruction for all children. As much as possible, we have confined ourselves to discussing changes, adaptations, and additions that, as classroom teachers, are within your power. You can decide that real reading and writing will take precedence in your classrooms and commit to providing the necessary time, materials, models, and motivation. You can decide to involve all children in comprehension and writing activities on a daily or weekly basis. You can decide that all children should learn to read and spell high-frequency words automatically and that they should develop effective strategies that help them figure out how to read and spell unfamiliar words. You can make sure that you include effective science and social studies instruction and expand your children's knowledge.

To some extent, you have control of grouping and scheduling. You can create larger blocks of time by integrating reading and writing with the knowledge subjects. You can help your children learn to work cooperatively with one another and can use a variety of partner, trio, and team groupings. You can pair up with another like-minded teacher and have big buddy–little buddy arrangements. You can coordinate with specialists and/or enlist the help of tutors so that your most needy students receive additional instruction.

The premise of this book is that you, as a classroom teacher who has control of almost 1,000 hours of learning time, can make and carry out decisions that result in greatly increased literacy levels for your children. Research and experience tells us that what the classroom teacher does, day in and day out and minute by minute, has the greatest effect on what children learn. For most children who "beat the odds," a teacher made that difference.

We know that other factors accelerate the achievement of struggling readers, but they are not within the power of classroom teachers. These changes, additions, and adaptations usually require a total school effort, an administrative decision, or some form of community action. Some require political action in legislative arenas. For more specifics on these beyond-the-classroom solutions, see our book *Schools That Work: Where All Children Read and Write* (Allington & Cunningham,

2002). Whereas the major efforts of a classroom teacher are rightfully expended within one classroom, we feel that you should know which beyond-the-classroom suggestions are worth whatever crusading efforts you are able to make. The remainder of this chapter is devoted to elaborating our list of "things worth fighting for."

SMALLER CLASS SIZE

Smaller class size, by itself, does not necessarily make a significant difference in children's learning, but smaller class size combined with the best instruction does. Recently, many large states have moved to reduce class size, particularly in the primary grades, but with increasing school enrollment, class size is creeping back up in many schools. McGill-Franzen and Allington (1991) note that we are now spending substantial sums of money on things that we know do not work, that is, retention in grade and transitional-grade programs, to name but two. If the money allocated to support these practices were redirected, class sizes could be reduced substantially in many schools.

The research available shows that smaller classes do facilitate better teaching and more personalized instruction (Achilles, 1999). The key to enhancing the quality of instruction lies in increasing teachers' expertise in effective reading instruction and in helping teachers act appropriately on that knowledge. With smaller classes, the latter is easier to accomplish, but not assured.

EARLY INTERVENTION

A variety of studies have demonstrated the effectiveness of early intervention programs (K–2) compared to interventions begun later (Pikulski, 1994). The best early intervention programs are targeted to the needs of children rather than designed for "one size fits all." All schools need effective early intervention programs in place, but especially schools that serve large numbers of children who arrive with few experiences with books, stories, and print. Early intervention efforts must be designed to provide each child with access to sufficiently intensive expert reading instruction. The available research indicates that an effective early intervention plan is comprised of three components: effective classroom reading instruction, targeted small-group support, and one-to-one tutoring (Allington, 2002).

Even if every classroom offered the effective classroom reading instruction we have described in this book, some students still need additional instructional support. The evidence indicates that a trained reading teacher can conduct small-group (two or three students) support lessons that often foster accelerated reading development. Larger-group remedial support does not work very well, nor does small-group instruction offered by paraprofessionals (Allington & Cunningham,

2002). The most effective small-group support is well coordinated with the classroom lessons and provides added opportunities for reading and writing and more expert and more personalized teaching.

Some children need very intensive one-to-one support if they are to become readers and writers. Tutoring those children can produce dramatically improved reading achievement (Shanahan, 1998). The Reading Recovery program is often criticized for being expensive, but it has the best track record for bringing struggling readers up to the average reading level of their classmates in a limited number of one-on-one tutoring sessions (Clay, 1993).

BETTER SCHOOL LIBRARIES AND BETTER ACCESS TO BOOKS

Perhaps it is not surprising that schools with large numbers of poor children often have wholly inadequate school libraries and nonexistent classroom libraries. We must provide all children with access to books. Currently, children in schools that are located in low-economic neighborhoods have about 50 percent fewer books in their schools than children going to schools located in wealthy communities (McQuillan, 1998). These poor schools serve the very children who are least likely to live in literate home environments and least likely to have access to public library facilities. These are the schools that should have (and must strive to have) the very best school libraries with the largest selection of informational texts, picture books, and multicultural literature. The classroom libraries in these schools need to include several hundred books.

These schools need to have the most liberal library policies for loaning books to students and their families. The school library needs to be open before and after school so children without books at home can have access to the resources at school. This library needs to invite children to drop in at virtually any time to browse, read, search for, study, and select books. These school libraries need multiple subscriptions to magazines so that they too can be loaned out. They even need to be open during the summer vacation period.

Upgrading the quality and quantity of library resources in schools with large numbers of disadvantaged children is worth fighting for. Enhancing access to the school library is also important. Expanding classroom library collections is necessary. Having wonderful books is of little use if access is limited!

RESPONSIVE SPECIAL PROGRAMS

Millions of dollars of federal, state, and local money are spent each year on children who fall in specific "categories." In many cases, the special education programs and remedial programs have simply established scores and levels that determine whether a child can receive any special help. Some children qualify for many programs and may be seen by several different special teachers each day. These different specialists (e.g., speech teacher, reading teacher, counseling psychologist) rarely coordinate what they do with each other. Some of these children receive minimal classroom instruction because they are seldom in the classroom. Despite this, their assigned classroom teacher is usually held accountable for their progress! Other children "fall through the cracks," often because they just miss the cutoff point on whatever test or tests have been selected to determine eligibility.

We hope to soon see more "responsive" programs and fewer children labeled and categorized. Responsive programs respond to children's needs as soon as they are evident, not after they finally test eligible for some available categorical program. We hope to see interventions that provide children with access to extra-instructional efforts on the day they first need them. For instance, if Maria misses 4 days of school because of illness, a school program should provide her with extra assistance on the day she returns and until she catches up with her classmates.

We hope to soon see schools design intervention programs that provide children with sufficient extra instruction to return them to the classroom at a level with their peers in a very short time. Too often today, at-risk children receive what is available, not what they need. Too often, special help comes too late—a year or more after it becomes apparent that a child is in trouble. A whole year may be spent waiting for the child to become eligible for some categorical program. By not providing immediate extrainstructional support, the problem is intensified and becomes more difficult to resolve.

The present system of categorizing children and specifying what kind of support various children can or must get is not meeting the needs of most struggling readers. Classroom teachers should work with administrators, parent groups, and others to develop ways to meet children's needs that do not require rigid entry standards and inflexible categories.

EXTENDING THE SCHOOL DAY OR YEAR

We are not in favor of the mandatory, for-everyone, more-is-better time extensions that many reformers are calling for. However, we would like to see optional extensions for children who want it or need it most. We believe after-school and summer school programs are needed to provide added expert instructional support for children who need it. We do not have enough hours in the present school day or year to provide every struggling learner with all the mind- and body-enriching experiences needed to effect optimal learning. In too many poor neighborhoods, as well as some not-so-poor neighborhoods, too many latchkey children are going home to empty houses and mindless hours in front of the TV. We would like these children to be able to stay at school and participate in extended-day activities that strive to increase their world knowledge and their motivation to learn. In addition, too many children in these and other neighborhoods spend all summer with little or nothing to read. The net result is a summer "reading loss" of several months, a loss that could be ameliorated if these children had access to the books and magazines locked away all summer in the neighborhood elementary school.

Many elementary schools could manage to provide extended school days with few additional personnel and with little additional funding. For instance, schools could schedule special teachers (art, music, computer, guidance, P.E., remedial reading, resource room, ESL, etc.) to begin their working day at 10:30 and end at 5:30. Some of their special classes would be scheduled between 11:30 and 3:30, but these classes would also be scheduled during the after-school programs. Thus, some children would receive their small-group remedial reading in the after-school program and perhaps afterward go to an after-school computer class to work on a related reading/writing activity. On other days those students might participate in an after-school art activity related to their reading or writing work in the after-school program. In addition to providing both intensive and enriching after-school activities, this arrangement would result in all classroom teachers having totally uninterrupted teaching time from 8:30–11:30 each day!

In schools with high concentrations of poor children, current federal program guidelines allow those schools to use categorical program funds to extend the school day or extend the school year into the summer months. Classroom teachers know that they do not have enough hours in the day or days in the school year to help all children achieve all their required learning goals. Some children simply need extended-day programs to keep up with or catch up to their peers.

AN END TO RETENTION AND TRACKING

An abundance of evidence reveals that many traditional "solutions" to the problems of underachievement actually contribute to the problems struggling learners face. For instance, in over 100 years of research, study after study shows that retaining struggling learners (usually struggling readers) has no positive effect on their achievement and increases the likelihood that retained students drop out of school (Shepard & Smith, 1989). In addition, retention is typically the most expensive school response to underachievement. The cost of an additional year of schooling far exceeds the cost of more effective interventions, including small-group remediation, tutoring, and summer school (Allington & McGill-Franzen, 1995).

Likewise, a long history of research shows the negative effects of tracking children by achievement levels (Wheelock, 1992). Filling a classroom with all the low-achieving students (or all the high-achieving ones) fails to have a positive effect on learning for many reasons, but, and even more important, tracked schools do not resemble the real world. Not all the people we know, work with, go to church with, or interact with were high-achieving students, nor were they all low-achieving students. One important goal of schools is to prepare students to participate in our society, which means learning to work productively with many different folks, all different from us. Additionally, creating classrooms with 20–25 children who have similar achievement levels across the range of subjects taught is almost impossible. Some kids may be low achieving in reading but above-average in math (and vice versa). Some may be good at recognizing words but not so good at understanding what they read, but they end up with the same reading level on an achievement test as the child who comprehends well but has problems with word recognition. In short, although tracking may narrow the achievement range a bit, tracking does not create classrooms in which one-size-fits-all instruction works to meet the needs of all students.

HEAD START/EVEN START

Head Start and Even Start are programs for economically disadvantaged 4-year-olds. Head Start has been around since the sixties and has been fairly successful in improving the school readiness of participating children. Even Start is a family literacy program that includes preschool children and their parents. Both children and parents go to school. Parents work to complete their high school education or receive adult literacy instruction. Children participate in a preschool program.

We know that children from high-literacy homes enter school with over 1,000 hours of informal reading and writing encounters, from which they develop an understanding about print that is essential to success in beginning reading. The literate home simulation kindergartens described in this book are designed to make up for some of the experiences many children have missed out on. Children who participate in Head Start or Even Start programs can be provided with many of the critical early literacy experiences, especially if the programs are modeled after the opportunities available in the literate home environment. When preschool programs immerse children in a print-rich and story-rich environment, the children acquire the same kind of knowledge about reading and writing as more advantaged children. When these programs also include effective parent support, we can begin to close the gap that now exists between children from different communities.

HELPFUL STANDARDS AND
THOUGHTFUL ASSESSMENTS

Across the United States individual states have been developing new standards for literacy learning. Much of this activity was stimulated by federal initiatives intended to raise achievement goals and to make clearer the grade-level competencies that are expected of all students (Rothman, 1995). Different states have taken very different approaches to standards development, and this seems to be one reason that standards vary widely from state to state. Some states prepare long lists of very specific grade-level standards:

Students will recognize words containing the *er, ir, ur* letter–sound patterns.

Other states have much broader, and far fewer, standards:

Students will use letter–sound relationships, onset-rime patterns, and the syntax of the sentence to arrive independently at the pronunciation of an unknown word.

Once standards are developed, states develop student assessments that, hopefully, match the standards. Again, different states seem to take different paths in developing assessments. Some states develop a variety of word-recognition tasks and traditional measures of comprehension using short passages and multiple-choice items. In contrast, several states use more authentic reading and writing tasks. In these states students read an actual book (e.g., an Eyewitness book in a content area) and then respond to some multiple-choice items and some extended-response items (i.e., items that involve writing a short or long essay). Typically, the extended-response items are weighted at least as heavily as the multiple-choice items.

The type of standards and assessments developed have wide-ranging effects on teaching and learning. If we want teachers to focus on important goals, and children to become thoughtful readers, we must fight against narrow standards and assessments that measure low levels of processing. We must fight for the development of standards and assessments that provide teachers with a clearer understanding of the important elements of a comprehensive, thoughtful literacy program and with better information on how student literacy is developing.

FAMILY AND COMMUNITY INVOLVEMENT

Schools that have unusually high success rates with struggling readers are usually schools with high levels of family and community involvement. These schools make superhuman efforts to reach out to the parents and surrogate parents—aunts, cousins, grandmothers—and involve them in the school. Getting the parents of at-risk children to come to school is often not an easy task. Many of the parents did not succeed in school themselves and their memories of school are not pleasant. Many of the parents have very limited literacy levels, and many are not proficient in English.

But all parents want the best for their children and, when they do feel welcome and included, can become a powerful source of support for teachers. Schools that want parental support provide a variety of school-based programs and services. They have monthly parent meetings in which the children "star" in a variety of productions. They send home weekly parent-friendly newsletters that have lots of pictures and announcements showing their children excelling! Administrators and home–school coordinators visit homes and bring along games, books, tape recorders, computers, and other activities that parents can borrow and use with their children. Catherine Snow and her colleagues (Snow, Barnes, Chandler, Goodman, & Hemphill, 1991) found that urban teachers who rated their parents as interested and involved were teachers who made 10–15 teacher-initiated parent contacts for every 1 contact made by teachers who reported uninterested parents. Parents of struggling readers often do not initiate contact with schools and teachers. However, they can be enticed to involve themselves in the school and their child's schooling. But the enticing of the involvement seems critical.

Many parents would like to help, and know they should, but do not know how. Patricia Edwards (1991), of Michigan State University, notes that she found that many less well educated parents simply did not know how to read *to their children,* even if they could read themselves (some could not). If parents never experienced lap reading themselves, how would they learn how to do it? In the case of the parents that Edwards worked with, they learned from a series of videos she prepared (available from Children's Press) that showed parents reading to and with their children and that explained what the parents were doing. These videos can be shown at parent meetings or loaned out to parents to review at home. Edwards demonstrated that just telling parents to read to their children or to help their children with school work is often insufficient.

Researchers at the Center for Disadvantaged Students, at Johns Hopkins University (Slavin, Karweit, & Wasik, 1993) delivered this same message after their work developing homework packets for parents. They found that low-income parents were very willing to work with their children, but they often needed more guidance than schools made available. These researchers worked with teachers to target key skills and strategies that parents could work on with their children and then organized homework packets with easy-to-follow directions. Not only were they surprised at the overwhelmingly positive response from parents, but also at the increase in student achievement that followed.

FAIRNESS IN FUNDING

Jonathan Kozol (1991), in *Savage Inequalities,* candidly describes the steady movement in this nation toward a two-tiered educational system—one system that serves our suburbs and the other our urban and rural areas. The former is substantially better funded than the latter. Why would we create an educational system in which schools with large numbers of poor children routinely receive 50 percent less funding per child than schools with virtually no disadvantaged children? Why would we have a system in which poor parents pay a substantially larger proportion of their paychecks to support schools but still cannot match the wealth generated in communities serving wealthier families? Why would we support a system in which New York City schools receive 50 percent less money than those in suburban Scarsdale, a system whereby some public schools spend three to four times as much per pupil as others in the same state? Why should we tolerate a system in which some children have carpeting and air conditioning whereas others have sewage and rats in the hallways?

Educating children costs money. Educating some children will inevitably cost more then educating others. Currently, our system is more likely to provide more funding to schools with few needy children than to schools with many. If we are serious about all children learning to read and write, we must seriously work to alter existing funding patterns and to provide some sort of modicum of fairness in funding. It is not that money will cure everything, but a good education does cost more than offering a bare minimum.

WELL-PLANNED PROFESSIONAL DEVELOPMENT

For too long, few states and few school districts developed any kind of comprehensive professional development initiatives. Instead, in-service sessions were scheduled, but often these sessions offered a generally haphazard and somewhat shallow approach to enhancing teacher expertise. What we know about teacher learning suggests that such approaches have little effect on improving (or changing) instruction. Instead, teachers need to develop their expertise in supportive, long-term professional relationships that focus on developing an understanding of how instruction impacts a child's learning in very specific ways (Duffy, 1997).

When activities such as Teachers As Readers conversation groups and participation in on-line listserves are combined with more traditional activities, such as membership in professional associations and attendance at these association conferences, as well as at workshops presented by invited professionals, and at professional journal readings, they can promote the kind of ongoing information needed to trigger reflection on personal practices. But teachers need to discuss their teaching professionally, not just read or hear about best practice. They need opportunities to observe others and to be observed in a nonevaluative setting and then to engage in professional conversations about teaching. Too few schools have institutionalized opportunities for productive professional conversations in the normal workday. But the most effective teachers have reported that just such opportunities led to the development of their teaching expertise (Day, 2001).

TEACHER INPUT ON THE BUSINESS OF RUNNING SCHOOLS

In many schools today, teacher committees have a say in how the money is spent, how special subjects are scheduled, and who are their administrators. This power has been entrusted to teachers not because of any new high regard for "regular" teachers, but because it is becoming increasingly clear that the top-down bureaucratic procedures of the past have not resulted in better schooling. In many schools, classroom teachers have the opportunity to effect changes beyond their classroom; they should seize the moment! The kind of decisions they make can determine whether they continue to have any power.

Whereas individual schools must set their own priorities, some general considerations apply to all schools. Teachers who want children to engage in lots of real reading and writing should see to it that a good chunk of whatever money is available for materials gets spent on books and magazines, both for the school library and for classroom libraries. Writing materials are generally not expensive, but a variety should be available. Paper for making books and a book binding machine should be as accessible as ditto paper and a ditto machine. Every classroom should have a few computers, a good printer, and some writing/publishing software.

The schedule is another area that classroom teachers should try to affect. In some schools, special teachers set their own schedules or have them set by a supervisor. Children come and go at all hours and classroom teachers seldom have an uninterrupted hour in which to teach anything to everyone. In other schools, a certain period of time—between 45 and 90 minutes—is designated for special subjects for each grade level. In addition to having only one time period each day when the children go somewhere and then come back again, scheduling special subjects by grade-level blocks provides the classroom teachers with some grade-level planning time each week. Other schools work in the reverse but still achieve a similar result. These schools have "safe" periods for each classroom every day—periods of 90–120 minutes when no child is to be pulled out for any special service.

Too many children, especially struggling readers, spend their school day moving from pillar to post, program to program, teacher to teacher, and subject to subject. Too often, teachers work in schools where their work is constantly interrupted by children leaving for support services (remedial reading, resource room, speech, etc.), children leaving for special subjects (art, P.E., music, computer, etc.), and loudspeaker announcements from the office. In some schools, classroom teachers rarely have more than 10–15 minutes of uninterrupted time with all the children in their classroom. No sane human being would design such an organizational plan if teaching and learning were high on the agenda!

It is important that teachers and children have large uninterrupted blocks of time to work together. We have found that when schools set a goal of providing these blocks, they can almost always be achieved. Two- or three-hour uninterrupted blocks are worth fighting for!

References

Achilles, C. M. (1999). *Let's put kids first, finally: Getting class size right.* Thousand Oaks, CA: Corwin Press.

Adams, M. J. (1990). *Beginning to read: Thinking and learning about print.* Cambridge, MA: MIT Press.

Allington, R. L. (1983). The reading instruction provided readers of differing reading ability. *Elementary School Journal, 83,* 549–559.

Allington, R. L. (2000). How to improve high-stakes test scores without really improving. *Issues in Education, 6,* 115–124.

Allington, R. L. (2001). *What really matters for struggling readers: Designing research-based interventions.* New York: Longman.

Allington, R. L. (2002). Research on reading/learning disability interventions. In A. Farstrup & S. J. Samuels (Eds.), *What research says about reading instruction* (3rd ed.). Newark, DE: International Reading Association.

Allington, R. L., & Cunningham, P. M. (2002). *Schools that work: Where all children read and write* (2nd ed.). New York: Longman.

Allington, R. L., & Johnston, P. (2001). Characteristics of exemplary fourth grade instruction. In C. Roller (Ed.), *Learning to teach reading: Setting the research agenda.* Newark, DE: International Reading Association.

Allington, R. L., & McGill-Franzen, A. M. (1995). Flunking: Throwing good money after bad. In R. L. Allington & S. A. Walmsley (Eds.), *No quick fix: Rethinking literacy programs in America's elementary schools* (pp. 45–60). New York: Teacher's College Press.

Beck, I. L., McKeown, M. G., Hamilton, R. L., & Kucan, L. (1997). *Questioning the author: An approach for enhancing student engagement with text.* Newark, DE: International Reading Association.

Caine, R. N., & Caine, G. (1991). *Teaching and the human brain.* Alexandria, VA: Association for Supervision and Curriculum Development.

Caldwell, J. (2002). *Reading assessment: A primer for teachers and tutors.* New York: Guilford.

Calkins, L. (1994). *The art of teaching writing.* Portsmouth, NH: Heinemann.

Carr, E., & Ogle, D. (1987). KWL plus: A strategy for comprehension and summarization. *Journal of Reading, 30,* 626–631.

Clay, M. M. (1993). *An observation survey of early literacy achievement.* Portsmouth, NH: Heinemann.

Cudd, E. T. (1989). Research and report writing in the elementary grades. *The Reading Teacher, 43*(3), 268–269.

Cudd, E. T., & Roberts, L. (1989). Using writing to enhance content area learning in the primary grades. *The Reading Teacher, 42,* 392–404.

Cunningham, P. M. (2000). *Phonics they use: Words for reading and writing* (3rd ed.). New York: HarperCollins.

Cunningham. P. M., & Cunningham, J. W. (1992). Making words: Enhancing the invented spelling–decoding connection. *The Reading Teacher, 46,* 106–107.

Cunningham, P. M., Crawley, S., & Mountain, L. (1983). Vocabulary scavenger hunts: A scheme for schema development. *Reading Horizons, 24,* 45–50.

Cunningham, P. M., & Hall, D. P. (1997). *Month by month phonics for first grade.* Greensboro, NC: Carson-Dellosa.

Cunningham, P. M., & Hall, D. P. (1997). *Month by month phonics for upper grades.* Greensboro, NC: Carson-Dellosa.

Cunningham, P. M., & Hall, D. P. (1998). *Month by month phonics for third grade.* Greensboro, NC: Carson-Dellosa.

Cunningham, P. M., Hall, D. P., & Cunningham, J. W. (2000). *Guided reading the four blocks way.* Greensboro, NC: Carson-Dellosa.

Cunningham, P. M., Hall, D. P., & Gambrell, L. (2002). *Self-selected reading the four blocks way.* Greensboro, NC: Carson-Dellosa.

Cunningham, P. M., Hall, D. P., & Sigmon, C. M. (1999). *The teacher's guide to the four blocks.* Greensboro, NC: Carson-Dellosa.

Day, J. P. (2001). How I became an exemplary teacher (although I'm still learning just like everyone else). In M. Pressley, R. L. Allington, R. Wharton-McDonald, C. C. Block, & L. Morrow (Eds.), *Learning to read: Lessons from exemplary first-grade classrooms.* New York: Guilford.

Day, J. P., Spiegel, D. L., McLellan, J., & Brown, V. B. (2002). *Moving forward with literature circles.* New York: Scholastic.

Duffy, G. G. (1997). Powerful models or powerful teachers? An argument for teacher-as-entrepreneur. In S. S. & D. Hayes (Eds.), *Instructional models in reading* (pp. 351–365). Mahwah, NJ: Lawrence Erlbaum.

Duke, N. K. (2000). 3.6 minutes per day: The scarcity of informational texts in first grade. *Reading Research Quarterly, 35,* 2.

Duthie, C. (1996). *True stories: Nonfiction literacy in the primary classroom.* Portsmouth, NH: Heinemann.

Edwards, P. A. (1991). Fostering early literacy through parent coaching. In E. H. Hiebart (Ed.), *Literacy for a diverse society: Perspectives, practices, and policies* (pp. 199–212). New York: Teachers College Press.

Ericson, L., & Fraser-Juliebo, M. (1998). *The phonological awareness handbook for kindergarten and primary teachers.* Newark, DE: International Reading Association.

Fall, R., Webb, N. M., & Chudowsky, N. (2000). Group discussion and large-scale language arts assessment: Effects on students' comprehension. *American Educational Research Journal, 37*(4), 911–941.

Faltis, C. J. (1993). *Joinfostering: Adapting teaching strategies for the multilingual classroom.* New York: Merrill.

Fitzpatrick, J. (1997). *Phonemic awareness: Playing with sounds to strengthen beginning reading skills.* Cypress, CA: Creative Teaching Press.

Gardner, H. (1993). *Multiple intelligences: The theory in practice.* New York: Basic Books.

Graves, D. H. (1995). *A fresh look at writing.* Portsmouth, NH: Heinemann.

Guthrie, J. T., McCann, A. D., Hynd, C., & Stahl, S. (1998). Classroom contexts promoting literacy engagement. In J. Flood, S. B. Heath, & D. Lapp (Eds.), *A handbook for literacy educators: Research on teaching the communicative visual arts.* Newark, DE: International Reading Association.

Guthrie, J. T., Van Meter, O., McCann, A. D., Wigfield, A., Bennett, I., Poundstone, C. C., Rice, M. E., Faibisch, F. M., Hunt, B., & Mitchell, A. M. (1996). Growth of literacy engagement: Changes in motivations and strategies during concept-oriented reading instruction. *Reading Research Quarterly, 31,* 306–332.

Hall, D. P., & Cunningham, P. M. (1997). *Month by month reading and writing for kindergarten.* Greensboro, NC: Carson-Dellosa.

Hall, D. P., & Cunningham, P. M. (1998). *Month by month phonics for second grade.* Greensboro, NC: Carson-Dellosa.

Hall, D. P., & Williams, E. (2000). *The teacher's guide to building blocks.* Greensboro, NC: Carson-Dellosa.

Harris, V. J. (Ed.). (1997). *Using multiethnic literature in the K–8 classroom.* Norwood, MA: Christopher Gordon.

Harvey, S., & Goudvis, A. (2000). *Strategies that work: Teaching comprehension to enhance understanding.* York, ME: Stenhouse.

Invernizzi, M., Juel, C., & Rosemay, C. A. (1997). A community volunteer tutorial that works. *The Reading Teacher, 50,* 304–311.

Ivey, G., & Broaddus, K. (2001). "Just plain reading": A survey of what makes students want to read in middle school classrooms. *Reading Research Quarterly, 36,* 350–377.

Johns, J. J. (2001). *Basic reading inventory* (8th ed.). Dubuque, IA: Kendall/Hunt.

Johnston, P., & Allington, R. L. (1991). Remediation. In R. Barr, M. Kamil, P. Mosenthal, & P. D. Pearson (Eds.), *Handbook of reading research* (Vol. 2, pp. 418–452). New York: Longman.

Keene, E. L., & Zimmerman, S. (1997). *Mosaic of thought: Teaching comprehension in a reader's workshop.* Portsmouth, NH: Heinemann.

Kozol, J. (1991). *Savage inequalities: Children in America's schools.* New York: Crown.

Langer, J., & Allington, R. L. (1992). Writing and reading curriculum. In P. Jackson (Ed.), *The handbook of curriculum research* (pp. 687–725). New York: Macmillan.

Leslie, L., & Caldwell, J. (2001). *Qualitative reading inventory—3.* New York: Longman.

Macon, J. M., Bewell, D., & Vogt, M. (1991). *Responses to literature.* Newark, DE: International Reading Association.

Manning, G. L., & Manning, M. (1984). What models of recreational reading make a difference? *Reading World, 23,* 375–380.

McGill-Franzen, A. M., & Allington, R. L. (1991). The gridlock of low achievement: Perspectives on policy and practice. *Remedial and Special Education, 12,* 20–30.

McQuillan, J. (1998). *The literacy crisis: False claims, real solutions.* Portsmouth, NH: Heinemann.

Moline, S. (1995). *I see what you mean: Children at work with visual information.* York, ME: Stenhouse.

Morrow, L. M., Pressley, M., Smith, J. K., & Smith, M. (1997). The effect of a literature-based program integrated into literacy and science instruction with children from diverse backgrounds. *Reading Research Quarterly, 32,* 54–75.

Ogle, D. (1986). K-W-L: A teaching model that develops active reading of expository text. *The Reading Teacher, 39,* 564–570.

Opitz, M. P. (2000). *Rhymes & reasons: Literature and language play for phonological awareness.* Portsmouth, NH: Heinemann.

Pearson, P. D., & Fielding, L. (1991). Comprehension instruction. In R. Barr, M. Kamil, P. Mosenthal, & P. D. Pearson (Eds.), *Handbook of reading research* (Vol. 2, pp. 815–860). New York: Longman.

Pikulski, J. J. (1994). Preventing reading failure: A review of five effective programs. *Reading Teacher, 48,* 30–39.

Pilla, M. L. (1990). *The best high/low books for reluctant readers.* Englewood, CO: Libraries Unlimited.

Pittleman, S. D., Heimlich, J. E., Berglund, R., & French, M. P. (1991). *Semantic feature analysis: Classroom applications.* Newark, DE: International Reading Association.

Pressley, M. (1998). *Reading instruction that works: The case for balanced teaching.* New York: Guilford.

Pressley, M., Allington, R. L., Wharton-McDonald, R., Block, C. C., & Morrow, L. (2001). *Learning to read: Lessons from exemplary first-grade classrooms.* New York: Guilford.

Raphael, T. E., Kirschner, B. W., & Englert, C. S. (1988). Expository writing program: Making connections between reading and writing. *The Reading Teacher, 41,* 790–795.

Rothman, R. (1995). *Measuring up: Standards, assessment, and school reform.* San Francisco: Jossey-Bass.

Routman, R. (1991). *Invitations.* Portsmouth, NH: Heinemann.

Shanahan, T. (1988). The reading–writing relationship: Seven instructional principles. *The Reading Teacher, 41,* 636–647.

Shepard, L. A., & Smith, M. L. (Eds.). (1989). *Flunking grades: Research and policies on retention.* Philadelphia: Falmer.

Slavin, R. E., Karweit, N. L., & Wasik, B. A. (1993). *Preventing early school failure: Research, policy, and practice.* Boston: Allyn & Bacon.

Smith, C., Constantino, R., & Krashen, S. (1997). Differences in print environment: Children in Beverly Hills, Compton and Watts. *Emergency Librarian, 24,* 8–9.

Snow, C. E., Barnes, W. S., Chandler, J., Goodman, I., & Hemphill, L. (1991). *Unfulfilled expectations: Home and school influences on literacy.* Cambridge, MA: Harvard University Press.

Spivey, N. (1997). *The constructivist metaphor: Reading, writing and the making of meaning.* New York: Academic Press.

Stanovich, K. E. (1991). Word recognition: Changing perspectives. In R. Barr, M. Kamil, P. Mosenthal, & P. D. Pearson (Eds.), *Handbook of reading research* (Vol. 2, pp. 418–452). New York: Longman.

Stauffer, R. G. (1980). *The language-experience approach to the teaching of reading* (2nd ed.). New York: Harper & Row.

Sudduth, P. (1989). Introducing response logs to poor readers. *The Reading Teacher, 42,* 452–454.

Taylor, B. M., Hanson, B., Swanson, K., & Watts, S. (1998). Helping struggling readers in grades two and four: Linking small-group intervention with cross-age tutoring. *The Reading Teacher, 51,* 196–209.

Van Allen, R. V., & Allen, C. (1966). *Language experiences in reading: Teachers' resource book.* Chicago: Encyclopedia Brittanica Press.

Visser, C. (1991). Football and reading do mix. *The Reading Teacher, 44,* 710–711.

Walp, T., & Walmsley, S. A. (1995). Integrating literature and composing into the language arts curriculum. *No Quick Fix, 90,* 251–274.

Wheelock, A. (1992). *Crossing tracks: How untracking can save America's schools.* New York: The New Press.

Wylie, R. E., & Durrell, D. D. (1970). Teaching vowels through phonograms. *Elementary English, 47,* 787–791.

Children's Books and Other Teaching Resources

(See also book lists on pages 11, 13, 16, 19, 184–185, 199)

Children's Books

Alphabet Annie Announces an All-American Album, Susan Purviance and Marcia O'Shell

Anastasia at Your Service, Lois Lowry

Are You My Mother? P. D. Eastman

Aunt Flossie's Hats (and Crabcakes Later), Elizabeth Fitzgerald Howard

Brown Bear, Brown Bear, What Do You See? Bill Martin

Caps for Sale, Esphyr Slobodkina

Cathedral, David MacCauley

Clifford the Big Red Dog, Normal Bridwell

Get On Out of Here, Philip Hall, B. Greene

Go Dog Go, P. D. Eastman

Goodnight Moon, Marcia Brown

Hattie and the Fox, Mem Fox

Hop on Pop, Theodore Le Sieg

How Things Work, Time-Life Books

I Went Walking, Sue Williams

Inside, Outside, Upside Down, Stan and Jan Berenstain

Island of the Blue Dolphins, Scott O'Dell

Missing: One Stuffed Rabbit, Maryann Cocca-Leffler

Once Upon a Sidewalk, Jean Craighead George

One Fish, Two Fish, Red Fish, Blue Fish, Theodore Le Sieg

Our Friend, the Sun, Janet Palazzo

Philip Hall Likes Me, I Reckon Maybe, B. Greene

Pyramids, David MacCauley

Robert the Rose Horse, Joan Heilbroner

The Beast in Ms. Rooney's Room, Pat Reilly Giff

The Biggest Tongue Twister Book in the World, Gyles Brandeth
The Carrot Seed, Ruth Krauss
The Clever Little Tailor (various authors)
The Little Engine That Could
The Little Red Hen (various authors)
The Sun Is On, Linda Michelle Baron
The Three Little Pigs (various authors)
There's a Wocket in my Pocket, Theodore Le Sieg
Treasure Island, Robert Louis Stephenson
What Makes the Weather? Janet Palazzo
When the Relatives Came, Cynthia Rylant

Children's Magazines

3-2-1 Contact, Children's Television Workshop
Chickadee, Owl Communications Group
Kid City, Children's Television Workshop
Magazines for Kids and Teens, Stohll, Donald
My Weekly Reader, Scholastic
Ranger Rick, National Wildlife Federation
Scholastic News
Sprint, Scholastic
Time For Children
Weekly Reader

Computer Software

Children's Writing and Publishing Center, The Learning Company
Language Experience Primary Series, Teachers Support Software
Monsters and Make-Believe, Queue
Once Upon a Time, Compu-Teach
Pow! Zap! Ker-Plunk! Queue
Print Shop, Broderbound
Snoopy Writer, American School Publishers
Story Builder, American School Publishers
Story Maker, Scholastic
Story Starters: Science, Pelican
Story Starters: Social Studies, Pelican
Thinking Networks for Reading and Writing, Think Network

Other Resources

Primary Reader's Theatre series, Curriculum Associates
Ripley's Believe It or Not, Time-Life Books
Take Part Plays, Grades 3–6, Sundance
Take Part Starters, Grades 2–3, Sundance
Tales and Plays collection, Rigby
The Baseball Encyclopedia, Time-Life

Index